BEFORE VIRTUE

BEFORE VIRTUE

Assessing Contemporary Virtue Ethics

Jonathan J. Sanford

The Catholic University of America Press
Washington, D.C.

Copyright © 2019
The Catholic University of America Press
All rights reserved
The paper used in this publication meets the minimum requirements of
American National Standards for Information Science—Permanence
of Paper for Printed Library Materials, ANSI Z39.48-1984.

∞

Library of Congress Cataloging-in-Publication Data
Sanford, Jonathan J., 1974–
Before virtue : assessing contemporary virtue ethics / Jonathan J. Sanford.
pages cm
Includes bibliographical references and index.
ISBN 978-0-8132-3262-1 (pbk : alk. paper)
1. Ethics. 2. Virtue. I. Title.
BJ1521.S26 2015
171'.3—dc23
2015001337

To my mother,
Ruth Marie (Dupuy) Sanford
Thank you

CONTENTS

Preface   ix

Introduction   1
    The Complexity of Contemporary Virtue Ethics, 5
    Some Preliminary Distinctions, 7
    Overview of the Project, 13

1. Moral Philosophy and Contemporary Virtue Ethics   21
    Contemporary Moral Philosophy: Competition and Incongruities, 22
    The Most Basic Questions of Moral Philosophy, 31
    Moral Philosophy and Metaphysics, 37
    Virtue Ethics and Moral Philosophy, 45

2. Origins of Contemporary Virtue Ethics   51
    Anscombe's "Modern Moral Philosophy," 60
    The Semantics of Obligation, 62
    Ceasing Moral Philosophy, 65
    Contemporary Virtue Ethics and Consequentialism, 69

3. All Anscombe's Children? The Varieties of Contemporary Virtue Ethics   81
    Identifying a Contemporary Virtue Ethicist, 85
    Classifying the Varieties of Contemporary Virtue Ethics, 89
    Taking Inventory, 111

4. Contemporary Virtue Ethics and Its Aspirations   114
    What Contemporary Virtue Ethics Promises, 121
    Does Mainstream Virtue Ethics Constitute a Cohesive Moral Theory? 126
    Does Mainstream Virtue Ethics Constitute a Comprehensive Moral Theory? 132
    Does Mainstream Virtue Ethics Provide a Coherent Virtue Theory? 139

5. Aristotle's Ethics and Contemporary Virtue Ethics — 143
   Whose Virtue Ethics? Which Aristotelianism?, 147
   Contemporary Virtue Ethics and Aristotle, 151
   Aristotle's Ethics Is Not a Virtue Ethics, 180
   A Way Forward, 182

6. Anthropology in Aristotelian Ethics: Every Virtue Needs a Home — 183
   Virtues Are Perfections of Human Beings, 187
   Skeletal View of Human Beings, 190
   Dependent Rational Animals, 199

7. Teleology in Aristotelian Ethics: Every Virtue Needs a Goal — 205
   Thinking about the Ends of Life, 206
   The Good Life for Man, 211
   Virtues as Ends, Virtues as Means, 216
   Happiness, 222

8. Natural Law in Aristotelian Ethics: Every Virtuous Action Needs Its Reason — 227
   Why Natural Lawyers and Contemporary Virtue Ethicists Have Not Been Friends, 228
   What Is Natural Law Theory? 231
   The Natural Law: Justice and the Common Good, 235
   The Natural Law: Virtues, Virtuous Actions, and Reasons, 253

9. Virtue Ethics, After and Before — 255

   Bibliography — 259
   Index — 275

PREFACE

If you are accustomed to the standard narrative communicated in most undergraduate ethics courses concerning the landscape in contemporary moral philosophy as consisting of three main camps—the deontological, utilitarian, and virtue ethical—or if you think each of those camps to be distinct and easily identifiable, or if you think that Aristotle's or Aquinas's moral philosophy can be described as virtue ethical, then this book may serve as a corrective. If you have already discerned the virtue ethics movement to be more complex than often presented, or if you are looking for ways to categorize and otherwise come to terms with the different sorts of virtue ethical approaches, or if you are interested in the history of virtue ethics, then this book will provide you with scholarly and argumentative resources to advance your research. If you are interested in the sort of questions that need to be answered in order to provide a foundation for moral philosophy, or the significance of Aristotelian ethics for contemporary moral philosophy, or if you wish to understand better the role of the virtues not only in moral philosophy but indeed in our lives, then this book will provoke what I take to be helpful progress on those matters. If none of the above interests you, then you should return this book to the shelf.

Writing a manuscript is a mostly solitary endeavor, and it requires considerable time and other resources. Solitude, time, and additional resources are harder to come by in some circumstances than others, and my own circumstances have taught me to be profoundly grateful for each portion of these instrumental goods I have received. The sabbatical I was given by the trustees of Franciscan University in the fall of 2009 freed me from teaching duties and enabled me to make a good beginning on this book. An Earhart Foundation Research Fellowship I was awarded in the summer of 2010 made possible the completion of a first draft of this manuscript. Without either of these two awards it is unlikely I would have been able to complete this book.

Several graduate assistants, Emily Hering, Kevin Kwasnik, and Samantha Bertrand, aided me in collecting some of the secondary literature utilized herein, and were helpful as critics of early drafts of chapters. I taught graduate courses dealing with elements of virtue theory and virtue ethics in 2007, 2010, and 2012, and I am grateful to each of the students in those seminars who helped me to shape better this book, especially to Brian Donahue, who read an earlier draft of this manuscript with great care and who critiqued aspects of it in a manner that proved significant to later drafts. Parts of several of these chapters were aired first at conferences, including those hosted by the American Maritain Association, the Center for Ethics and Culture at the University of Notre Dame, the American Catholic Philosophical Association, and colloquia at my own institution. I am grateful to each of those in attendance, and particularly to those who provided criticisms.

More recently I have had reason to be grateful to James Kruggel, acquisitions editor at the Catholic University of America Press, whose encouragement and support have been of essential importance. I am also grateful to Theresa B. Walker, managing editor of the press; Trevor Lipscombe, its director; the editorial committee; Carol A. Kennedy for her extensive work in copyediting; Alice Ramos; and three anonymous reviewers.

I owe my wife, Rebecca, a special debt of gratitude.

BEFORE VIRTUE

INTRODUCTION

It makes no small difference, then, whether we form habits of one kind or another from our very youth; it makes a very great difference, or rather all the difference.

Aristotle, NE II 1, 1103^{b}24–26

A good case can be made that the most exciting work done in moral philosophy over the last fifty years is that set of inquiries collected under the title of "contemporary virtue ethics." In its infancy it was not always clear that this would be so, and indeed, it used to be the case that the proponents of contemporary virtue ethics could rightfully complain that they did not receive the respect they deserved. But this has changed. Current handbooks on moral philosophy include significant entries on virtue ethics, there has been a proliferation of articles and books on it, and there are job postings seeking virtue ethicists for hire. Its leading figures are easily recognized by our newest generation of aspiring philosophers, with names like Elizabeth Anscombe (the movement's grandmother), Philippa Foot, Alasdair MacIntyre, Martha Nussbaum, and many others making regular appearances on college syllabi. By the accounts of those with

---

Quotations follow Aristotle, *Nicomachean Ethics* (hereafter *NE*), trans. W. D. Ross, in *The Complete Works of Aristotle*, vol. 2, ed. Jonathan Barnes (Princeton, N.J.: Princeton University Press, 1984), with a few emendations based on Bywater's Greek edition in the Oxford Classical Texts.

a stake in classifying the varieties of ethical theories, virtue ethics is treated as a cohesive movement unified by a common aim and methodology, and it prospers.

There is perhaps no clearer evidence that the contemporary virtue ethics movement has been endorsed as a coherent and significant contributor to debates at the heart of moral philosophy than its recent treatment in Cambridge University Press's companion series.[1] The arrangement and variety of chapters in the companion make evident the appealing features of virtue ethics: it focuses on the fundamental Socratic question of how one ought to live, draws from the wisdom of both ancients and moderns, is theoretically rich, and makes significant contributions to applied ethical questions of great importance.[2] *The Cambridge Companion to Virtue Ethics* also reveals some of the ways in which the controversies concerning virtue ethics over the last fifty years have shaped the movement and made it relevant to debates across the field of moral philosophy generally. To be sure, virtue ethics has not achieved universal sanction, but it is widely regarded as a legitimate approach to moral philosophy, indeed one that has a seat beside the two other main approaches most discussed in contemporary moral philosophy, deontology and conseqentialism. In short, the movement has grown into a popular way of addressing questions at the fore of contemporary moral debates and cannot be ignored.

A review of the chapters composing *The Cambridge Companion to Virtue Ethics* reveals, as well, some of the challenges to making sense of contemporary virtue ethics and assessing its value. There

---

1. Daniel C. Russell, *The Cambridge Companion to Virtue Ethics* (Cambridge: Cambridge University Press, 2013), hereafter *CCVE*.
2. For an analysis of some different ways in which virtue ethics approaches applied ethics see Liezl van Zyl's "Virtue Ethics and Right Action," *CCVE*, 172–96. The *CCVE* also contains chapters dealing with bioethical issues (Justin Oakley, "Virtue Ethics and Abortion," 197–220), environmental ethics (Matt Zwolinski and David Schmidtz, "Environmental Virtue Ethics: What It Is and What It Needs to Be," 221–39), and business ethics (Edwin Hartman, "The Virtue Approach to Business Ethics," 240–64).

are included chapters describing the virtue ethics of Aristotle,[3] Plato and the Stoics,[4] Confucius,[5] various medieval authors,[6] Hume,[7] and a number of contemporary authors. There are of course significant differences between these various classical, medieval, modern, and contemporary approaches. How can contemporary virtue ethics draw from each of them and remain unified and distinctive? This is a question at the forefront of adherents to virtue ethics, and both the editor and several other authors address it over the course of the companion volume. But one discovers in the various attempts to answer that question additional difficulties. Daniel C. Russell, the editor of the companion volume, whose *Practical Intelligence and the Virtues* provides an impressive defense of the centrality of practical wisdom to each of the virtues and forges on it a relatively narrow definition of what he calls Hard Virtue Ethics,[8] argues in his introduction to *The Cambridge Companion to Virtue Ethics* that it is impossible to provide a definition of virtue ethics that is brief, specific, and inclusive.[9] Nevertheless, he contends that all approaches to virtue ethics include a focus on one's character and whole way of life. Christine Swanton, whose chapter in *The Cambridge Companion to Virtue Ethics* is the

---

3. Daniel C. Russell, "Virtue Ethics, Happiness, and the Good Life," *CCVE*, 7–28.

4. Rachana Kamtekar, "Ancient Virtue Ethics: An Overview with an Emphasis on Practical Wisdom," *CCVE*, 29–48.

5. Philip J. Ivanhoe, "Virtue Ethics and the Chinese Confucian Tradition," *CCVE*, 49–69.

6. Jean Porter, "Virtue Ethics in the Medieval Period," *CCVE*, 70–91.

7. Paul Russell, "Hume's Anatomy of Virtue," *CCVE*, 92–115.

8. Daniel C. Russell, *Practical Intelligence and the Virtues* (Oxford: Oxford University Press, 2009), hereafter *PIV*. "My view therefore stands in stark contrast to the trend towards increasing indifference to the notion of phronesis in recent through about the virtues of character. Some virtue theorists argue that phronesis is important for some virtues, but certainly not all (Swanton, 2003); others.... Consequently, I distinguish between two basic varieties of virtue ethics: those on which phronesis is part of every virtue, which I call 'Hard Virtue Ethics', and those on which it is not ('Soft Virtue Ethics')."(*PIV*, xi). Later, he contends that only Hard Virtue Ethics is real virtue ethics (*PIV*, 71).

9. He contends the best one can arrive at is to incorporate two of those three criteria (*CCVE*, 3). His preferred strategy is to provide a definition that is brief and specific. The exclusivity of Russell's position on virtue ethics is what motivates objections such as Swanton's to it.

last, explicitly rejects Russell's definition of Hard Virtue Ethics as too narrow, and endorses instead a view that collects all virtue ethical approaches as united by virtue notions.[10] The notional approach to defining virtue ethics has advantages of inclusivity, but, like other notional solutions, is susceptible to claims that it lacks substance. We will have occasion to address this and other matters addressed by the companion volume and other literature in the pages to follow. At this early stage, what is to be noted is that even though virtue ethics is evidently regarded as a coherent and comprehensive approach within moral philosophy, it is not free of internal conflicts. Those internal divisions may indicate vitality within the movement, or may point to serious problems. It is perhaps not surprising, given the nature of most movements in philosophy, that we will discover the contemporary virtue ethics movement to be complex, a mixture of both vitality and, seen from at least some perspectives, decay. It is one of the tasks of the book before you to sort through this mixture in the hope of advancing a virtue-focused approach to moral philosophy that draws from the strengths and not the weaknesses of recent work in virtue ethics in combination with features of classical, and particularly Aristotelian, moral philosophy. For reasons that will become evident, I hesitate to describe my favored approach as a virtue ethics.

A note on terminology is in order before we begin in earnest. One of the claims of many adherents of virtue ethics, and indeed many of the approach's opponents, is that virtue ethics is as old as Plato, or if not Plato, then at least as old as Aristotle. It is indisputable that virtue theory has its origins in classical philosophy. But, as Julia Driver has pointed out,[11] a virtue theory does not necessarily imply a virtue ethics. It is one of the claims that I will advance later in this book that what one finds in Aristotle is not what is typically thought of as virtue ethics in its contemporary use. Therefore the expression "contemporary

---

10. Christine Swanton, "The Definition of Virtue Ethics," in *CCVE*, 332–33.

11. Julia Driver introduces this in her first footnote to "The Virtues and Human Nature," in *How Should One Live?* ed. Roger Crisp (Oxford: Clarendon Press, 1996), 111–29.

virtue ethics" will generally be used to specify the movement ushered in by Anscombe near the beginning of the second half of the twentieth century, and especially when it is necessary to signal discontinuities between the ethics of Aristotle and virtue ethics as it is employed in contemporary moral theorizing. Further distinctions between various strategies within contemporary virtue ethics will be introduced as we progress through an analysis and assessment of this movement.

The Complexity of Contemporary Virtue Ethics

Thinking about virtue ethics seems not unlike Augustine's description of the challenge of thinking about time: one seems to know what it is until challenged to describe it. Students before they are led through some of the literature on it, interested laypersons, and indeed even philosophers tend to assume virtue ethics to be easily describable. However, the pedestrian descriptions of the movement tend to be rather too general to specify it in such a way as to distinguish it from others, such as virtue ethics being about one's whole way of life, or about being rather than doing. Often there is more familiarity with some of the key figures usually identified with the movement, such as Aristotle or MacIntyre, than there is with the movement itself. And indeed, if Russell is right that it is impossible to have a definition of the movement that is brief, specific, and unified, then there is good reason why commonplace descriptions of the movement generally do not encapsulate it.

My own initial experiences of thinking about virtue ethics, at least, fall under this description of a commonplace view of the movement. Perhaps they can serve as an instructive point of entry for advancing upon a preliminary description of contemporary virtue ethics, especially for those readers of this book who are interested in the movement but have not been tutored by an adherent of contemporary virtue ethics. When in 2001 I completed my dissertation, which focused in large part on the foundations for Aristotle's ethics, I saw my project working in the same direction as the efforts of contemporary virtue ethicists. I had, naturally, worked closely on the ethical and political writings of Aristotle himself, and took in the contemporary, and some of the classical, commentaries on those works. I had also begun a close reading of Alasdair MacIntyre's work, and MacIntyre, I was given to understand, was a virtue ethicist by virtue of being an Aristotelian on the virtues. Many of the other virtue ethicists I had read also looked to Aristotle for some inspiration, and so I concluded that contemporary virtue ethics was a revival of Aristotelian ethics, and a much needed one at that.

A more thorough review of the movement has revealed a much more complicated, and in some respects more sophisticated, approach to moral philosophy than I had anticipated. A closer examination of the movement's literature reveals that there is no common set of principles or strategies for grounding the virtues, but rather a variety of competing eudaimonistic, agent-basing, and agent-centered theories of the virtues. Moreover, it reveals that the movement is not in fact consistently Aristotelian in orientation or methodology since sometimes different virtue ethicists look to competing philosophical systems as foundational, and that even some of those works that have claimed to be Aristotelian (or more often neo-Aristotelian) have departed quite far from Aristotle's approach, sometimes without acknowledging those points of departure.[12] In many ways, at least the mainstream of contemporary virtue ethics seems not to represent a radical departure from what Anscombe characterizes as "modern moral philosophy," and given the origins of the contemporary move-

---

12. Daniel C. Russell's *Practical Intelligence and the Virtues*, and Julia Annas's *Intelligent Virtue* (Oxford: Oxford University Press, 2011), are notable exceptions. Russell and Annas, both classical philosophers, have endorsed versions of virtue ethics that draw more heavily from Aristotle than from features in the mainstream of contemporary virtue ethics. In this work Russell several times mentions his distance from the mainstream of the movement and, as we have seen already, is registered as an outlier by Christine Swanton in her chapter in the Cambridge Companion volume that Russell edits.

ment this is a great irony. Moreover, recent literature on the virtues often employs theories of the virtues that bear little resemblance to the accounts given them by their classical originators. These were, as I have said, surprising discoveries for me. My hunch, based on conversations with and studies of other philosophers with an interest in virtue theory, is that it will also be a matter of surprise for others. Since many readers with an interest in virtue theory tend to think of contemporary virtue ethics as a reintroduction of Aristotelian ethics in a modern context, identify Anscombe, Foot, MacIntyre, or Nussbaum as some its leading lights, and assume a general coherence of doctrine and philosophical direction, it will be useful to them to see why these assumptions do not bear up well under closer scrutiny. For those already informed on this point, there is much this book offers by way of analysis and critique to advance positions within debates surrounding virtue ethics that will be of use. For all readers, both the critical and constructive dimensions of this book offer a perspective on the role of the virtues in moral philosophy that, though certainly indebted to the insights of many past and present philosophers, offers a fresh perspective on the role of virtue within moral theorizing.

Some Preliminary Distinctions

Since contemporary virtue ethics is a complex movement, it is necessary to determine if there are some significant divisions implicit within the whole if we are to analyze it successfully. Movements, unlike arguments, theories and doctrines, do not typically yield distinctions that have hard edges. The historical and situational conditions vary between the many authors of any movement, as do their degrees of responsiveness to the work of other thinkers and their unique formulations of central features of the movement. For these reasons, we should not expect anything more than distinctions with soft boundaries, or trends as we might call them, which compose the broader categorical divisions within the virtue ethics movement.

David Solomon describes one such set of trends. Some virtue ethicists engage in what he calls "routine" virtue ethics—an approach that emphasizes the importance of the virtues within the typical strictures of the way in which moral philosophy is currently pursued, particularly in the analytic tradition.[13] It was not and is not always the case, however, that all of those who identify as virtue ethicists adopt the strategies and preoccupations that are more typical of current mainstream moral theorizing. Much of early virtue ethics literature, for instance, was polemical in nature, disparaging Mill and Kant as wrongheadedly rule-based ethicists. In place of the rule-based approaches, those virtue ethicists Solomon calls "radical" proposed various alternatives.[14] For reasons that will become more apparent later in this book, Solomon seems to have described a genuine division. Although many of the radical virtue ethicists' solutions bear little in common with each other, there is among them a more or less unified turn away from the mainstream of modern moral philosophy. On the other hand, more recent works in virtue ethics have sought to show the pillars of modernity, including Hume, to have a genuine concern with character development, which is taken to imply they are contributors to an ethics of virtue.[15] The distrust early virtue ethical lit-

---

13. David Solomon, "Virtue Ethics: Radical or Routine?" in *Intellectual Virtue: Perspectives from Ethics and Epistemology*, ed. Michael DePaul and Linda Zagzebski (Oxford: Clarendon Press, 2003): 57–80. It is a shame that this insightful chapter has not received more attention. One notable exception is Christine Swanton's mention of it in "The Definition of Virtue Ethics," in *CCVE*, 315–38, 318, though she does not engage his main thesis there.

14. Timothy Chappell in "Virtue Ethics in the Twentieth Century," (*CCVE*, 149–71) emphasizes the revolutionary character of the work of Anscombe and the early Foot. He contends that everything that has followed, including the work of MacIntyre, Bernard Williams, and Charles Taylor, has been a matter of seeking to fill in the details of Anscombe's and Foot's research project.

15. For just a few prominent examples of this strategy, see Michael Slote's efforts at a Humean virtue ethics in *Morals from Motives* (Oxford: Oxford University Press, 2001), Kwame Anthony Appiah's declaration of J. S. Mill as a great virtue ethicist in *Experiments in Ethics* (Cambridge, Mass.: Harvard University Press, 2008), and Christine Swanton's effort at arguing that all major moral theories contribute elements of a virtue ethics in *Virtue Ethics: A Pluralistic View* (Oxford: Oxford University Press, 2003).

erature directed toward the leading lights of modern philosophy has not simply been softened in the cases of some recent contributors, it seems in some cases to have become admiration. The process of accommodation to the more narrow range of concerns and methodology typical of modern moral philosophy is one that Talbot Brewer helpfully characterizes as the "normalization of virtue ethics."[16]

There are some disadvantages to the terms preferred by Solomon, Brewer, and some other observers of the movement,[17] to describe these trends. The adjective "routine" can be taken pejoratively, and "normalized" admits of several interpretations depending on the norms specified. So, when referring to this trend, I will usually employ the terms "conventional" or "mainstream." "Conventional" is useful insofar as it points to the ways in which this trend in contemporary virtue ethics has adopted many of the conventions of current moral theorizing, and "mainstream" is useful for pointing out the ways in which this approach has become dominant in more recent virtue ethical literature. The term "radical" is somewhat less clear as a label, if only because of the variety among those thinkers marginal to mainstream virtue ethics. Several of the significant figures whom Solomon counts as radical virtue ethicists do not describe themselves as virtue ethicists at all. These include those philosophers I mentioned in the first paragraph of this introduction as usually associated with the movement. Anscombe never claimed to be one, and judging from the radical departure from modern moral philosophy she advocated, there is little doubt that she would not claim to be one now were she still alive to witness what she is so often credited by mainstream virtue ethicists with starting. MacIntyre never intended his project to be seen as a contribution to contemporary virtue ethics, and has made it clear that he does not in any way wish to be seen

---

16. Talbot Brewer, *The Retrieval of Ethics* (Oxford: Oxford University Press, 2009), 7.
17. Especially notable for drawing out the distinctions between radical and routine varieties of virtue ethics is Christopher Miles Coope's "Modern Virtue Ethics," in *Values and Virtues: Aristotelianism in Contemporary Ethics*, ed. Timothy Chappell (Oxford: Clarendon Press, 2006), 20–52.

as a proponent of the movement.[18] Foot seems to have done much to develop the movement with a series of articles later collected in *Virtues and Vices*, but has gone in a different direction, that of re-grounding ethics in general and not just contributing a third way to engage in the projects of modern moral philosophy, with *Natural Goodness*.[19] Nussbaum, always resistant to categorization, published a paper in 1999 in which she argued that "virtue ethics" is a misleading category and ought to be jettisoned altogether.[20] For these reasons, I usually will refer to these thinkers, and others in a similar situation with respect to mainstream virtue ethics, as "unconventional" or "marginal" virtue ethicists.

We find in virtue ethics a multifaceted contemporary moral philosophical movement, some of the parts of which—generally, those represented in more recent literature—accommodate themselves to status quo moral philosophizing; others of which—generally, those produced in the first and second generation of the contemporary movement—depart radically from status quo moral philosophizing. We also find in virtue ethics a movement not always sensitive to its rebellious origins, so that those thinkers credited by many of the movement's current adherents as being the movement's founders—Anscombe and MacIntyre most notably—would not or do not wish to see their own work as contributing to the contemporary movement at all. On the contrary, and as I will argue in the second chap-

---

18. This is clear enough from his writings. This is why nearly all of his post *After Virtue* writings are ignored (with the occasional exception of *Dependent Rational Animals*) by virtue ethicists. *Whose Justice? Which Rationality?* is, in many respects, a defense of an Aristotelian-Thomist approach to ethics, and is not the work of a virtue ethicist. In addition, MacIntyre graciously answered by email some questions I had about how he sees his relationship to the virtue ethical movement, and he made it abundantly clear in our exchanges that he does not identify with the movement in the least.

19. Philippa Foot, *Natural Goodness* (Oxford: Oxford University Press, 2001). Moreover, in his review of her book in *Mind* 112 (2003): 130–39, Michael Slote claims that Foot made clear to him in a personal communication that she does not identify herself as a virtue ethicist.

20. Martha Nussbaum, "Virtue Ethics: A Misleading Category?" *Journal of Ethics* 3 (1999): 163–201.

ter, there is good reason to characterize conventional virtue ethics as developing in part from the rejection of that influential and rebellious observation submitted by Anscombe that the whole project of modern philosophy has gone off the rails and from Anscombe's advice to cease doing moral philosophy until we have retrieved something like an Aristotelian philosophical psychology. Seen from this historical perspective, the most institutionally successful variety of virtue ethics, mainstream virtue ethics, has achieved its current status only after reversing the course of its initial impetus.

The developmental stages leading to success in the mainstream of contemporary virtue ethics might have been different if those who celebrate the inspiration Anscombe provided to the movement acknowledged the ways in which they disagree with her. We cannot say in retrospect whether a different set of developmental stages might also have met with the sort of success contemporary virtue ethics now enjoys as a major contributor to contemporary moral inquiry. What we can observe is that current encyclopedic, anthological, textbook, and companion entries on virtue ethics tell the story of vibrancy in the movement, and it is this story that has become the defining narrative for the way the next wave of moral philosophers has been taught to consider virtue ethics—as one more alternative for solving the questions that define contemporary moral philosophy. Even though Anscombe is in these entries generally acknowledged as the founder of the movement, the core of her teachings has often been jettisoned without comment. If the core of Anscombe's analyses and recommendations is sound, as I will argue in the second chapter that it is, the fact that it has been set aside is a significant indication that something may be amiss in what otherwise appears to be a healthy and rich movement in ethics.

This is not to suggest that criticisms of contemporary virtue ethics is uncommon. In the critical literature a standard set of objections to the approach of virtue ethics has emerged. The most common of these is that virtue ethics does not provide sufficient guidance for action. The second most common is that a concern with the development of one's virtues is self-centered, and renders one unsuitably prepared to come to the aid of others in need. More recently, situationists have challenged the very notion of there being something like stable character traits, and this is often hailed as the situationist challenge. Other, less common but significant, objections include the charge of cultural relativity; the circularity problem of determining grounds by means of which a character trait can be claimed a virtue when virtues are taken as already epistemologically basic; and, the so-called conflict problem, where two or more virtues suggest different courses of action for resolving a moral conundrum. Standard criticisms of contemporary virtue ethics press one or more of these objections.[21]

These objections, and the mainstream virtue ethical responses to them, take for granted a shared set of assumptions about the tasks of moral philosophy: first, that moral philosophy ought to be action guiding; second, that one ought to be altruistic; third, that our actions are not merely the products of our situations; fourth, that there are universal ethical principles; fifth, that there is some way to derive first moral principles from which to build an account of the virtues; and sixth, that there simply are some insoluble moral dilemmas. In standard virtue ethical attempts to respond to these objections, it is the shared set of assumptions between objectors to and adherents of virtue ethics that has served to bring the two parties together, indeed, on many points they are indistinguishable.

This book does not fit neatly into the model represented by this list of standard virtue ethical objections and assumptions, and the reasons for it failing to do so are twofold: on the one hand, my critical appraisal is, unlike standard criticisms and defenses of contemporary virtue ethics, attentive to the basic difficulty in specifying just what contemporary virtue ethics is so that the target, or rather

21. Rosalind Hursthouse discusses the standard criticisms, in different order, in her "Virtue Ethics," *Stanford Encyclopedia of Philosophy*, ed. Edward N. Zalta, Fall 2007 ed., http://plato.stanford.edu/archives/fall2007/entries/ethics-virtue/.

targets, for criticism are adequately described. Second, I find significant flaws with several of the standard assumptions concerning the basic tasks of moral philosophy subscribed to by most critics and defenders of virtue ethics alike. I am not unique in pointing out these flaws. Some of them have been most ably described by those thinkers Solomon names radical proponents of virtue ethics. In the pages to follow, some of the arguments used to criticize features of the virtue ethics movement will be drawn from the work of thinkers who may or may not, depending on what view of virtue ethics is being taken, be regarded as proponents of the virtue ethics movement. The complexities of the first task, those related to specifying what virtue ethics is, necessarily create complexities for the second task, that of critically evaluating the movement. It certainly does not serve a genuine philosophical purpose to avoid tackling these complexities if we are to gain a more thorough understanding of this important movement. It is hoped that this critical appraisal of the movement will yield some worthwhile conclusions not just about virtue ethics, but also about the basic tasks of moral philosophy itself.

Overview of the Project

This book includes both critical and constructive arguments concerning virtue ethics. Regarding the critical position advanced, I intend to argue that contemporary virtue ethics, considered as a unified movement in ethics, does not present an altogether promising alternative to the strategies and preoccupations characteristic of what Anscombe describes as modern moral philosophy, but is rather, in many respects at least, an extension of them. It is important to highlight the qualification employed in this thesis, that it regards contemporary virtue ethics considered as a whole. There is much variety between the parts of this movement, and especially between those virtue-focused thinkers lying outside the virtue ethical mainstream. Both philosophers in the mainstream of virtue ethicists and those more marginal to the movement provide help for advancing the constructive thesis that a virtue-focused approach is essential to an adequate moral theory.

The critical thesis should not then be taken to imply that the contemporary virtue ethics movement is a worthless philosophical dead end, for, despite some of what I will describe as failures to advance a genuine alternative to modern moral philosophy, contemporary virtue ethics has successfully reintroduced some of the perennial questions essential to a classical and medieval approach to ethics, questions that are comprehensive in scope, putting a concern with one's overall way of life at the center of focus. Moreover, if contemporary virtue ethics as a whole has failed to be a comprehensive alternative to other popular approaches to philosophical ethics, and one of the reasons for its failure is the inadequate manner in which it has recovered the Aristotelian tradition of moral inquiry, then there are still reasons to think that the survival of some form of an Aristotelian approach to ethics is viable, and, moreover, that a discussion of some of the more significant failures of the contemporary virtue ethics project can advance that Aristotelian project in both negative and positive ways. Negatively, by indicating what to avoid. Positively, by pointing out the directions in which philosophical ethics, I will argue, needs to move. In addition to its polemicizing then, this book seeks to indicate new directions to pursue in philosophical ethics, albeit new directions that take their bearings from ancient maps.

This book includes both a description of the virtue ethics movement and a defense of an Aristotelian strategy for moral philosophizing. The initial articulation of this Aristotelian strategy takes place in chapter 1, wherein I examine the competing claims of modern moral philosophy and the contemporary virtue ethics movement. I then examine the origins of the contemporary virtue ethics movement (chapter 2); consider its many varieties (chapter 3); look to the central claims and promises of especially mainstream virtue ethics to provide an adequate alternative to other leading modern moral

INTRODUCTION 15

theories and the failure to make good on those promises (chapter 4); and then I turn in chapter 5 to a consideration of the ways in which especially the Aristotelian varieties of contemporary virtue ethics have too aggressively censored the Aristotelian project, and add to that claim the further one that Aristotle's approach ought not to be named a virtue ethics. Then in chapters 6, 7, and 8 I argue that not just deontology, consequentialism, and contractualism, but conventional virtue ethics and many of its unconventional proponents as well, have failed to provide as successful a strategy for answering the basic questions of moral philosophy—the answers to which, though taking many varieties, must nevertheless be given—as that provided by a more thoroughgoing Aristotelian approach. Chapter 9 looks to draw a last conclusion from the inquiry.

For a number of reasons, my claim that the Aristotelian approach to moral philosophy provides a more promising alternative to modern moral philosophy, whether in its rule- or its virtue-based varieties, is far more controversial than pointing out the taxonomical difficulties in describing virtue ethics as well as the shortcomings of the movement. If all I have to offer is a set of observations to the effect that contemporary virtue ethics, like the rest of modern moral philosophy, fails to be Aristotelian in the scope of its inquiry and its methodology, and yet nevertheless use Aristotelianism as a normative standard for judging the adequacy of other moral philosophies, then this work could fairly be criticized as a sustained but unreflective argument from authority—even a misguided effort in circular argumentation. But it is not that, as I hope to make clear in summary fashion now and extended argument later.

Though not every adherent of an ethics of virtue advanced in recent years identifies with the Aristotelian project, it is certainly the case that the greater part of them has done so in one way or another. Most, like Foot, Nussbaum, Gabrielle Taylor, or Hursthouse, prefer to refer to their adoption of Aristotle's approach as selective, and so name their approach neo-Aristotelian. Such selection is normally characterized as a matter of leaving out the rotten bits—like Aristotle's views about women and slaves—and keeping the rest. Because of the prominence of claims to be philosophizing according to the mind of Aristotle, which implies a deference to essential facets of the Aristotelian project, it is significant to my criticism of especially mainstream virtue ethics to point out that there is far more "neo" than "Aristotelian" in their neo-Aristotelianism.[22] More significant, however, is it to point out and argue for the position that many of the facets of the Aristotelian project that are typically left out by virtue ethicists are by no means marginal, but rather are at its heart.[23]

It is my contention that there is far more Hume, Mill, and Kant at work in the neo-Aristotelianism of many contemporary virtue ethicists than there is Aristotle, and that at the critical points of disagreement mainstream virtue ethicists reveal themselves to be adherents to the modern moral project rather than the Aristotelian. I further argue that Aristotle's project fails to fit into any of the leading mainstream contenders for what is to count as virtue ethics.[24] Moreover, Aristotle's project is non-reductionistic in the way that most contemporary virtue ethical projects are reductionistic, insofar as Aristotle does not seek to derive an ethics meant to answer the main concerns at work in the project of modern moral philosophy of justifying claims to right action from universally acceptable intu-

22. To borrow Peter Simpson's expression in "Contemporary Virtue Ethics and Aristotle," *Review of Metaphysics* 45 (1992): 503–24.

23. The areas of fundamental discontinuity between Aristotelian ethics and mainstream contemporary virtue ethics, to be discussed in chapter 5, include the special concern with moral motivation, the role of consequentialist reasoning, the significance of contemplative wisdom, the logical relation between the virtues and happiness, the significance of practical wisdom, the unity of the virtues, the supposed significance of altruism and benevolence, the significance of friendship, the significance of justice, and the political nature of the human person.

24. Recent works by Daniel C. Russell and Julia Annas are generally Aristotelian in the more robust sense I am using it here. Moreover, as they themselves note in several places in their respective works, *Practical Intelligence and the Virtues* and *Intelligent Virtue,* their approaches to eudaimonism and their treatments of *phronesis* and the unity of the virtues put them at odds with the mainstream of contemporary virtue ethics.

itions about either virtue or happiness. Aristotle, instead, assumes what many modern moral philosophers take it as their task to prove: the goodness of certain actions or traits of character. It is the openness of Aristotle's ethical project to the riches of his own tradition that makes such a starting point possible, and it is not the case that such openness to the riches of his cultural tradition makes Aristotle's project a cultural relativistic one. Aristotle's ethical project is multifaceted in its principles, and shows itself to be answering a different set of questions than those occupying the efforts of most contemporary virtue ethicists. To be sure, the virtues play a central role in Aristotle's ethics, but not the role of a set of core principles from which all other principles come to be derived. This is in fact one of the advantages of the Aristotelian project, as well as one of the reasons why it should not be characterized as a virtue ethics.

I contend that the main reason for the superiority of the Aristotelian approach to moral philosophy is its ability to do a better job of answering what I argue to be the fundamental background questions of moral philosophy than do its rivals, virtue ethical or otherwise. These questions are: What is a human being? What is the end of human life? By means of what criteria does one measure successful progress toward the end of human life? I argue in chapter 1 that these questions are explicitly the subject of philosophical anthropology, natural philosophy, and natural theology, and that those disciplines are necessarily foundational to a more adequate moral philosophy. This funneling of other disciplines into ethics is possible only in a moral philosophy that is non-reductionistic with respect to its foundational principles. The lack of an insistence to begin with a "pure" moral philosophy, and openness to including the fruit of intersecting disciplines,[25] is just one of the many virtues of the Aristotelian ethical project.

25. Consider the contrast between Michael Slote's efforts to generate a pure ethics in *Morals from Motives* and Kwame Anthony Appiah's celebration of the intersections between moral philosophy and the social sciences, especially psychology, in *Experiments in Ethics*.

It is my contention that the Aristotelian ethical project is superior to others because of its ability to address these questions more adequately than do other ethical approaches. I argue that marginal virtue ethics has already done a sufficient job of showing that the leading approaches of modern moral philosophy have failed to answer these questions adequately. My specific concern in these chapters is to argue that mainstream virtue ethics has also failed to do so. There are several stages to this line of argumentation. First, I argue that these are, indeed, questions the answers to which must be either assumed or argued for by any moral philosophy. Those approaches that have sought to ignore these questions have done so at their own peril, for in ignoring them one is destined to provide unexamined answers to them at critical junctures of moral inquiry.

Second, I argue that Aristotle's project is at least free of this error of willfully ignoring questions that must be answered to proceed with a sufficiently well-examined ethical project. These questions, in fact, become thematic in the Aristotelian project, and Aristotle himself brings his project as a whole to be measured against the success with which it brings greater clarity to these foundational concerns. It is because of the central role that these questions have for ethics, including an ethics of virtue, that I have called this work *Before Virtue*.

Third, it is not just that Aristotle explicitly answers these questions that makes his ethical inquiry superior, but I argue further that Aristotle's answers are correct, at least in their general structure and in a way that is left open for further clarifications by later Aristotelians—most notably in this regard, by Aquinas. Arguing for this claim, that Aristotle's answers to these questions are correct, has proven to be the most challenging aspect of my project, and it is at those points that my argumentation is especially indebted to MacIntyre's works.

In making the case for the verity of the general features of Aristotle's ethical inquiry, I argue that it is impossible adequately to answer questions about what a human being is without some account of what a human being is for—a position in line with the relationship Aristotle discovers between formal and final causes. I follow MacIntyre in arguing that absent some version of an Aristotelian sort of answer to what the purpose of human life is, one is left with the Nietzschean alternative that life is mere will to power; and further, that on this central question of moral philosophy, and so with respect to mature and competing moral philosophies, the only real alternative is that between Nietzsche and Aristotle. As valuable as MacIntyre's account in *After Virtue* of a sociological teleology is, this account does not go far enough. First, MacIntyre is wrong to dismiss so hastily what he calls Aristotle's "metaphysical biology." I am not in a position to defend at length in this project, even if I could, the principles (as distinct from the details, many of which are known to be false) of Aristotle's biology, though I do in general think its basic principles not without merit, and I provide some reasons for deploying the full array of Aristotelian causality to make sense of human life and action. Moreover, MacIntyre himself has corrected this dismissal with his often overlooked but significant account of the central role of the virtues of acknowledged dependency in *Dependent Rational Animals*. These arguments will help to show, as well, the superiority of an ethical approach that recognizes that we social animals only can flourish in relation with others.

Finally, I argue that Aristotle himself is at his weakest in answering the third fundamental question articulated above, that concerning the criteria for assessing progress toward one's end. It is from one of the most formidable of Aristotle's heirs, Aquinas, that we find more adequate means to address that question. Aquinas's Aristotelian project enables us to fill in those features of Aristotle's account of practical wisdom that remain opaque in his own writings. It is with a broadly conceived Aristotelian account of the workings of right reason, that is to say his account of the natural law, that we find adequately articulated those criteria needed for sufficient assessment of progress toward the goal of life.

These, then, are the main features of my defense of the Aristotelian ground of my project. It is from this ground that I will, indeed, be judging the successes and failures of the contemporary virtue ethics movement. Not all of that assessment need rely as explicitly on my claims regarding the superiority of the Aristotelian ethical project as do others. For instance, it will not be necessary always to invoke Aristotle to point out that contemporary virtue ethics has not delivered on its central promises. Those central promises, as I take them, are to provide a comprehensive ethical approach that proves a rival to the other moral philosophies in vogue today, including its ability to settle matters of applied ethics; to provide a single unifying account of what virtue is; and to be able to articulate and use as touchstone a more or less universally acceptable tabulation of which character traits are to count as virtues and which as vices. I will, however, need to invoke the Aristotelian approach to argue at length for why virtue ethics does not present a comprehensive approach to ethics, and that it is because of virtue ethics' failure sufficiently to address the foundational questions of ethics that it fails to deliver on the second two promises mentioned above; a failure that, I will argue, Aristotle's approach does not suffer.

The central claims of this book's argumentation are, then, the following: virtue ethics arises from critiques of the modern moral project; mainstream virtue ethics suffers from the very same defects that unconventional virtue ethics has pointed out in modern moral philosophy; mainstream virtue ethics has failed to achieve what it has promised even when evaluated on its own terms; unconventional virtue ethics has failed to provide a constructive path out of the problems of the modern moral project that it has often so successively described; sufficient recourse to the Aristotelian approach to ethics has not yet been made by mainstream virtue ethicists, despite some claims to the contrary; the Aristotelian approach to ethics is in fact the superior approach to ethics because it is more successful than all rivals, virtue ethical and otherwise, at addressing the foundational questions for ethics; we ought to make recourse to an Aristotelian approach to ethics.

Chapter 1

MORAL PHILOSOPHY AND CONTEMPORARY VIRTUE ETHICS

It is a necessary feature of consequentialism that it is a shallow philosophy.

G. E. M. Anscombe, "Modern Moral Philosophy"

Before a critical appraisal of any philosophical system can be provided, one needs to have made sense of the system. The more familiar work involved in that process is a set of inquiries with the goal in mind of providing a detailed examination of the main features internal to the system. Less familiar, but no less important, is the work of understanding that system's situational features with respect to the history of investigations concerning the questions that the system is meant to answer and the status of that system relative to competing explanations. No one working in the field of virtue ethics refers to virtue ethics as a system, for the associations between the various virtue ethical approaches are too loose to merit the label. However,

G. E. M. Anscombe, "Modern Moral Philosophy"; first published in *Philosophy* 33 (1958): 1–19; my page numbers in the quotations follow one of its many anthologized printings in *Virtue Ethics,* ed. Roger Crisp and Michael Slote (Oxford: Oxford University Press, 1997), 26–44.

movements are analogous to systems, and the same sort of work is required for critically appraising a philosophical movement as is for making sense of a philosophical system.

There are advantages to beginning with a consideration of some of the ways that contemporary virtue ethics is situated within moral philosophy before turning to an examination of its main features. This chapter seeks to understand contemporary virtue ethics within the wider context of contemporary moral philosophy. It is also the task of this chapter to identify the foundational questions of moral philosophy and to argue for their priority and their importance for judging the relative strengths of different approaches to moral philosophy. These two tasks are related insofar as both require reflection on the state of contemporary moral philosophy and the relation between moral theorizing and metaphysics.

Contemporary Moral Philosophy: Competition and Incongruities

What exactly is contemporary virtue ethics? Both adherents and detractors of the movement have an interest in providing a relatively straightforward answer to this question: an adherent, to clarify what it is that her efforts are advancing; a detractor, to set up the target at which she will take aim. If, however, we attempt to take on the perspective of a mere observer of this movement, one whose interests in it have been attracted because she wants to know what motivates its adherents and detractors, say a perceptive graduate student, what will she say after working through the literature of those usually identified as its major proponents? Sarah Conly, I think, accurately describes one likely reaction: "One's first impression on reviewing literature on virtue is that here, more than most places in philosophy, anything goes."[1] Conly could make that claim in 1988, short-

---

1. Sarah Conly, "Flourishing and the Failure of the Ethics of Virtue," *Midwest Studies in Philosophy* 13 (1988): 83–96, 83.

ly before a swift acceleration in the number and variety of virtue ethical approaches that were produced in the next two decades. On the one hand, mainstream elements in the movement have become more unified since the late 1980s by developing a set of strategies for responding to its critics; on the other hand, the fissures between competing virtue ethical approaches have become deeper. On both hands, the variety of virtue ethical approaches and the divisions between them reflect variety and divisions within contemporary moral philosophy in general.

The level of disagreement about basic issues in moral philosophy is staggering. There is no shortage of evidence on this point: simply open any anthology or handbook of moral philosophy and read through the table of contents. Sentimentalism is pitted against deontology, both of which are pitted against utilitarianism, all of which are contrasted with divine command theory, which is again contrasted with contractarianism, which are all again opposed to virtue ethics, and so on. Add to this the striking contrast between the sorts of inquiries that ancient and medieval philosophers pursued and those pursued by philosophers today, and the picture of the state of ethics is even more complex. There simply are no questions settled once and for all in contemporary moral philosophy.

Still more unsettling, there is not even basic agreement about what it is that a philosopher engaged in ethical inquiry ought to be doing. Some contend that the task of the ethical philosopher is to clarify the principles by means of which people are already living their lives. Others contend that the task of ethics is to bring clarity to what ought to be the main goals of human life, as well as to the means by which we attain it. Others seek to unearth the foundations from which sure and certain rules governing human action are derived. Others, with the significant addition of a sense of moral obligation, seek to find the foundations from which sure and certain principles that ought to govern human action are derived. Those producing textbooks often seem to take it as the basic task of moral philosophy to compare and contrast the varieties of ethical theories, and then either to argue for the superiority of one of those approaches over others or to leave it to one's readers/students to select their own preferred approach. One can forgive a student who has received instruction along these lines if he develops a consumer's mindset about ethical theories, not unlike a shopper surveying a shelf full of perfumes and selecting one on the basis of the leading principles of appeal—like its smell (hedonism), its effects on the opposite sex (consequentialism), its ability to bring to greater perfection natural aromas (eudaimonism), or its popularity (contractualism).

Judged by normal standards for distinguishing between disciplines, moral philosophy's status as a discipline would seem in jeopardy. Imagine physicists who deny the existence of atoms, or astronomers who contend the earth to be at the center of the solar system, or chemists who continue to promote the phlogiston theory of combustion, with all of them regarded as respectable members of their disciplines who, far from being censured, are given major grants to continue their research and teaching. The degree of disagreement between these researchers and their familiar counterparts—subatomic physicists, post-Copernican astronomers, and post-Boylean chemists—is no greater than that between different partisans of opposed ethical theories. The glaring difference, of course, is that in those other disciplines the theories proposed have all been proven false, and have been accepted as such by reputed members of the discipline, whereas no manner of experimentation or argumentation has proven sufficient to mark similar progress in ethics. In fact, by some measures, moral philosophy has degenerated rather than progressed over the course of its history.[2]

Compounded with the general failure of moral philosophy to

---

2. Leo Strauss's *Natural Right and History* (Chicago: University of Chicago Press, 1953); and Alasdair MacIntyre's *After Virtue*, 2nd ed. (Notre Dame, Ind.: University of Notre Dame Press, 1984) can each be read as advancing that conclusion, albeit in very different ways.

have as yet sorted out its basic principles is the proximity of this discipline to the lives we all lead. "Ethics" has at least two main senses: it is often used as a byword for "philosophical ethics" or "moral philosophy"; but "ethics," outside of academic circles, means those customs and principles by which a person attempts to guide his or her life. We can make do without philosophical ethics, but not ethics. Human action, which is acting with reasons, however underarticulated they may be, is as common as pulling on some clothes in the morning; in fact, doing that, and any other mundane matter about which we may deliberate, such as whether to brush our teeth and for how long and with what sort of substance, implies some degree of choice and so is, I would argue, ethical. Although determining how the academic discipline of moral philosophy relates to our everyday lives, which are necessarily fraught with moral deliberation, remains a matter of dispute for moral philosophers, there is no denying the fact that moral philosophy seems the most easily accessible field of philosophy, at least from the perspective of initiating students into the sorts of questions that philosophers ask and the strategies employed to answer them.

It is because of the proximity of praxis to theory in ethics that the issues pertinent to moral philosophy are those about which we take special care, and often do so with great passion. The conclusions arrived at by moral philosophers can, and often do, have a tremendous impact on the sorts of decisions we make in our everyday lives, and the stakes of those decisions are often exceedingly high: Should I abort the radically dependent human being within me, especially when my formal education will be imperiled if I do not? Should I lie to my employer to seek advancement, especially when he is an oppressive boss? Should I put my failing mother in a nursing home, especially when having her live with me will cause tension in my marriage? It is, as we will see Anscombe argue next chapter, a sign of our times that many of the moral theories most popular today could be used to justify both a positive and negative answer to each of these questions, and not a few moral philosophers would count that feature in their favor. In addition to these questions of a discrete and thorny dimension, there is also a holistic and personal dimension to the grounding question of moral philosophy, at least of classical moral philosophy, which is "how ought I to live?" Pressing an answer to this question reveals the most expansive and pertinent dimensions of moral reflection: it is a field of inquiry that concerns our whole way of life.

There seem to be, then, two seemingly incompatible features of moral philosophy: on the one hand it is a discipline in disarray, with first principles, aims, and methodology all still very much in dispute; and on the other hand it is a discipline in which the stakes are especially high and about whose conclusions academics and nonacademics alike care very much, even if many people seem not to care particularly about the philosophical strategies employed to arrive at those conclusions. Of all the fields of inquiry in which one could expect the best minds to have devoted themselves to good effect, it would seem that moral philosophy should hold preeminent place. Yet no field of inquiry, judged in terms of its status as a unified discipline, seems in a worse state than moral philosophy.

Not every moral philosopher finds the current state of moral philosophy problematic, and for reasons that extend beyond the overused joke about philosophers being put out of business should solutions be found. Some claim it is a sign of health for a discipline to be fraught with conflict, pointing to the degree of passion to which many of its practitioners approach its subject matter. Others take the stance of the cool-headed skeptic who looks to moral philosophy as the most striking example of our inability to secure knowledge about important matters. It is also the case that in ethics, more than other areas in philosophy, students are encouraged to develop what is sometimes called their own "personal philosophy," and variety in ethics could be looked on simply as an indication of the variety of persons who write and think about philosophical ethics.

Against such reasons, imagine a young and earnest aspiring philosopher who is deeply concerned about issues pertinent to ethics. She thinks that through studying philosophical ethics she will be helped in her reflections on issues important to her. Now imagine the alarm she feels after surveying the moral philosophical landscape and discovering what a jumble of theories, methodologies, questions, and presuppositions it actually is. She is no longer sure that the different characters in this philosophical drama are talking about the same things. She wonders if there are any principles or even aims shared across the whole spectrum of positions, and whether there could be any legitimate means to claim that genuine progress is achievable in this field. As disturbing as her experience may be, it is only once she has analyzed the broad framework of ethics and grasped its confusions that she can more fully appreciate and adopt the Socratic strategy of pressing for answers that reach deeper than conventional ones.

What is perhaps most discomforting for those students of moral philosophy who avoid the temptations to specialize too early and who study a wide array of ethical approaches, hopefully with some sensitivity to differences between ancients and moderns, is that there appears to be no golden thread weaving through the labyrinth of the history of moral philosophy. The reason for this is that moral philosophy is not composed of just one maze; there are many, and each has its own parameters and motivating questions. Nietzsche is the better guide, not Rawls, for recognizing that what is at work in the history of moral philosophy is that there are different moralities. Though hardly Nietzscheans in the conventional sense, Anscombe, MacIntyre, and a few others often counted in the early virtue ethical camp extend this Nietzschean insight in their own distinctive critiques of modernity.[3] Not only are there different moralities, but

---

3. "This book (1886) [*Beyond Good and Evil*] is in all essentials a *critique of modernity,* not excluding the modern sciences, modern arts, and even modern politics, along with pointers to a contrary type that is as little modern as possible—a noble,

there are opposing moralities—opposing scales of values, opposing descriptions of practical rationality, and opposing descriptions of foundational virtues, such as justice. Some moral philosophers, including some virtue ethicists, seek to downplay these oppositions. Often, the strategy in such efforts is to paint the opposing side in colors drawn from one's own favored palate. Consider how Rawls, for instance, presents his *Theory of Justice* as an extension in important ways of Aristotle's project; this is possible because he reads Aristotle as endorsing a notion of practical rationality as tantamount to enlightened self-interest, and justice a matter of fairness.[4] Close readers of Aristotle, I will argue in chapter 8, will not find him in Rawls's descriptions.

The reaction of those attentive to basic oppositions between different moralities ought not to be, Bernard Williams's nuanced reflections notwithstanding, that of the cynic. Although it is the case that there are foundational conflicts within moral philosophy, and not much in it to teach us how to live well (for that is left to parents), there is nevertheless much to gain from studying moral philosophy. Yet, it can be gained only if we are attentive to the cross-purposes at play between different theories, as well as to the deeper reasons for such oppositions. I think it the case that the most significant reasons for conflict between different moral theories lie outside the boundaries of moral theory itself. These are the cultural, historical, political, and religious presuppositions that inform a person's, or a people's, ethics in the first place, and give shape to distinctive ethical theories in the second. Though there are still many who insist on a presuppositionless approach to moral theorizing, the works of MacIntyre,[5]

Yes-saying type." Friedrich Nietzsche, *Ecce Homo* in *Basic Writings of Nietzsche*, trans. Walter Kaufmann (New York: Modern Library, 1968), 766.

4. John Rawls, *A Theory of Justice*, rev. ed. (Cambridge, Mass.: Harvard University Press, 1971, 1999), 10, 22, 372–80.

5. This claim is explored in detail in MacIntyre's *Whose Justice? Which Rationality?* (Notre Dame, Ind.: University of Notre Dame Press, 1988), and *Three Rival Versions of Moral Enquiry: Encyclopaedia, Genealogy, and Tradition* (Notre Dame, Ind.: University of Notre Dame Press, 1990).

Rist,[6] Adams,[7] Appiah,[8] and others, though different from each other in other respects, show that moral philosophy must rely upon additional theoretical and nontheoretical resources for its own vitality. Attention to the background sources for differences in moral theories does not prevent one from judging that some moral theories have got things more right than others, or that there are better and worse resolutions to moral conundrums. What it does preclude, however, is the attempt to make such a judgment from a neutral perspective, for any would-be adjudicator of philosophical disputes is always shaped by a distinctive set of historical, cultural, political, and religious presuppositions.

If we are to take the traditional approach to distinguishing one discipline from another and look for the common subject matter, aim, and methodology at work across all varieties of moral theories, our search will be in vain. Moore and Hare were engaged in a different inquiry than were Plato and Aristotle, for the former were seeking to explain the meanings of moral articulations, and the latter to describe how best to organize one's life as a whole. Similarly, Rawls and Singer have advanced a different sort of project than had Augustine or Aquinas, for the former have sought to clarify the procedures for the successful use of instrumental reason without making any recourse to principles transcending a naturalistic perspective, and the latter insisted that human reason fails to be fully rational if not nurtured by eternal reason. All eight of these thinkers are counted moral philosophers, but aside from consideration given to voluntary action little else remains to unite their efforts under a single inquiry.

An approach to moral philosophical inquiry that employs careful reading, sensitivity to historical context, and the shifting meaning of key terms, as well as attunement to the most basic questions

---

6. John Rist, *Real Ethics: Rethinking the Foundations of Morality* (Cambridge: Cambridge University Press, 2002).

7. Robert Merrihew Adams, *Finite and Eternals Good* (Oxford: Oxford University Press, 1999).

8. Appiah, *Experiments in Ethics*.

animating moral philosophy, is necessary to move beyond the impasses that are readily apparent between different approaches to foundational questions. Though Aristotle was perhaps less attuned to points of conflict between different moral traditions than we are, it is false to say, as some do, that Aristotle had no historical sense or ear for genuine conflict between moral traditions. And it is from Aristotle that we learn "it is the mark of an educated man to look for precision in each class of things just so far as the nature of the subject admits: it is evidently equally foolish to accept probable reasoning from a mathematician and to demand from a rhetorician demonstrative proofs."[9] Moral philosophy cannot be judged by the standards used to judge another discipline, so our study of it requires a hermeneutic shaped by the subject matter rather than one imported from other fields. However, one of the points I have tried to emphasize is that not all moral philosophies, at least at first glance, share the same subject matter. Nor do they employ the same methodology. Nor are they pursued with the same aims in view. Once again one can ask, what justifies the claim that they are members of a single discipline?

It is the commonality of the foundational questions animating all traditions of moral inquiry, no matter how opposed they may be, that justifies grouping such disparate inquiries together. In some traditions of moral inquiry, these questions are made explicit, whereas in others they lie below the surface, but are no less motivating. Whereas it is the questions that unite different moral theories, it is the different answers to them, and the subsequent questions to those first set of answers, that account for variety and conflict between different traditions of moral inquiry. So for example, even though inquiring into the foundations for a metaphysics of morals is very different from inquiring into what it means to be truly flourishing as the sort of creatures we are, there is nevertheless a common set

9. *NE* I. 3, 1094^{b}24–27

of questions behind inquires like Kant's or Plato's and Aristotle's that makes comparison between their respective approaches possible. What are the questions?

The Most Basic Questions of Moral Philosophy

These basic questions are not always articulated in the same way, and it is much better to think of them in terms of categories of questions, of which, I argue, there are three. It is not always the case that particular adherents of a moral tradition recognize their answers to these questions as being in conflict with the answers provided by adherents to other moral traditions; it is not even always the case that such adherents recognize their approach as having adopted a particular answer to these questions. Answers to these questions, nevertheless, are always implied, even if only tacitly, by every party to moral inquiry.

The first category of question has to do with what a moral philosopher takes a human *being* to be. What is a human being? There is always both a particular and a universal dimension to this class of question: "What am I?" and "What is it to be a human being?" are two different, but related, questions. In contemporary discussions, this sort of question often takes the form of, "What is a person, as opposed to a mere human being?" Theories about human nature, whether it is good or bad at root, whether it is end-directed or open-ended, whether we find in it the basis for norms that we live by, whether it is the product of evolutionary development or a special act of creation or some combination thereof, whether there really is a human nature or if we misleadingly speak of human nature to describe beings who only come to be defined after they are acting, and more besides, all wrestle with questions that belong to this class. It is not only moral philosophers who worry about these questions—there are many philosophers working in philosophy of mind, personal identity, ethnology, and other subdisciplines who take a special interest in these questions—but worrying about these questions, or at a minimum adopting a set of positions with respect to them, is necessary for one to engage in moral philosophy. Why so?

Whether one takes the basic task of ethics to explain what we are to *do*—a decision-centered approach to moral philosophy, or how we are to *live*—an integrated approach to moral philosophy often identified with an ethics of virtue, it is impossible to proceed without exercising some conception of what *we* are. It is *human* action and life at issue in moral inquiries, and no matter of attempting, for the sake of avoiding controversy, to avoid positing a theory of what a human being is can eradicate the logical priority of employing one.

The second category of question pertains to what a moral philosopher takes a human life to be about. What is my purpose? What is the purpose of human life in general? Is there some overarching purpose to human life? This can be thought of as the teleological—in the widest sense of the term—class of questions. Ancient and medieval answers to these questions typically point to virtuous activity as in some way providing a solution insofar as it is tantamount to living a flourishing or happy life. So too do many contemporary virtue ethicists. One of the marks of the transition into modernity, as many of the more unconventional virtue ethicists have emphasized, is a rejection of classical answers to teleological questions. Some modern moral philosophers have taken great efforts to avoid formulating a careful answer to the question of what life is all about in order to deny an overarching purpose to life. Others have shifted the very meaning of the term "teleological" to construct a framework that emphasizes the consequences of actions as opposed to the classical emphasis on activity as its own end—in fact, in contemporary analytic circles of moral philosophy "teleological" is usually taken as a synonym for "consequentialist."

We can set the classical versus modern controversy regarding this category of question aside for the moment, for here it suffices merely to point out that denying that there is some overarching purpose to my life in particular, or to human life in general, *is* in fact an answer to this category of question. So too is living as though life is about the pursuit of pleasure, or the easing of other people's suffering, or the having of many far-ranging experiences, or the acquisition of a good will, or the exercising of one's will to power, or the enjoyment of aesthetic experiences, or the respecting of other people's points of view, or any other number of platitudes that one hears when one is pressed to say something summative about the purpose of human life. When plain persons describe,[10] often in a jocular fashion, the activities of philosophers, it is with philosophers' engagement with this set of questions in mind—as in "Philosophy? That's when professors talk about the meaning of life." The "professors" in question often conjure images of bearded men, canes, pipes, and jargon-laden discourse. It is ironic then that one seldom finds contemporary philosophers taking up this set of questions in an extensive fashion; perhaps they, too, find the activity somewhat ridiculous.[11] But, is there a more pressing set of questions than the teleological—pressing, that is, if we are to care for how we act and live?

Whether put under the spotlight of philosophical scrutiny or not, whether carefully developed or merely presupposed, one's answers to the questions in this class are necessary to the activity of moral philosophy. There is no thinking about what we are to do without thinking about ends. Action cannot help but be goal-directed, no matter how discretely we limit the goal in a particular decision-theoretic framework. What goes for particular actions goes as well for organizing our lives; one needs an organizational principle, and organizational principles are by definition telic. There is no thinking

---

10. I am using "plain person" in the sense employed by MacIntyre in "Plain Persons and Moral Philosophy: Rules, Virtues, and Goods," *American Catholic Philosophical Quarterly* 66 (1992): 3–19.

11. Talbot Brewer suggests that questions about the overall purpose of life have become a matter of some embarrassment for philosophers as violations of good taste. See *The Retrieval of Ethics*, 6–7.

about how to live our lives without thinking about its overarching purpose, no matter how fastidiously we strive to scrub our view of life's purpose of any definite dimensions.

The third class of questions pertains to what a moral philosopher takes as the source of normativity in ethics. Why should I live this way rather than that? Why should I acquire this virtue rather than that vice? What are the reasons for comporting myself in this manner rather than that? By what rule ought I to determine what to do in this or that situation? Is God the source of normativity? Or nature? Or evolutionary determinism? Or our will to outdo all others? Or reason alone? Or society? It is on questions of this sort that modern moral philosophers have trained their attention with nearly single-minded focus.[12] One can find answers to questions about the human being and human life merely presupposed by modern moral philosophers, but no modern moral philosopher fails to give special attention to normative questions. Ancient and medieval philosophers certainly deal with these normative questions, but not in the same way. The question for Aristotle or Aquinas, for instance, is not so much "How do I come to know the right thing to do?" as "Why is this action I know to be right, right?" The facts of our moral life, what counts as good or right, as noble or ignoble, were not in dispute for premodern moral philosophers as they are so often for us.[13]

This difference is one of the more salient reasons why so much of modern and contemporary moral philosophy has been focused on moral conundrums, a process in which one proposes a purported

---

12. The twentieth-century preoccupation in Anglo-Analytic philosophy with meta-ethics falls under this set of questions. For a history of that preoccupation, and one that reveals the very narrow focus of many contributors to it as well as the interminability of the debates within it, see Stephen Darwall, Alan Gibbard, and Peter Railton's "Toward Fin de siècle Ethics: Some Trends," *Philosophical Review* 101 (1992): 115–89. See also John Rist's reflections on this article in his *Real Ethics*, 140–44. .

13. The reasons for this difference are many, and one way to regard the projects of Anscombe and MacIntyre, as well as Charles Taylor, Bernard Williams, Philip Rieff, Leo Strauss, Eric Voegelin, and others, is that the exploration of those reasons are a central feature of modernity with which to wrestle.

dilemma, looks to the intuitions we have about how to answer it, and then tries to find which principles need to be employed to solve it. Worries about whether Jim should shoot an Indian, or whether we should pull a trolley lever, or shove a fat man onto some tracks, to name a few of the more vivid examples of thought-experimentation in the literature, have a prominence in current literature that is not to be found in classical. This is not to suggest that questions of applied ethics are sidestepped in classical philosophy, for we do find Aristotle, and especially Aquinas, dealing with issues of applied ethics, but they do so to show how to apply their moral principles, not to discover what those principles are.

The constant disputativeness among modern moral philosophers about the basic facts of human life and action suggests to some contemporary observers that moral philosophy is in disarray. Often, too, inferences are made between the state of moral philosophy and the state of culture under the principle that as moral philosophy goes, so goes culture. It is not, however, so certain that the state of things today is that different than in the time of moral philosophy's infancy. Socrates faced a similar set of challenges when confronting the sophists, those busybodies seeking to subvert what every good Athenian took to be right. Against the false perception that philosophy is simply the product of an advanced civilization, it is worth noting that ancient philosophy thrived at the nadir of Athenian culture, at that point at which classical Greece rent itself to pieces in the Peloponnesian War and its aftermath. A good case can be made that we have reached a similar cultural low point, in which case it is natural to ask: who are our Socrateses and who are our sophists? If we are to follow Plato's strategy, we can discern the veracity of normative positions only by weighing them against truths concerning human nature and its intrinsic purpose.

Discovering how a particular moral philosopher answers questions belonging to the three categories of questions sketched above, whether they do so explicitly or not, proves essential to making sense of his or her moral theory. The descriptive role of this way of inquiring into moral theories yields the principles we can assess as being either strengths or weaknesses of various moral theories. Such assessment cannot proceed without making recourse to a set of standards, standards that are built from what one considers the correct answers to these same basic questions of moral philosophy. The evaluative work of judging moral theories cannot, then, be done from some neutral point of view, but rather must be done from the position of the moral tradition of inquiry we identify, more or less explicitly, as our own.

This butts us up against one of the significant challenges for those who would approach moral philosophy in the way I have recommended: Are we justified in working from the position of our own—and with the use of this "our" I do not suppose yours is mine—tradition of moral inquiry and using it as a standard from which to judge others? If there are so many conflicting moral traditions of inquiry on offer today, how does identifying largely with one of them even come about? Is this merely a matter of the accidents of one's life, of moral luck?[14] Is it simply accidental that you have had this upbringing, in this country, went to these schools, had those teachers, and so on? Of course the whole of human life is hemmed all about by such accidents, but it would be wrong to think we are simply the product of these accidents. One of the central tasks of any philosophical approach is that of bringing to light the beliefs that have already shaped our perspectives, and determining whether or not they ought to be held on to. It is Plato who first teaches us how to do this, inviting us to sort through our false and true beliefs and striving to "give an account of the reason why" for our true beliefs, tying them down so they don't wander off like a statue of Daedalus.[15] Such Platonic

---

14. I mean this in Nussbaum's sense of the term as explored in *The Fragility of Goodness: Luck and Ethics in Greek Tragedy and Philosophy* (Cambridge: Cambridge University Press, 1986).

15. See Plato's discussion in *Meno* 96d–98b.

efforts are, loosely speaking, metaphysical, which is to say foundational in a way that goes beyond the efforts typically identified as metaethical.

Moral Philosophy and Metaphysics

To appreciate the sense of "metaphysical" applied in the last sentence, it is helpful to consider some features of practical judgments. To be human is to face difficult practical decisions with life-changing consequences. On such occasions, principles of practical reasoning are applied, even when not fully grasped or justified. Such principles are often little more than unexamined beliefs about how one ought to act when circumstances have forced us to apply them. Sometimes they appear in the form of exhortative idioms: "Always be kind," "Do unto others as you would have them to do to you," "Do the right thing," "Don't be dishonest," "Don't murder," and so on. More often, as many virtue ethicists have pointed out, they are prepropositional and emulative; we are animated by a desire to be like the courageous person, the just person, or the practically wise person, and so are motivated primarily by a desire to imitate those whom we admire. These principles are available to us sometimes as prepropositional and sometimes as propositional beliefs about the world and how beings like us are supposed to respond to it.

It is not that we carry such principles around like tools in our action-making toolbox. Rather, they are embodied beliefs that are experienced as though proceeding from our nature because each contributes to our second nature, that is to say, our ethical character. Such embodied beliefs themselves depend on still other background assumptions about how the world works, who is more and who less deserving of our attention, why the Golden Rule should be applied, what honesty's connection is to truth and being, what justice entails in the person we admire, and so on. It is these more basic presuppositions, presuppositions informing the presuppositions of practical deliberation, which I am identifying here as metaphysical. For moral philosophers and plain persons alike, it makes a tremendous difference what sort of metaphysical principles they hold, for they give shape and scope of application to the basic principles informing moral action.

It should be clear that nothing too austere or precise is intended by "metaphysics" here. What metaphysics as a discipline is, whether it is a legitimate discipline in philosophy, if it is then how it is to be conducted, and other related questions do not need to be answered to justify the claim that one's metaphysics, in the sense outlined above, is of the greatest importance for one's moral philosophy.[16] The modest and everyday sense of metaphysics is nevertheless at the same time surprisingly bold, even audacious, for it stakes out positions on how things stand with respect to the world. Is the universe ordered, or disordered? Was it created, or has it always been? Are beings end-directed, or merely the product of a vast number of efficient causes? Is there a God, or no God? Are goodness, truth, and beauty properties of beings, or only fabrications of our own evaluative powers? Plain persons may not ask these questions in precisely this way, but they do indeed wonder about such matters and hold views on them.

In fact, I would go still further and contend it is impossible to be human and not to have at least some vague set of beliefs about these and related issues. We are, as Etienne Gilson frequently pointed out, metaphysical animals. For most people, the positions held on these issues are in large measure a matter of inheritance—that is, they are received passively and inhaled in the cultural air we breathe. For

---

16. I do consider such metametaphysical questions important, and address them elsewhere, including in "An Aristotelian Critique of Gracia's View of Metaphysics," in *Revisiting Metaphysics: Essays on Jorge J. E. Gracia's* Metaphysics and Its Task, ed. Robert Delfino (Amsterdam, Netherlands: Rudopi, 2006); and "Categories and Metaphysics: Aristotle's Science of Being," in *Categories: Historical and Systematic Essays,* ed. Michael Gorman and Jonathan J. Sanford (Washington, D.C.: The Catholic University of America Press, 2004).

those striving to live reflectively, inherited positions are scrutinized in the effort to build a considered set of answers to these metaphysical questions. For all, holding a position on metaphysical issues supplies a background for the answers given to the questions pertaining to anthropology, teleology, and normativity that were just specified as basic to efforts in moral inquiry. To be sure, one can argue about the meaning of moral propositions, the status of moral claims, and the difficulty of certain moral conundrums without seeming to make recourse to ultimate positions, but moral philosophers do themselves and others a disservice when they pretend their metaphysics does not matter for their moral philosophy. Moral philosophy is concerned with reflective action, with our interactions with the world and those beings that compose it, and one cannot envisage deliberating about different courses of action without some ideas about the ways things are within the arena of the world in which actions occur.

Metaphysics is then being used here to designate one's positions on first causes and principles, even when one thinks that such first causes and principles can be discerned from an exclusively natural scientific investigation of the world. With this sense of metaphysics in mind we can see that for the greater number of moral philosophers writing today, "naturalism" is the preferred term used to encapsulate their basic metaphysical commitments.[17] Naturalism takes many forms, but in recent usage it entails the belief that there simply are no explanations that extend beyond the field of observable phenomena. Naturalism takes, then, Aristotelian second philosophy, physics in the sense of natural philosophy, to be in fact first philosophy. Although it is often triumphantly hailed as an anti-metaphysical position, it nevertheless entails a view of how things stand with respect to the world, and so is a metaphysical position in the sense of the term meant here.

---

17. One measure of the prevalence of naturalism is to be found in the 2009 Philpapers survey of what philosophers believe, see http://philpapers.org/surveys/. The prevalences of atheism, naturalism, and physicalism among philosophers are all notable.

So too are idealism, realism, skepticism, theism, physicalism, and the other -isms that entail pronouncements about first things.

Though broad, this use of "metaphysics" does not conflate one's views about first things with religious commitments. One's metaphysics are a matter of judgments about ultimate causes and principles that, at least in theory, are defendable by means of rational scrutiny. The principles of one's religion are received in faith and, though open to philosophical scrutiny and potentially rationally defendable, ultimately are a matter of holding beliefs about what one owes God. I think it important to maintain the distinction between metaphysics and religion, in part because I think that metaphysics names a legitimate philosophical discipline whereas religion, strictly speaking, names a virtue, that of justice toward God. Neither is metaphysics the same as theology, at least not sacred theology, even though theology bears a closer kinship to metaphysics than does religion.

Nevertheless, it is the case that theological doctrines do entail a set of positions about first things, such as: there is a God, the world is created, and our lives are directed toward union with God. The objects of metaphysical inquiry are canvassed in theology, and it must be this shared range of concern about ultimate causes and principles that is the source of the popular confusion of metaphysics with religious views. However, theological doctrines extend beyond the metaphysical scope of concerns with the special attention given to understanding the interrelations between grace, sin, and salvation. Moreover, theology draws its principles from revealed texts, rather than from rational inquiry into the nature of reality.[18] The special concern with salvation and the distinctive methodology of theology make it clear that it is a distinctive mode of inquiry, a distinctive science, from metaphysics. Nevertheless, one's religious views, that is to say the beliefs that inform one's religion, do have a profound impact on one's metaphysics in the more general sense in which the word

---

18. *Summa theologiae* I, q.1,a.1, *resp.*

is being used here. In a similar way, among those who identify as nonreligious one finds a connection between those beliefs informing their nonreligion and their metaphysics.

It would be a mistake, then, to pretend that one's religious views, or lack thereof, are irrelevant to one's moral philosophizing. Thinkers as diverse as the cultural anthropologist René Girard,[19] the sociologist Philip Rieff,[20] and philosophers Robert Merrihew Adams and Alasdair MacIntyre[21] have all made clear both the historical and the ongoing connections between religion and moral theorizing. No great perceptive powers are needed to observe that it makes a tremendous difference for the positions one holds with respect to the three foundational classes of questions specified above whether one is committed to a secular or to a religious way of life.[22]

This connection is even more easily observed when philosophy is viewed not merely as a specialized activity, but as a whole way of life.[23] This all-encompassing conception of philosophy is prevalent not just in the ancient Greek philosophers, but in those of the Hellenistic period as well. Even in the early Christian church, for example, the Christian way of life was commonly called a philosophy, or, as St. Justin Martyr calls it, the true philosophy.[24] Whatever one thinks about Justin's claim, there is something admirable in his bold honesty. He was a philosopher, which meant he was committed to

---

19. See Girard's *Violence and the Sacred*, trans. Patrick Gregory (Baltimore, Md.: Johns Hopkins University Press, 1977); *The Scapegoat*, trans. Yvonne Freccero (Baltimore, Md.: Johns Hopkins University Press, 1986); and *I See Satan Fall Like Lightning*, trans. James G. Williams (Maryknoll, N.Y.: Orbis Books, 2001).

20. See Rieff's seminal *Triumph of the Therapeutic* (New York: Harper & Row, 1966), and his posthumous work *Sacred Order/Social Order: My Life among the Deathworks* (Charlottesville: University of Virginia Press, 2006).

21. See Adams's "Saints," *Journal of Philosophy* 81 (1984): 392–401, and *Finite and Eternal Goods*; and MacIntyre's *After Virtue*.

22. The reasons why philosophers often have acted as though that is not the case is a subject worthy of analysis, some of which is pursued in the works just mentioned.

23. See Pierre Hadot's *Philosophy as a Way of Life: Spiritual Exercises from Socrates to Foucault*, trans. Michael Chase (Malden, Mass.: Blackwell Publishing, 1995).

24. *Dialogue with Trypho*, 8,1.

a way of life in search of wisdom that entailed the highest standards of ethical conduct, just as it did for Socrates, Plato, and Aristotle before him. He encounters Christianity as a man already committed to the philosophic life. Never once does he imagine his embrace of Christianity as the abandonment of his life of philosophy, but rather only its fulfillment.

We contemporary philosophers tend to be more narrow-minded than St. Justin Martyr in this regard. Philosophy is often treated as something we do, as opposed to an all-encompassing way of life. Pressures on philosophers in the academy to justify their tenured existence has no doubt played a part in our efforts to make it seem like we are doing the same sorts of things that our colleagues in the sciences do: investigating narrow questions, collecting data, collaborating with other specialists, and developing ever more precise—and so often obtuse to outsiders—terminology. Of course, many of these efforts are fruitful, but only if they are properly regarded as limited contributions to the grander aims of philosophy.

One way or another, the classical and expansive approach to philosophy will have its due. Try as we might to contain the contents of the different compartments of our lives, the demands for consistency and integrated living cannot be denied. Putting aside the demands for reflective integration leaves us at a disadvantage, whereas we are better served when we strive to be attentive to the ways in which the principles we rely upon in our moral inquiries are nurtured by our views concerning how things stand with respect to the world. In fact, it seems that no solution to the apparent multitude of moral conundrums discussed in the literature of moral philosophy today can be given without recourse to metaphysical presuppositions. Consider one relatively simple test of this that we will have occasion to revisit in more detail next chapter, the question of moral absolutes.[25] If one

---

25. I do not mean that supporting a position on moral absolutes is a simple affair, but rather that one's position on moral absolutes provides a simple test for showing the relation between metaphysics and applied ethics.

thinks there is no point at which one can rightfully abandon a moral absolute, that is because of some view about the metaphysical status of moral absolutes and their source that one has. If one argues for some nuanced points at which one can abandon a moral absolute, then one does not really think that there are moral absolutes, and that too is a position on the metaphysical status of moral absolutes. One's views on the metaphysical status of moral absolutes have profound effects on the conclusions one arrives at with respect to questions of applied ethics.

The case of one's position on moral absolutes brings to light another feature regarding the relationship between moral philosophy and metaphysics, and that is the significance of religious belief to one's metaphysics. Though there is not necessarily a causal relationship between religious belief and the endorsement of moral absolutes, it does tend to be the case that religious believers identify and rely upon moral absolutes at a far higher rate than nonbelievers. The prevalence of atheists in professional philosophy and a prevailing tendency to think of religious belief as a blind act of faith notwithstanding,[26] the differences with respect to religious or secular positions on moral absolutes is not indicative of a seriously religious believing philosopher being any less of a philosopher than an unbelieving one. If it were, we would have to say the same for the seriously secular or naturalistic philosopher, whose embrace of the secular or naturalistic worldview demands his or her allegiance to certain principles that have not been demonstrated because they are, necessarily because of their status as first principles, indemonstrable. Fortunately we do not need to sort through the claims to greater reasonableness on both sides of the religious and secular aisles to stress the importance one's ultimate views of reality make for one's moral philosophizing.

26. For the prevalence of atheism among professional philosophers, see again the 2009 Philpapers survey cited above. Brian Leiter's popular blog, leiterreport.typepad.com, provides a useful gauge of the status quo attitude about Christianity in academic philosophy.

The difference between a seriously religious and a seriously secular moral philosopher does not come through in the degree of analytical acuity either achieves,[27] for one is not in a better or worse position than another on this score, but rather it is in the metaphysical principles that inform one's moral philosophizing that we find these differences most pronounced. Is human life sacred? Do human beings have a destination beyond the natural world? Is God the ultimate foundation for our moral principles? Jewish and Christian philosophers, with of course all the appropriate qualifications, would answer "yes" to these questions, whereas those committed to a secular worldview, again with a bevy of qualifications, would answer "no." To be sure, much common ground can be found between the two camps on issues pertaining to what sometimes goes by the name of metaethics, or a consideration of the formal features of virtues, or the proper application of one or another principle. And perhaps this common ground, and the hope of achieving consensus, explains why there has been so much attention paid to such issues in recent moral philosophy. But, on the questions I have argued to be most fundamental to ethical inquiry, the questions pertaining to anthropology, teleology, and the sources of normativity, one's deepest commitments make the greatest difference. This is a matter of the metaphysical presuppositions undergirding one's ethics, and to pretend either that they are not there or that they do not matter can only serve to perpetuate one of the leading causes of what can seem intractable disagreements in moral philosophy today.

The metaphysical presuppositions undergirding this book are for the most part identified with the Aristotelian tradition, particularly the thread in the Aristotelian tradition that grants to Aquinas a preeminent place. There are of course many varieties of both Aristotelianism and Thomism, and so one should not imagine that adherence to this multifaceted tradition will yield results necessar-

---

27. By "seriously" is meant a position held with so significant a degree of conviction that consistency is sought between one's views on first things and all other principles.

ily acknowledged as true by other adherents of this tradition—far from it. Neither does adherence to this tradition render it an unsuitable resource to other philosophers not working in this tradition. The resurgence of Aristotelian studies in the last century, to which important additions have been made by those working in the analytic, various continental, and other traditions and the ways in which philosophers from so many different backgrounds have been able to learn from each other belie the claim that one must embrace a tradition of inquiry to really learn from it. Nor does being an adherent of the Aristotelian tradition yield ready-made answers to the challenges facing contemporary moral philosophers—even if one accepts a basic set of Aristotelian principles and his methodology, there is no assurance from the outset that one can use these to address adequately the challenges that face us today. What we do, however, have from this tradition are not only exemplars to model, principles to rely upon, and some tools to work with, but an approach to fundamental questions in which we can have some confidence for a number of reasons, not the least of which that Aristotelianism has withstood the test of time, and from which we can begin to go to work on current challenges.

Virtue Ethics and Moral Philosophy

The attention given in this chapter to the current state of moral philosophy, the fundamental questions of moral inquiry, and moral philosophy's necessary reliance on extra-moral principles has been sought to establish the basis for a critical evaluation of contemporary virtue ethics. Focus has been given to some of the deep-seated problems in contemporary philosophy because it is precisely the claim, first and most forcefully articulated in G. E. M. Anscombe's "Modern Moral Philosophy," that something has gone terribly wrong with modern moral philosophy, combined with her suggestion that we return to the sort of philosophical ethics advanced by Aristotle, which set the contemporary virtue ethics movement on its course. Anscombe's claims will be examined in some detail in the next chapter, but the point needs to be underlined at this stage of the argument that the initial momentum of contemporary virtue ethics, and that which garnered the interest of other moral philosophers similarly disenchanted with modern moral philosophy, was to find a way to jettison the dominant preoccupations and methodologies that have given shape to modern moral philosophy and to seek either to retrieve a classical approach to moral philosophy or to develop a new one. It was by and large this revolutionary impetus that defined contributions in the early stages of the contemporary virtue ethics movement. What happens to a revolutionary philosophical movement after its initial energetic period? One of three things generally occurs: either it fades away because it lacks the depth necessary to sustain itself, or it successfully establishes itself as a new paradigm, or it loses its rough edges and accommodates itself to the prevailing paradigm. We have already previewed how it is the latter two options that characterize the difference between unconventional and conventional virtue ethics.

The distinction between unconventional and conventional virtue ethics is not readily discernable in the early works of this movement.[28] The ethical writings of Elizabeth Anscombe,[29] G. H. Von Wright,[30]

28. James D. Wallace's *Virtues and Vices* (Ithaca, N.Y.: Cornell University Press, 1978) perhaps provides an exception. His intention, he tells us in the introduction, had been to follow Anscombe's recommendation and provide an account of the virtues that is not reliant on a normative structure. He found, however, that he cannot, at least not for some of the virtues. The normative structure he employs, however, is variously Kantian, Humean, and Rawlsian. Some other features of his work, however, are on the unconventional side of the divide, such as his view of life as fundamentally normative—a teleological perspective that one finds in general disfavor in modern and contemporary moral philosophy.

29. Several collections of these can be found. See *Ethics, Religion, and Politics*, vol. 3 of *The Collected Papers of G. E. M. Anscombe* (Minneapolis: University of Minnesota Press, 1981); *Human Life, Action, and Ethics*, ed. Mary Geach and Luke Gormally (Charlottesville, Va.: Imprint Academic, 2005); and *Faith in a Hard Ground: Essays on Religion, Philosophy, and Ethics*, ed. Mary Geach and Luke Gormally (Charlottesville, Va.: Imprint Academic, 2008).

30. *The Varieties of Goodness* (London: Routledge and Kegan Paul, 1963). Von Wright is less well known now than the other writers in this list. His seventh chapter takes up the

Philippa Foot,[31] Peter Geach,[32] Alasdair MacIntyre,[33] Bernard Williams,[34] and others were all regarded with a high degree of suspicion by dominant voices in moral philosophy because of the radical nature of their proposals. One of the things they all share in common is a deep suspicion of that notion at the heart of the modern moral project, that acting in a morally right manner is dependent on the correct application of a particular rule. Whether that rule is Kant's categorical imperative or Mill's Greatest Happiness Principle, what the modern project shares in common is the insistence that there is a special class of human actions that can be described as moral, and only those rule-grounded actions belong to it. This, the unconventional defenders of virtue insisted, inappropriately narrows the range of ethical reflection and so forestalls inquiry into areas of moral philosophical reflection that are in fact of central importance.

More conventional virtue ethical approaches tend to be marked by a similar narrowing of focus characteristic of the modern moral project. The development of these approaches that accommodate themselves to the prevailing paradigm in modern moral philosophy is gradual and eclectic. There remain, moreover, significant efforts to establish the revolutionary elements as a new paradigm while combining these features with elements of the conventional approach, such as Russell's defense of a Hard Virtue Ethics in *Practical Intelligence and the Virtues*.[35] The mainstream virtue ethical movement is

---

problem of virtue, but the whole is an attempt to think through a new way to approach doing moral philosophy by recognizing the priority of nonmoral senses of "good."

31. *Virtues and Vices, and Other Essays in Moral Philosophy* (Oxford: Clarendon Press, 1978).

32. *The Virtues* (Cambridge: Cambridge University Press, 1977).

33. By any stretch a voluminous writer before the publication of *After Virtue*, MacIntyre is a relative latecomer to the virtue theoretic scene.

34. *Ethics and the Limits of Philosophy* (Cambridge, Mass.: Harvard University Press, 1985).

35. There are elements both of an unconventional approach to virtue ethics in this work, such as his strong defense of the unity of the virtues, and of a conventional approach to virtue ethics, such as a focus on making the case that virtue ethics can be action-guiding.

epitomized in one way by Rosalind Hursthouse's *On Virtue Ethics*,[36] and in another by two of Michael Slote's works, *From Morality to Virtue*,[37] and *Morals from Motives*. Their work has awakened thinkers to a number of overlooked but important issues in moral philosophy, especially by bringing to mind again the importance of dealing in a rigorous philosophical manner with questions pertaining to human nature and the ends of human life. They have also developed a largely successful set of polemical responses to many features of the other moral theories popular today. Many well-fashioned critiques of deontology and consequentialism have been forged in the polemical fires of these and other thinkers who see themselves, or at least are seen by others, as proponents of the virtue ethics movement. A critical evaluation of the contemporary virtue ethics movement considered as a whole is pursued in this book, but claims made with respect to marginal virtue ethics often cannot be applied to mainstream, and vice versa. Care will be taken throughout to specify whether it is virtue ethics considered as a whole, as unconventional, or as conventional, that is under consideration in particular discussions.

The status virtue ethics has achieved in contemporary moral philosophy is itself enough to warrant an assessment of its strengths and weaknesses. The fact that this movement does not have the sort of theoretical cohesion evident in the other dominant moral theories, such as consequentialism, deontology, sentimentalism, or contractualism, makes this assessment particularly challenging. This is, perhaps, one reason why no other book-length critical appraisal of this movement has yet to appear. Most criticisms of virtue ethics, and there are many, do not criticize it from a perspective within the Aristotelian tradition, but there have been a few to do so,[38] and we will have occasion to reflect on some insights from articles by Peter

---

36. Rosalind Hursthouse, *On Virtue Ethics* (Oxford: Oxford University Press, 1999).
37. Michael Slote, *From Morality to Virtue* (Oxford: Oxford University Press, 1992).
38. Though I think it fair to describe each of these three thinkers as Aristotelians, they are Aristotelians of very different types.

Simpson,[39] Martha Nussbaum,[40] and Christopher Miles Coope in the pages to follow.[41]

※

It will be helpful to keep four questions before us as we seek to understand the particular features intrinsic to the contemporary virtue ethics movement. First, what exactly is contemporary virtue ethics? We have already canvassed some of the reasons why answering this question is difficult. There are many varieties of virtue ethicists who look to a variety of sources for their inspiration. Among these varieties, there are significant disagreements about what precisely virtue is, what makes a virtue a good for a human being, and what the connection is between a good human life and the virtues.

Second, does contemporary virtue ethics provide a viable alternative to the two most prominent ethical theories adhered to by contemporary moral philosophers, consequentialism and deontology? We will find that describing itself as such a third, and better, way is one of the hallmarks of virtue ethics literature. The common strategy, and one that certainly seems on the right track, is to argue that contemporary virtue ethics is positioned to answer the central question of ethics—how ought one to live?—in a far more suitable manner than the other two approaches. But does one in fact find the resources within the mainstream virtue ethics literature to answer this question suitably? It is a negative answer to this question that prompts the third.

Third, why is it that contemporary virtue ethics fails to provide the resources necessary to respond sufficiently to the central questions of ethics? It is certainly not my position that either consequentialism or deontology, or sentimentalism or contractualism for that matter, has theoretical or normative advantages over contemporary virtue ethics. Of the alternatives, one must give the nod to contem-

---

39. Simpson, "Contemporary Virtue Ethics and Aristotle."
40. Nussbaum, "Virtue Ethics: A Misleading Category?"
41. Coope, "Modern Virtue Ethics."

porary virtue ethics. But, in its attempts to reconstruct facets of the Aristotelian legacy of the virtues, contemporary virtue ethicists have for the most part not made sufficient use of the underpinnings of Aristotle's own account of the virtues. The measure by means of which this judgment is defended is the degree of success that contemporary virtue ethics has had in addressing what have been described in this chapter as the foundational questions of moral philosophy.

This prompts a fourth question: is a virtue-focused approach to moral philosophy viable? I argue that it is, and that its success depends upon an approach that incorporates something more akin to the anthropological, teleological, and normative underpinnings found in the broadly conceived Aristotelian tradition of moral inquiry.

Chapter 2

ORIGINS OF CONTEMPORARY VIRTUE ETHICS

But not every action nor every passion admits of a mean; for some have names that already imply badness, e.g. spite, shamelessness, envy, and in the case of actions adultery, theft, murder; for all of these and suchlike things imply by their names that they are themselves bad, and not the excesses or deficiencies of them. It is not possible, then, ever to be right with regard to them; one must always be wrong. Nor does goodness or badness with regard to such things depend on committing adultery with the right woman, at the right time, and in the right way, but simply to do any of them is to go wrong.

Aristotle, *NE* II 6, 1107^{a}9–17

We need to understand more clearly what contemporary virtue ethics is, and this entails a more detailed focus on its relatively short history. Even a movement with a short history, however, cannot incorporate every detail of its development, and so one's historical focus must be selective. Of what are the following two chapters a selective history?

Julia Annas points out that virtue ethics has long been the default position of ethical theorists, with the notable exception of the modern moral theorists.[1] Because of the dominance of modern moral philosophy, those approaches inspired by Hume, Kant, and Mill, and the significant differences in focus and methodology between modern and classical approaches to ethics, the point of entry for virtue ethicists has been polemical: they seek to point out the failures of the modern moral project in order to reintroduce the classical and default position. Annas's observation on the default ethical position brilliantly reverses the tables so that it is the other camp, that of the modern moral theorists, that bears the burden of proof to establish their approach as representative of moral philosophy. A history of contemporary virtue ethics might be thought, then, to begin with Aristotle, or earlier with Plato; and, in some ways, it does. However, characterizing contemporary virtue ethics as a return to classical moral philosophy in the way that Annas does in *The Morality of Happiness* and other works tends to overlook those features in the contemporary virtue ethics which are unlike classical moral philosophy.[2] Contemporary virtue ethics is not simply a revival of Ancient Greek and Hellenistic virtue-centered moral philosophy, but a movement shaped by the very questions and methods of the domi-

---

1. Julia Annas, "Virtue Ethics," chapter 18 of *The Oxford Handbook of Ethical Theory*, ed. David Copp (New York: Oxford University Press, 2006), 515.
2. Julia Annas, *The Morality of Happiness* (Oxford: Oxford University Press, 1993). I do not mean to suggest that Annas thinks all modern virtue ethics successfully revives the classical approach. She notes, for instance, the distinctively modern, and she thinks wrongheaded, attempt of some modern virtue ethicists to take a reductionistic approach to virtue ethics: "Ancient virtue theories, at any rate, do not aspire to be hierarchical and complete. In them, the notions of the agent's final end, of happiness and of the virtues are what can be called *primary* as opposed to basic. These are the notions we start from; they set up the framework of the theory, and we introduce and understand the other notions in terms of them. They are thus primary for understanding; they establish what the theory is a theory of, and define the place to be given to other ethical notions, such as right action. However, they are not basic in the modern sense: other concepts are not derived from them, still less reduced to them" (9). Nevertheless, she argues that ancient theories of virtue line up with modern concerns with morality, rather than claiming that the modern concerns with morality are on the wrong track (120).

nant moral theorizing that it seeks to displace. This is the case even in its most unconventional varieties when it is precisely the dominant approach to moral theorizing that is being rejected. This is due to the fact that criticism of the prevailing focus and methodology of modern moral philosophy dictates the form that contemporary virtue ethical literature has taken.

The early stage of the virtue ethics movement in the late 1950s is, then, in important ways, something new: an Anglo-American response to the dominant features of Anglo-American moral philosophy. The ways in which this movement recovers features of classical virtue theory are partial at best,[3] and its critical engagements with emotivism, prescriptivism, consequentialism, contractualism, and deontology continue to give shape to what it focuses on not just in its polemical mode, but in its attempts at constructing a positive approach to moral theorizing. It is the well-intentioned attempt to be relevant, to engage the mainly analytic adherents of modern moral philosophizing in debate in order to disabuse them of their fundamental moral philosophical commitments and to persuade them to adopt a neoclassical set of commitments that leads contemporary virtue ethics to bear the marks of the modern moral project. It is the intended audience addressed by the literature of contemporary virtue ethicists, and the anticipated objections they will make to the virtue ethical project, that have given the virtue ethical literature the particular shape it has.

It is not the case, however, that only philosophers working in the analytic tradition have produced significant recent scholarship on the virtues. On the one hand, there has been an explosion of research

3. Julia Driver's distinction between "virtue ethics" and "virtue theory," mentioned in the introduction, is helpful in this context, for it provides a way to distinguish between revivals of interest in the virtues within the broader context of modern moral philosophy and attempts to found moral philosophy on notions of the virtues. "Virtue ethics" she takes to mean "basing ethics on virtue evaluation." Virtue theory is concerned with providing a theory of the virtues. Every virtue ethics employs virtue theory, though not every virtue theory is tied to a virtue ethics (as in Driver's case).

on Aristotle's ethics in the twentieth and twenty-first centuries by historians of philosophy.[4] The questions these historians of philosophy ask and seek to answer are of the sort "What did Aristotle mean by X?" "Does Aristotle have a consistent theory of Y?" and so forth; these are very different sorts of questions than asking whether an Aristotelian notion provides a better answer to a contemporary concern in moral philosophy. It is, however, the case that a number of virtue ethicists, indeed the majority of them, have sought to bring Aristotle's ethical notions to bear on the problems of contemporary moral theory. The degree to which these efforts have been successful in reintroducing Aristotle is addressed in chapter 5.

On the other hand, the twentieth and twenty-first centuries have seen a growing number of Thomistic scholars who combine the resources of historians of philosophy with a concern to make the case that the Thomistic account of the virtues and other elements of his moral philosophy provides a better alternative to its rivals. Students of Jacques Maritain are especially to be noted here, such as Yves Simon, but also Ralph McInerny, John Finnis, and Alasdair MacIntyre; each has contributed in very different ways to the tradition of Thomistic thinking.[5] Though there are various points of intersection between these thinkers and contemporary virtue ethicists, and some of the more notable contemporary virtue ethicists (such as Philippa Foot and Rosalind Hursthouse) have claimed inspiration from Aquinas,[6]

---

4. See the extensive bibliography compiled by Thornton C. Lockwood, "A Topical Bibliography of Scholarship on Aristotle's *Nicomachean Ethics*: 1880–2004," *Journal of Philosophical Research* 30 (2005): 1–116.

5. McInerny was a prolific Thomist, MacIntyre is one, and the contributions of the new natural law theorist John Finnis are many and well known, but Yves Simon—student of Jacques Maritain who taught both at Notre Dame and at the Committee for Social Thought at the University of Chicago—is less well known; see his *The Definition of Moral Virtue*, ed. Vukan Kuic (New York: Fordham University Press, 1986).

6. Of course G. E. M. Anscombe and Peter Geach would be the two most prominent examples of a convergence of analytic philosophy, Aristotelianism, and Thomism in the virtue ethics movement, if they were virtue ethicists. It is my contention that though Anscombe inspires the movement, she does not belong to it, and that neither does Geach.

the aims of Thomism and the aspirations of contemporary virtue ethicists are quite different, as are their respective histories.[7]

One does find many scholars of Aristotle's ethics and analytic Thomists who see their work as advancing the goals of clarity and precision, pursuing the hallmarks of analytic philosophy as well as making progress in our understanding of Aristotle or Aquinas.[8] There are, moreover, many points of intersection in topic and focus between the three movements. It is because of these intersecting points of interest—with defining virtue, cataloguing the virtues, and situating the virtues within the overall structure of moral theory—that the three movements are sometimes regarded as one. However, it would obscure the task of describing the contemporary virtue ethics movement if it were not disentangled from its older siblings whose projects have been inspired by a very different set of concerns and who judge their success by different standards. Scholars of Aristotle's texts share the peripatetic aim of interpreting his texts. Thomists seek to defend a comprehensive natural law–based ethics against its detractors. Contemporary virtue ethicists of the unconventional variety seek to show that an approach grounded in the virtues ought to replace the dominant modern moral philosophies, while those of the conventional variety argue that virtue ethics ought to share the main stage with the other dominant moral theories.[9]

---

7. Moreover, one does not find the same interruption of the default position in moral philosophy in the Thomist camps that one finds in modern moral philosophy—Thomists have, more or less continuously since the time of Aquinas, but certainly in a much more focused manner since the publication of Pope Leo XIII's *Aeterni Patris* in 1879, striven to think according to the mind of St. Thomas. They have been affected, to be sure, by the vicissitudes of modern moral philosophy, but theirs is a different history from that of the contemporary virtue ethicists.

8. See John Haldane, ed., *Mind, Metaphysics, and Value in the Thomistic and Analytic Traditions* (Notre Dame, Ind.: University of Notre Dame Press, 2002).

9. A third significant area of focus on the virtues has been developed within the growing field of Eastern philosophy. See, for instance, Philip J. Ivanhoe's "Virtue Ethics and the Chinese Confucian Tradition," 49–50. Particularly notable are those works that have woven together Confucian and Aristotelian ethical approaches; see especially May Sim's *Remastering Morals with Aristotle and Confucius* (Cambridge: Cambridge

There are additional reasons why Aquinas and his Thomist successors are marginal figures not just to virtue ethics but to contemporary moral philosophy in general. Aquinas is a theologian, and a Catholic theologian at that. He argues at length that the activities enabled by the virtues identified by Aristotle are brought to their full perfection only through the working of the divinely infused (rather than habitually acquired) theological virtues of faith, hope, and charity. So Aquinas's approach is not merely a modified Aristotelian ethics, it is an ethic that deliberately seeks to surpass in a way that completes rather than negates that proposed by Aristotle. Aquinas agrees with Aristotle that the acquired virtues are able to be identified and articulated and that each of them is a perfection of our nature; however, he thinks that our final perfection is something more than natural and that we can achieve it only should we accept the redeeming infusion of God's grace.

These are claims that one does not find in any major corners of the contemporary virtue ethics movement. They are found, however, in some varieties of what might be called a contemporary Christian virtue ethics, which has been championed by Stanley Hauerwas,[10] Gilbert Meilander,[11] and Jean Porter,[12] among others. The connections between these Christian theologians and those in the secular virtue ethics movement has, however, been mostly a one-way street—Christian virtue ethicists have been eager to engage and

---

University Press, 2007), and Jiyuan Yu's *The Ethics of Confucius and Aristotle: Mirrors of Virtue* (New York: Routledge & K. Paul, 2007). The fact that the Confucian and Aristotelian traditions are not developmentally connected but come to be compared only later makes the history of Aristotelian-Confucian virtue ethics unique.

10. Stanley Hauerwas, *Character and the Christian Life* (San Antonio, Tex.: Trinity University Press, 1975); and, with Charles Pinches, *Christians among the Virtues: Theological Conversations with Ancient and Modern Ethics* (Notre Dame, Ind.: University of Notre Dame Press, 1997).

11. Gilbert Meilander, *Theory and Practice of Virtue* (Notre Dame, Ind.: University of Notre Dame Press, 1984).

12. Jean Porter, *The Recovery of Virtue: The Relevance of Aquinas for Christian Ethics* (Louisville, Ky.: Westminster/John Knox Press, 1990); *Moral Action and Christian Ethics* (Cambridge: Cambridge University Press, 1999).

draw from the arguments of contemporary virtue ethicists, but not vice versa. Most contemporary virtue ethicists have completely ignored their work, and others have denounced Christian intrusions onto what they consider exclusively secular territory.[13]

These points distinguishing contemporary virtue ethics from Aristotelian and Thomistic ethics are stressed because of the frequency with which they are compounded. As true as it is that the majority of contemporary virtue ethicists have identified their approach with some variety of Aristotelianism, contemporary virtue ethicists look as well to other traditions for inspiration, such as the Stoic and more recently, the Humean, Kantian, and Nietzschean traditions. The fact that different contemporary virtue ethicists can harvest from these different traditions, each of which is in conflict with another on some central claims, and still count themselves as contemporary virtue ethicists, is a significant clue to discovering what contemporary virtue ethics is.

Despite the verity of Annas's claim that some sort of ethic of virtue has always been the default position of moral philosophy, contemporary virtue ethics is best understood as a very recent movement in moral philosophy.[14] As we will see in the next chapter, it has

---

13. Annette Baier argues that the distinctively Christian notions of original sin, divine law, grace, and supernatural happiness are fundamentally opposed to a legitimate virtue ethics in *Postures of the Mind: Essays on Mind and Morals* (Minneapolis: University of Minnesota Press, 1985). See also Richard Taylor's *Virtue Ethics: An Introduction* (Amherst, N.Y.: Prometheus Books, 2002). Given the historical continuity between the classical and contemporary world provided by Christian moral theorizing, calls to jettison Christian-influenced moral philosophy are, among other things, paradoxical.

14. Though *The Cambridge Companion to Virtue Ethics* includes chapters detailing a long history of virtue ethics, the manner in which this history is compiled points to the newness of the contemporary movement. Dorothea Frede's chapter, "The Historic Decline of Virtue Ethics" (in *CCVE*, 124–48), supplies an account of a rupture in the philosophical tradition of virtue-focused moral philosophizing, and Timothy Chappell's "Virtue Ethics in the Twentieth Century" (in *CCVE*, 149–71) provides an analysis of its reemergence. The narrative of rupture and rebirth is given a very new synthesis in the last chapter of the volume, when Christine Swanton, in "The Definition of Virtue Ethics," (in *CCVE*, 315–38) argues for a notional definition of the virtues that is intended to unite all virtue ethical theories and that is uniquely identified with no single approach in the tradition.

developed in a variety of ways, and has been variously described by its different adherents. Its origins are easier to discern than its later permutations, since we can trace its initial inspiration to a single and truly remarkable essay, Anscombe's "Modern Moral Philosophy."[15] Yet even in its first generation, one finds a curious division between two leading figures, both analytic philosophers associated with virtue ethics in the 1970s, Philippa Foot and Peter Geach.[16]

Philippa Foot's *Virtues and Vices and Other Essays in Moral Philosophy*, is a collection of essays, all of which but two were previously published, the earliest of them in 1957.[17] This collection represents, as she tells us in her introduction, her preoccupation with two themes, "opposition to emotivism and prescriptivism, and the thought that a sound moral philosophy should start from a theory of the virtues and vices."[18] The polemical character of her efforts is prominent throughout, and she herself remarks on the ways her early work was given shape by its attempts to distance itself from the Kantian project—as when reflecting on what she considers now her justly critiqued "Morality as a System of Hypothetical Imperatives," for proposing interest and desire to do the work that Kant's categorical imperative does and that Foot now thinks that a naturalized practical rationality does.[19]

Peter Geach's *The Virtues* is not primarily concerned to make the case that emotivism and prescriptivism are failed ethical theories, although Geach certainly agrees with Foot on that score. His main

---

15. The page numbers in what follows are from the most easily accessible printing, chapter 1 of *Virtue Ethics*, ed. Roger Crisp and Michael Slote, *Oxford Readings in Philosophy* (Oxford: Oxford University Press, 1997).

16. It should also be noted that G. H. von Wright devoted a chapter to the virtues in his 1963 book, *The Varieties of Goodness*.

17. Philippa Foot, *Virtues and Vices and Other Essays in Moral Philosophy* (Berkeley: University of California Press, 1978).

18. Ibid., xi.

19. Ibid., 157–73. She remarks on this work in *Natural Goodness* (Oxford: Oxford University Press, 2001), 60–61. The retrospective character of much of *Natural Goodness* provides a fascinating example of philosophical maturation over the course of a lifetime.

concern is to make the case that human beings need the virtues—and by "need" he tells us he has in mind something like what "need" meant for Aristotle, as a condition for flourishing. Geach thus employs an Aristotelian notion of teleology, and insists that it can be used in a way that is safe from the failures embedded in Aristotle's natural theories, which are poorly informed by flawed empirical evidence.[20] He also provides a fairly traditional Aristotelian and Thomistic account of the virtues, responding to real and hypothetical critics of such an account along the way. Geach's work is, then, a hybrid of sorts, combining elements from the three movements of scholarly Aristotelianism, Thomism, and the burgeoning virtue ethics movement.

Foot's metaethical and ethical efforts are secular in their metaphysical cast, even though they are acknowledged by her to have found inspiration in the works of St. Thomas Aquinas.[21] Her commitment to atheism motivates her attempts to provide an exclusively naturalized account of practical rationality. Geach's work on the virtues, also inspired by the works of Aquinas, embraces the Catholic tradition to which Aquinas is seen as a major contributor, and *The Virtues* is remarkable for its unapologetic theological commitments. Significantly, it is Foot's rather than Geach's investigation that provides the template for many of the virtue ethical investigations to follow. Yet both of them, and the many others to follow, can be seen to have drawn impetus for their very different projects from G. E. M. Anscombe—friend and colleague to Foot, friend and wife to Geach.

---

20. Significantly, Foot takes up this theme, and in an extensive manner, in *Natural Goodness*.

21. Philippa Foot remarks, "it is best when considering the virtues and vices to go back to Aristotle and Aquinas.... It is my opinion that the *Summa Theologica* is one of the best sources we have for moral philosophy, and moreover that St Thomas's ethical writings are as useful to the atheist as to the Catholic or other Christian believer"(*Virtues and Vices and Other Essays in Moral Philosophy*, 1–2). Though Foot begins her essay with these remarks, her contention that it is possible to use virtue wrongly could not be further from the Aristotelian and Thomistic claim that a virtue is such as never to be used wrongly.

Anscombe's "Modern Moral Philosophy"

"What is now called 'virtue ethics' is everywhere said to owe its origin, or at least its revival, to Elizabeth Anscombe's article 'Modern Moral Philosophy,'" remarks Christopher Coope in his perceptive and acerbic reflection on the vicissitudes of contemporary virtue ethics.[22] It is worth noting, however, that not every interpretation of Anscombe's essay arrives at the conclusion that she means to be founding a movement in virtue ethics. Julia Driver, for instance, notes there to be an alternative *modus tolens* interpretation of Anscombe's essay in her *Stanford Encyclopedia* entry, which, instead of pressing the standard *modus ponens* argument and arriving at the conclusion that virtue ethics should be pursued in the absence of religious-based ethics, proceeds as follows: "(1) If religiously based ethics is false, then virtue ethics is the way moral philosophy ought to be developed. (2) It is not the case that virtue ethics is the way to develop moral philosophy. (3) Therefore, it is not the case that religiously based ethics is false." Driver continues, "Thus, according to the alternative reading, one can conclude that Anscombe is arguing that the only suitable and really viable alternative is the religiously based moral theory that keeps the legalistic framework and the associated concepts of 'obligation.'"[23] Driver finds support for the *modus tollens* interpretation in Anscombe's doubts about whether we can at present find a nontheistic account of human flourishing. Driver does, however, note that Anscombe's own daughter, herself a philosopher, Mary Geach, endorses the standard *modus ponens* interpretation:

---

22. Coope, "Modern Virtue Ethics," 20–52, 21.
23. Julia Driver, "Gertrude Elizabeth Anscombe," in *The Stanford Encyclopedia of Philosophy*, ed. Edward N. Zalta, winter 2011 ed., http://plato.stanford.edu/archives/winter2011/entries/anscombe.

Note that this reading of the article is at odds with that of Mary Geach, who maintained in a letter to the *Times Literary Supplement*, in response to Simon Blackburn's 30 September 2005 review of *Human Life*, that her mother was "... proposing, in an atheistic culture, a study of the psychology of the virtues with a view to finding a clear and non-theistic method by which one could come to see the objective truths of morality." This view, though, doesn't seem well supported by Anscombe's clearly expressed doubts about developing a normative account of human flourishing that was naturalistic, and that would stand up to scrutiny.[24]

My reading of Anscombe favors Mary Geach's interpretation, but such an interpretation of Ancombe's intentions in this watershed essay does not imply that virtue ethics took shape in the manner Anscombe would have wished.

To wit, as Coope explains, Anscombe never referred to what she was doing as "virtue ethics." Her main focus was on practical rationality, seeking to revive a robust account of *phronesis*. Her work, and that of other early thinkers in this movement, is better described as contributing to what Coope contends is more aptly called "good sense ethics." The irony of mainstream contemporary virtue ethicists looking to Anscombe's essay as their inspiration is striking when one contrasts the radical nature of her views about modern moral philosophy against virtue ethical efforts to accommodate the virtues to modern moral philosophy. Coope remarks:

> At first—way back in the late 1950s—a virtue ethicist would have been someone who found more of interest in "Modern Moral Philosophy" than in modern moral philosophy. That article was disconcerting, and hence one expected to learn something from it. Turning to modern virtue ethics, what a contrast we find. It can be called concerting. Modern virtue ethics has become something soothing, edifying and familiar. It has grown up in the polluted atmosphere of contemporary expectations (assumptions, presuppositions, confusions, distractions) and naturally enough has quickly become tarnished by them.[25]

---

24. Ibid., note 2.
25. Coope, "Modern Virtue Ethics," 31.

In order to appreciate Coope's perspective on contemporary virtue ethics, we should first try to see Anscombe's remarkable essay with fresh eyes.

Anscombe posits three theses:

> The first is that it is not profitable for us at present to do moral philosophy; that should be laid aside at any rate until we have an adequate philosophy of psychology, in which we are consciously lacking. The second is that the concepts of obligation, and duty—*moral* obligation and *moral* duty, that is to say—and what is *morally* right and wrong, and of the *moral* sense of "ought," ought to be jettisoned if this is psychologically possible because they are survivals, or derivatives from survivals, from an earlier conception of ethics which no longer generally survives, and are only harmful without it. My third thesis is that the differences between the well-known English writers on moral philosophy from Sidgwick to the present day are of little importance.[26]

We see immediately the point of Coope's claim that the essay is disconcerting: if Anscombe is right, we need to cease and desist from engaging in moral philosophy in its current mode because we lack a coherent anthropology to support it; there is something profoundly amiss with our contemporary and prevalent use of "moral"; and the great variety we find in contemporary Anglo-American ethics is of no consequence—and that because of its near obsession with consequences. Anscombe intends her article to serve as an obituary for modern moral philosophy, and it is an obituary that lacks an encomium.

The Semantics of Obligation

Of the three, it is the second thesis that seems to have had the most effect on the literature to follow, and it helps to explain why so much early virtue ethical literature begins from the viewpoint of a

---

26. Anscombe, "Modern Moral Philosophy," 26.
27. For two such examples, see Kathleen Wilkes, "The Good Man and the Good for

critique of deontology.²⁷ It is sometimes overlooked, however, that Anscombe does not seek to do away with every notion of "ought" or "obligation." This could not be clearer than in her use of a non-deontological "ought" in the very formulation of her thesis that claims that the use of "the *moral* sense of 'ought,' ought to be jettisoned." What she means is that the special sense of "ought" that seems so interwoven within the very fabric of contemporary ethics, that which goes by the name of the "moral ought," needs to be rejected. Remove this thread, and the garment has lost its shape.

Nevertheless, "should," "ought," "needs," and related terms are needed to refer to ordinary senses of good and bad. For instance, for a lawnmower to be good—to cut well—you ought to sharpen its blades. Anscombe remarks that such terms as these are indispensable, and do not evoke any sort of "moral" connotations. The application of these terms in such a way as to harness connotations that indicate being bound by law is, she says, the result of history. It was Christianity's Torah-derived conception of divine law that gave "should" and its equivalents their obligatory bite. The modern world is no longer dominated by a Judeo-Christian worldview, and yet it is precisely a belief in God as lawgiver that is required to make intelligible a law conception of ethics. Nevertheless, the terminology of our predecessor culture remains intact. Anscombe remarks:

It is as if the notion "criminal" were to remain when criminal law and criminal courts had been abolished and forgotten. A Hume discovering this situation might conclude that there was a special sentiment, expressed by "criminal," which alone gave the word its sense. So Hume discovered the situation in which the notion "obligation" survived, and the word "ought" was invested with that peculiar force having which it is said to be used in a "moral" sense, but in which the belief in divine law

---

Man in Aristotle's Ethics," in *Essays on Aristotle's Ethics*, ed. Amélie Oksenberg Rorty (Berkeley: University of California Press, 1980), 355; Bernard Williams's chapter, "Morality, the Peculiar Institution," in *Ethics and the Limits of Philosophy* (London: Penguin Books, 1985), 174–96; which is also anthologized as chapter 2 in *Virtue Ethics*, ed. Roger Crisp and Michael Slote (Oxford: Oxford University Press, 1997), 45–65.

had long since been abandoned: for it was substantially given up among Protestants at the time of the Reformation. The situation, if I am right, was the interesting one of the survival of a concept outside the framework of thought that made it a really intelligible one.[28]

Where worldviews crumble, language remains—retaining the semblance of intelligibility but bereft of meaning. Hume, on Anscombe's reading, exposes what Kant seeks to clothe—namely, the vapidity of our language of obligation once stripped of its metaphysical underpinnings.

Anscombe argues that one can indeed accept the "bruteness" of facts, as Hume sees them, and nevertheless find transitions from "is" to "owes"—you owe your grocer an agreed-upon sum of money for the potatoes he delivered to your house;[29] and from "is" to "needs"—a machine needs oil to run well.[30] Yet she posits that Hume is right to point out that, absent a divine lawgiver, no implication can be made from "is" to the "ought" of the alleged moral type.[31] She concludes her thoughts on Hume's naturalistic fallacy in the following way: "I should judge that Hume and our present-day ethicists did a considerable service by showing that no content could be found in the notion 'morally ought,' if it were not that the latter philosophers try to find an alternative (very fishy) content and to retain the psychological force of the term."[32] It is precisely the attempt to wiggle their way out from the implications of Hume's observation, the attempt to continue to employ an unintelligible concept that nevertheless retains its "mesmeric force," an attempt to clothe what in essence remains a naked imposter, that leads modern moral philosophy to run amok.

This is just the place, Anscombe protests, where the lesson of Aristotle ought to have been remembered—that one can do ethics without

---

28. Anscombe, "Modern Moral Philosophy," 31. It is precisely this "interesting situation" that MacIntyre elaborates on in the opening chapter of *After Virtue,* 2nd ed. (Notre Dame, Ind.: University of Notre Dame Press, 1984).
29. Anscombe, "Modern Moral Philosophy," 28–29.
30. Ibid., 30.   31. Ibid., 33.
32. Ibid.

the notion "morally wrong" through the employment of aretaic terminology, such as "untruthful," "intemperate," and "unjust." With varying degrees of successful avoidance of the notion "morally wrong," contemporary virtue ethicists have striven to follow Anscombe's suggestion and to utilize elements of Aristotle's aretaic investigations.

Ceasing Moral Philosophy

Anscombe's first thesis, that regarding the need to desist from moral philosophizing in its current mode, has not been widely heeded. Anscombe argues that following Aristotle's path of describing actions using the language of virtue and vice requires far more than a well-heeled aretaic vocabulary—it requires an adequate and comprehensive account of human action: "In present-day philosophy an explanation is required how an unjust man is a bad man, or an unjust action a bad one; to give such an explanation belongs to ethics; but it cannot even be begun until we are equipped with a sound philosophy of psychology."[33] We cannot explain what injustice is without providing an account of what sort of characteristic a virtue is, and how it is related to the actions in which we find it. Anscombe contends that such an account is a matter not for ethics, but rather for a conceptual analysis that must be done before an ethics that highlights the virtues can be deployed. Before virtue, one needs a philosophical anthropology. Her insistence on this point explains the motivation for Anscombe's own work in intention and action theory.[34]

Some marginal virtue ethicists, most notably Alasdair MacIntyre, have evidently taken Anscombe's second thesis to heart. Most, however, have undertaken the task of reviving the language of virtue without supplying the philosophical psychology she calls for. Instead of painstaking conceptual analysis trained on action theory, we have seen in the mainstream virtue ethics movement the explosion

33. Ibid., 30.
34. *Intention* (Oxford: Basil Blackwell, 1957; 2nd ed., 1963).

of descriptions of the virtues, the effect of which, Coope complains, has been concerting. Instead of shedding light on key concepts in order to fill the explanatory gap described by Anscombe,[35] we find, Coope claims, obscurantism on key notions such as happiness, and the elevation of a reshaped and vague virtue. Coope again:

> The key notion of good fortune or *eudaimonia* was given a moral slant: "Eudaimonia in virtue ethics is indeed a moralized concept" writes Hursthouse (2003: 7). Goody virtues were soon being invoked (or invented or emphasized) by the dozen.... The new generation of virtue ethicists however all went for charity or benevolence.... Yet charity had inexplicably been left out by Aristotle.... Why this curious omission? How could Aristotle (to say nothing of Plato and the rest) have failed to notice what now seems to so many to be the most vivid and obvious of all the virtues? What have we learned since his day, and how did we learn it? There seems to be an enormous change—not to be characterized as a difference of emphasis! About all this there has arisen a not-to-worry complacency.[36]

Coope goes on to note that although Anscombe's fellow traveler, Peter Geach, emphasizes charity in his work on the virtues, the word for him names a supernaturally infused theological virtue, not the general benevolence celebrated by the standard-bearers of mainstream contemporary virtue ethics, such as Rosalind Hursthouse and Michael Slote.[37] For this and other reasons Geach simply does

---

35. "It can be seen that philosophically there is a huge gap, at present unfillable as far as we are concerned, which needs to be filled by an account of human nature, human action, the type of characteristic a virtue is, and above all of human 'flourishing.' And it is the last concept that appears the most doubtful. For it is a bit much to swallow that a man in pain and hunger and poor and friendless is flourishing, as Aristotle himself admitted" ("Modern Moral Philosophy," 44).

36. Coope, "Modern Virtue Ethics," 33.

37. Rosalind Hursthouse elevates charity to a master virtue when she writes, "From the perspective of virtue ethics, one can say that it is 'absolutely required' that one does not 'pass by on the other side' when one sees a wounded stranger lying by the roadside, but the requirement comes from charity rather than justice" (*On Virtue Ethics*, 6); and claims that every virtue ethicist recognizes this central role of charity: "Charity or benevolence, for example, is not an Aristotelian virtue, but all virtue ethicists assume it is on the list now"(ibid., 8). These claims leave undetermined such questions as: Which justice? Which charity? Which benevolence? There seems to be a Kantian notion of

not fit into the mainstream virtue ethical category and, if anything, remains marginal to the movement.

The point about competing definitions of charity is significant. Christian charity is a gift from God, the basis of our friendship with God and neighbor, and the organizing and motivational point of unity for all the other virtues.[38] It leads one to love others—and such love has both a unifying and a beneficent dimension; that is, it seeks to do good to others and it seeks union with them because they are seen as fellow brothers and sisters in a spiritual family of which God is the Father. Like Anscombe's observations about the philosophical cum theological account that renders obligation intelligible, charity is an intelligible concept only if its theological core holds true.

What becomes of charity when this theological underpinning is rejected, or at least considered irrelevant? Secular charity demands that we do good to others, but the important question of "Why should we?" has received very few attempted answers, and they are not especially inspiring. Consider Michael Slote's reflections on secular charity, or as he terms it, a "generalized concern for other people":

> The moral philosophies that today dominate the philosophical scene, (utilitarian) consequentialism and Kantianism, are both ready with answers as to why we must be concerned, at least to some extent, with all other human beings. And it has become difficult to accept any overall moral philosophy, like Aristotle's, that offers no defense of generalized concern for (other) people. Such a moral philosophy now strikes most philosophers as retrograde, and, more particularly, it seems to be unhelpful in regard to one of the great and central moral issues of contemporary (or modern) life, namely: how *much* concern or help do we owe to those, half a world away, whose troubles or sufferings we hear about and can do something to relieve.[39]

---

justice competing with a secularized version of Christian charity in the first quotation. Michael Slote writes: "I hope to persuade you thereby that basing morality ultimately in a motive like caring or (universal) benevolence or even love makes a good deal of sense" (*Morals from Motives*, x).

38. Aquinas, *ST* II-II, qq.23–46.
39. Slote, *Morals from Motives*, vii–viii.

To Slote the matter appears settled: charity, benevolence, or its particularized "warm" agent-based "care" variety, as Slote will have it in this work, is fundamental.[40] Everyone, Slote suggests, knows this, or if they do not they are retrograde. Aristotle is retrograde and unhelpful with respect to the primary tasks of our age, and in fact no moral philosophy that fails to make secular charity or benevolence central is acceptable.

But Slote's explanation does not sufficiently explain why we should exercise charity. Slote tells us we should because consequentialism and Kantianism are ready with answers for why we should. He also tells us that it is retrograde not to express this concern for others. Slote's insinuation seems tantamount to a claim that charity is popular, other moral theories are endorsing it, and so should those who adhere to an ethics of virtue. If Anscombe is to be heeded and so an adequate philosophical psychology provided, then it would seem a much richer account of the justification and motivation for charitable action should be provided by Slote or others endorsing the secular version of charity. But that justification simply seems unneeded to Slote, and the pressing question for him is not why we should be charitable. Rather, he is concerned with such questions as whether we should care for distant and personally unknown persons, how we are to determine how much to donate, and how to balance universal benevolence with the particular care we should have for those we know and are responsible for. What Slote seeks in this work of his is not an account that charity is required, but of how we are to be charitable, and he looks to our sentiments for an answer.

What would a Hume, or more pointedly a Nietzsche, make of Slote's efforts? They would point out that the reasons that charity or benevolence seem so central have to do with the force the word retains from its formerly Christian context. Absent that context, we find a notion that retains motivational force without the content to

---

40. Ibid., 114–37.

justify that motivation. Here is Coope again: "Clearly, a reasonable virtue ethic needs either be Geachean or Nietzschean. In the early days of its revival it was more or less so. But what a falling away there has been. Nietzsche would have talked of decadence: meaning here the replacement of good sense by goodyness."[41] The concerting, consoling effect of the sort of virtue ethics championed by Hursthouse and Slote uses to its advantage a notion of "charity" whose continued force is merely accidental to the religious and historical context that invest it with meaning. Like the "present-day ethicists" described by Anscombe, they make use of a notion that has a noble heritage and retains motivational force but that is no longer motivationally justifiable. If Anscombe and Coope, and Hume and Nietzsche too, are correct regarding the way in which key terms can live on beyond the theological context that gives them their meaning, then attempts to employ those terms, like obligation and charity, outside of those contexts are suspect, and, to the extent that their moral theories rest upon those key terms, they are susceptible to devastating criticism.

Contemporary Virtue Ethics and Consequentialism

Anscombe's third thesis, that the differences between the many Anglo-American moral philosophies that can be observed today are negligible, is not the sort of claim to endear Anscombe to those with a stake in articulating those differences. What justifies this thesis? Has it had an impact on the contemporary virtue ethics movement inspired by Anscombe's article? To answer this question, we need first to look at her characterization of modern moral philosophy.

On Anscombe's view, what ties together the various dominant ethical theories in such a way as to justify calling them as a whole "modern moral philosophy" is their united anti-absolutist stand,

---

41. Coope, "Modern Virtue Ethics," 36.

which is put to the service of ends that justify means. "Consequentialism" is the term Anscombe coins for this. She observes that in moral philosophy since Sidgwick, it is considered legitimate to conclude that there are circumstances wherein it can be "morally right" to do something that is simply and absolutely unjust, like punishing an innocent man when one knows he is innocent. Anscombe reflects on these attempts to legitimize what both the Bible and the Greeks consider nefariousness in these terms:

> It is clear that a good man is a just man; and a just man is a man who habitually refuses to commit or participate in any unjust actions for fear of any consequences, or to obtain any advantage, for himself or anyone else. Perhaps no one will disagree. But, it will be said, what *is* unjust is sometimes determined by expected consequences; and certainly that is true. But there are cases where it is not: now if someone says, "I agree, but all this wants a lot of explaining," then he is right, and what is more, the situation at present is that we can't do the explaining; we lack the philosophic equipment. But if someone really thinks, *in advance*, that it is open to question whether such an action as procuring the judicial execution of the innocent should be quite excluded from consideration—I do not want to argue with him; he shows a corrupt mind.[42]

Anscombe is no Pollyanna. She acknowledges the significant role that the consideration of consequences should play in moral deliberation. She also readily admits we have yet to do the work, and even to develop the tools necessary to do the work, to explain why it is the case that the good man is the just man. She also does not have explanations for why a just man is one who would never perform an unjust action or why every violation of a moral absolute is an unjust action. Indeed, the metaphysical bases for Anscombe's own reliance on the inviolability of certain moral principles are never communicated, much less defended. Nevertheless, like Aristotle remarking that philosophical ethics can really be pursued only by those who have been properly educated about the basic facts of the ethical

---

42. Anscombe, "Modern Moral Philosophy," 41–42, footnote excluded.

life,[43] there is no philosophizing with those who do not recognize that there are certain actions that can never be considered just or good or right.

Why does Anscombe not provide reasons for why she thinks that violations of moral absolutes are never just? She of course tells us that we currently lack the philosophical tools to provide an explanation for why her position on moral absolutes is true. But philosophical explanations are one thing, and reliance on presuppositions is another. What are the reasons for Anscombe's presupposition regarding moral absolutes? We can only speculate, but it is likely that some of those reasons are nourished by her faith. It is not the case, however, that one needs to embrace Judeo-Christianity to think there are moral absolutes; Plato remains the counterexample to that supposition. It is also likely then that Anscombe is relying on insights about the very structure of the universe. In any event, the presupposition of moral absolutes is widely shared throughout the history of moral philosophy, and has long held a firm position in the legal structures of all variety of political communities. Anscombe may simply have thought it unnecessary to defend what she takes as an obvious point.

One implication of Anscombe's claim regarding corrupt minds is that on her view those who are willing to consider the suspension of moral absolutes for the obtainment of so-called good results are not in fact engaging in moral philosophy. Instead, they are engaging in a variety of sophistry that might more properly be called rationalizing. Such an insinuation is of course highly inflammatory for those who embrace the Platonic distinction between philosophy and sophistry but nevertheless are willing to set aside absolute prohibitions on actions traditionally described as unjust, but it is not one of Anscombe's goals to avoid giving offense.[44] No opponents were more odious to Plato or Aristotle, and none fought against more fiercely,

---

43. *NE* I 4, 1095^{a}31–1095^{b}12.

44. The charge of "a corrupt mind" indicates one is past the point of being persuaded. Aristotle reflects on such as these in the following: "Now if arguments were in

than those "wise ones" willing to give rhetorical cover to the corrupt. Anscombe is cut from this same cloth, and her essay is a contemporary assault on the sophistry of her day.

A good case can be made that identifying modern moral philosophy as consequentialism and exposing it as sophistic provides the primary motivation of Anscombe's entire essay. Her exhortation to cease and desist from moral philosophy as it is currently practiced and to rebuild foundations for ethical philosophy through developing a "philosophical psychology" needs to be understood as the response to the crisis she has discovered and named. Those other two theses are weapons meant to battle against the sophistical arms wielded by those she has grouped together and identified as her adversaries.

Consider further the manner in which Anscombe peels back the armor of some terms of central importance to moral philosophy in order to reveal what she considers the true nature of her enemy:

> It is left to modern moral philosophy—the moral philosophy of all the well-known English ethicists since Sidgwick—to construct systems according to which the man who says—"We need such-and-such, and will only get it this way" *may* be a virtuous character: that is to say, it is left open to debate whether such a procedure as the judicial punishment of the innocent may not in some circumstances be the "right" one to adopt; and though the present Oxford moral philosophers would accord a man *permission* to "make it his principle" not to do such a thing, they teach a

---

themselves enough to make men good, they would justly, as Theognis says, have won very great rewards, and such rewards should have been provided; but as things are, while they seem to have power to encourage and stimulate the generous-minded among the young, and to make a character which is gently born, and true lover of what is noble, ready to be possessed by excellence, they are not able to encourage the many to nobility and goodness. For these do not by nature obey the sense of shame, but only fear, and do not abstain from bad acts because of their baseness but through fear of punishment; ... What argument would remould such people?" (*NE* X 9, $1179^{b}4$–16). In this and other quotes from the *Nicomachean Ethics*, W. D. Ross's translation in *The Complete Works of Aristotle*, vol. 2, ed. Jonathan Barnes (Princeton, N.J.: Princeton University Press, 1984). It is for such as these that political institutions need to use force, not just the art of persuasion practiced on the few who are truly persuadable. Few things were more worrying to Plato or Aristotle than legislators who lack the requisite excellent character needed to govern well.

philosophy according to which the particular consequences of such an action *could* "morally" be taken into account by a man who was debating what to do; and if they were such as to accord with his ends, it might be a step in his moral education to frame a moral principle under which he "managed" (to use Nowell-Smith's phrase) to bring the action; or it might be a new "decision of principle," making which was an advance in the formation of his moral thinking (to adopt Mr. Hare's conception), to decide: in such-and-such circumstances one ought to procure the judicial condemnation of the innocent. And that is my complaint.[45]

It is passages such as this that justify seeing Anscombe as a champion of absolutism against a new barbarism of consequentialism. Moreover, one cannot appreciate the reasons for her call to recover elements of an Aristotelian approach to ethics without taking stock of her position on the inviolability of certain moral precepts. That is, she turns to Aristotle precisely because modern moral philosophy has proven itself unwilling to do justice to a moral theory's requisite reliance upon moral absolutes.

There is a notable disconnection between the departure of those Anscombe deems "consequentialists" from the foundation of moral philosophy and the reputations they enjoy. Consequentialists are to be found in nearly department of philosophy. They enjoy good reputations, are entrusted with the education of the youth of society's leaders, and one finds those they have educated running universities, hospitals, cabinets, congresses, and countries. If Anscombe is right, then the situation of consequentialism she unmasks is a problem that extends far beyond the pages of academic journals. Consequentialism is, moreover, symptomatic of a deep problem in the modern moral philosophy not just of Anscombe's day, but of much of the mainstream contemporary virtue ethics movement that takes its inspiration from Anscombe.

How can that be, especially when we find rule-based approaches to ethics, including those of the utilitarian variety, regularly criticized

---

45. "Modern Moral Philosophy," 44, footnote excluded.

in much of the contemporary virtue ethical literature? One reason is that there are a number of ways to critique a rule-based approach to ethics other than on the basis of its willingness to consider the occasional suspension of moral absolutes. The core of Anscombe's critique of consequentialism is not, however, that it is rule-based, but that it is willing to suspend moral absolutes.[46] And indeed, the evidence shows that it is possible to have a virtue-based approach to moral philosophy that endorses a version of consequentialism. For example, Michael Slote takes the side of Anscombe's opponents when he writes, "If killing an innocent person is necessary in order to avoid a large-scale human catastrophe, then one may and even should perform the killing. In such a case, we think a certain sort of moral shift occurs because large-scale humanitarian concerns enter the picture."[47] What is this "certain sort of moral shift"? It is the shift from considering the care of one's own character to considering the general welfare of a larger community. Echoing Machiavelli, Slote urges that on occasion we need to lay aside our own moral well-being for the well-being of the whole by committing an intentional killing of an innocent man or group of persons who are tragically at the wrong place at the wrong time.

Providing further evidence of mainstream virtue ethical complicity with consequentialism, Slote goes on to argue that affecting such a "moral shift" is incumbent on those who have taken on a role of public service: "For when a person has to decide whether to kill an innocent person in order to prevent a great human catastrophe, it is natural to think of her as having been effectively but unofficially *thrust into* a public or political role.... Political roles should override considerations of personal or family advantage in those who have a

---

46. "It is noticeable that none of these philosophers displays any consciousness that there is such an ethic, which he is contradicting: it is pretty well taken for obvious among them all that a prohibition such as that on murder does not operate in face of some consequences. But of course the strictness of the prohibition has as its point *that you are not to be tempted by fear or hope of consequences*" (ibid., 35).

47. Slote, *Morals from Motives*, 96.

deep and genuine love of their own country."[48] It is unclear how else to read this passage than that Slote is arguing that caring for large numbers of people obligates you to lay aside your care and concern for your own good—even the good of maintaining a just character, as well as your care and concern for your family and friends—such as not sacrificing them on the consequentialist altar of the public good. The underlying presupposition is that care for one's country requires one to sacrifice care for what is in fact just. The good and the just have been put at opposite poles in this passage, and yet strangely Slote hardly seems to notice. Slote's admonition is reminiscent of Adeimantus's interpretation of the wisdom literature of his day in the second book of the *Republic*, and a contemporary Adeimantus would be justified in interpreting Slote as having provided political leaders carte blanche for otherwise heinous actions that have been determined as necessary for securing the common good.

Rosalind Hursthouse, justly regarded as one of the most significant contemporary virtue ethicists, is more conflicted on the topic of whether one can suspend a moral absolute than is Slote. Consider Coope's interpretation of the underlying meaning of Hursthouse's discussion of absolutism in the context of "Irresolvable and Tragic Dilemmas" in *On Virtue Ethics*:

> Rosalind Hursthouse thinks that one would be "seriously lacking in virtue" if one has come to consider the world to be such that one is forced quite often—"not infrequently"—to lie or to kill ([*On Virtue Ethics*] 1999: 86). Again she maintains that "a too great readiness to think that 'I can't do anything but this terrible thing, nothing else is open to me' is a mark of vice, of a flawed character" ([*ibid.*] 1999: 87, footnote, italics omitted). All this suggests a consequentialist attitude; for after one has checked, and double checked, to be quite sure one has not been "too ready," one is presumably to go ahead. One is not to lie or to kill the innocent *too often*.[49]

Is Coope's interpretation unfair?

---

48. Ibid., 98.
49. Coope, "Modern Virtue Ethics," 51.

Hursthouse is very sensitive to claims that virtue ethicists are all too ready to throw moral principles to the wind, and she explicitly argues that virtue ethics is wrongly accused of doing away with absolutism in ethics, at least doing away with it easily or too quickly.[50] Nevertheless, her own account does not seem successfully to respond to the charge she intends it to. The whole point of an absolute prohibition on certain actions, at least as the term is generally applied, and as Ancombe takes it, is that it is always binding. A lack of appreciation for that common sense implication concerning the reach of a moral absolute becomes evident when considering an example offered by Hursthouse that is intended by her to make clear her endorsement of moral absolutes. This example comes at the end of a dialogue she pursues over several pages, in which she concludes with modest support for the absolutist position on ethical foundations: "I am quite willing to stick my neck out and say that we find the world to be such that no genuinely virtuous person would ever sexually abuse children for pleasure."[51] But is this, in fact, an absolute? The "for pleasure" qualification is rather unsettling. It is clear enough that she thinks that sexually abusing children for pleasure is always wrong (or at least it is not what the virtuous agent *would* do). However, is this meant to leave open the possibility that doing so for the sake of saving lives, or educational purposes, or whatever, just *might* be the right thing to do in some circumstances? Hursthouse's standard way of dealing with dilemmas is to ask whether a particular choice is in accord with what a virtuous person would do, and it is of course hard to imagine any virtuous person ever sanctioning the torture of children for any reason whatsoever. Nevertheless, her qualification is, to say the least, troubling.[52] In any event, there

---

50. "The preceding discussion of tragic dilemmas ... should serve as a corrective to another misunderstanding of virtue ethics: the idea that it denies that there are any absolute prohibitions, some particular actions that one is categorically required not to do" (Hursthouse, *On Virtue Ethics*, 83).

51. Ibid., 87.

52. For a more recent reflection on dilemmas and moral absolutes, see Hursthouse's

are no examples of unqualified absolutes that I have discerned in Hursthouse's works, whereas endorsing absolutes with qualifications is consistent with her other works. This suggests that Hursthouse endorses a weak variety of consequentialism.[53] At the very least, we can conclude that Hursthouse's defense of absolutism is atypical because it avoids both theistic and deontological principles, and because the absolutes she offers are not without qualification.[54]

Perplexingly, given her own position, Hursthouse's qualified prohibition against the sexual abuse of children is directly preceded with what seems a note of approval of that quote from Anscombe regarding the consequentialist to be one who shows "a corrupt mind." Hursthouse puts stress on the corruption being due to thinking *in advance* that there can be conditions under which violating an absolute can ever be just, and this would seems to entail endorsement of Anscombe's claim that the mark of a "modern moral philosopher" is

---

"Discussing Dilemmas," *Christian Bioethics* 14 (2008): 141–50. Her position in this article is, as far as I can tell, unchanged from her position in *On Virtue Ethics*. In remarking on an anecdote regarding a lecture by Anscombe that Hursthouse attended she writes: "One need not share her [Anscombe's] belief that lying is always a sin, nor her belief that God's Providence ensures that an agent will be confronted with a forced choice between forbidden acts only through previous wrongdoing of his own, to accept her point. I do not believe either" ("Discussing Dilemmas," 143). Lying is not always wrong, and neither is killing, as Hursthouse argues in her important work on abortion in which she recognizes that abortion is the killing of a living being, that there is something fundamentally wrong with a callous approach to abortion, but also that there are a number of circumstances that can make abortion the right action to perform ("Virtue Theory and Abortion," *Philosophy and Public Affairs* 20 [1991]: 223–46); for a discussion of the circumstances in which abortion may be justified see 236–42).

53. This is taking consequentialism in broad terms to include varieties of moralities grounded on self-interest, to encompass Hursthouse's conclusion: "My conclusion, in this chapter, is that it offers a distinctively unfamiliar version of the view that morality is a form of enlightened self-interest, a version *so* unfamiliar that probably, as things are at the moment, that is a dangerously misleading way to describe it." (*On Virtue Ethics*, 190). What makes her position on self-interest, which she notes is similar to those of Hare, Gauthier, and Singer, different from theirs is that unlike defending enlightened self-interest from a neutral point of view she does so from the distinctive perspective of the work she sees *phronesis* performing (ibid., 191).

54. The whole of chapter 3 of *On Virtue Ethics* deserves careful reading on this topic, especially 83–87.

one who considers that "in such-and-such circumstances one is to procure the judicial condemnation of the innocent," or the killing of defective children, or the telling of lies, or the sexual abusing of children. Nevertheless, Hursthouse's modest defense of absolutism seems to leave open the possibility that there are conditions in which a virtuous person may have to violate an absolute, and that seems to be a matter of envisioning such possibilities *in advance*.

Additional evidence for this consequentialistic cast of mind when it comes to looking at issues of applied ethics within mainstream virtue ethics is found in Justin Oakley's entry in *The Cambridge Companion to Virtue Ethics*.[55] Oakley posits the claims that virtue ethics has both illuminated a number of bioethical issues and that "its applications to bioethics have, in turn, arguably helped to develop virtue ethics as an approach more generally."[56] To defend both of these claims Oakley considers significant virtue ethical approaches to several of the most sensitive life-and-death issues. On euthanasia, for example, he commends the manner in which Foot's treatment applies charity in such a way as to show when it requires us to kill another person,[57] remarking: "Thus, in reminding us that euthanasia is death brought about *for the good of* the person who dies rather than merely at the request of the person (competent or otherwise) who dies, Foot is able to bring out the relevance of the virtue of charity to the question of when acts of euthanasia are ethically justifiable."[58] Euthanasia is a good for a person when the condition of that person includes significant disability and suffering, depriving, on Foot's view of flourishing, the individual of the basic goods constituent of a flourishing life. Unlike the theologically informed virtue of charity, this secular variety of charity is not anchored to an absolute prohibition against killing. Foot's position is further expounded upon by Liezl van Zyl,[59]

---

55. *CCVE*, 197–220. 56. Ibid., 198.
57. Philippa Foot, "Euthanasia," *Philosophy and Public Affairs* 6 (1977): 85–112.
58. *CCVE*, 200.
59. Liezl van Zyl, *Death and Compassion: A Virtue-Based Approach to Euthanasia* (Burlington, Vt.: Ashgate Publishers, 2000).

who utilizes additional virtues like compassion, benevolence, and respectfulness to help determine when terminating or significantly shortening a person's life is justifiable. Oakley himself endorses the view that euthanasia does not undermine a health provider's obligation to heal rather than harm because terminating a patient's life, in certain circumstances, brings a wholeness or completion to it.[60]

On the question of abortion, Oakley credits Hursthouse with shifting focus away from the question of whether or not women have the right to terminate their pregnancy, or whether or not an unborn child has an inalienable right to life, to a focus on the question of whether in the particular circumstances in which a woman finds herself it would be virtuous or vicious for the woman to abort her unborn child. Hursthouse describes ways in which abortion can be wrong when it is a callous, selfish, or cowardly act. However, there are times when a woman's decision to abort can be an expression of deep humility.[61] Hursthouse's virtue-centered approach to abortion is taken up by other virtue ethicists to address the question of prenatal testing and the decision to abort those unborn children discovered to have significant impediments to the possibility of flourishing in the ways in which healthy individuals typically flourish.[62]

Although there should be no doubt that a virtue-rich approach to patient-doctor care is of great value and has improved the medical profession,[63] there should also be little doubt that when faced

60. Justin Oakley and Dean Cocking, *Virtue Ethics and Professional Roles* (Cambridge: Cambridge University Press, 2001); *CCVE*, 200.

61. *CCVE*, 209.

62. Oakley focuses in particular (*CCVE*, 211–14) on Rosalind McDougall's recent articles, "Acting Parentally: An Argument against Sex Selection," *Journal of Medical Ethics* 31 (2005): 601–5; "Parental Virtue: A New Way of Thinking about the Morality of Reproductive Actions," *Bioethics* 21 (2007): 181–90; "Impairment, Flourishing and the Moral Nature of Parenthood," in *Disability and Disadvantage*, ed. K. Brownless and A. Curenton (Oxford: Oxford University Press, 2009).

63. Edmund D. Pellegrino's work has been particularly helpful in advancing this richer approach to medical practice. See especially his *A Philosophical Basis of Medical Practice*, with David C. Thomasma (Oxford: Oxford University Press, 1981), and *For the Patient's Good: The Restoration of Beneficence in Health Care* (Oxford: Oxford University

with difficult life-and-death issues, the mainstream virtue ethical approach endorses a view that is willing to consider those, admittedly narrow, times when it is incumbent on the virtuous agent to set aside a moral absolute. It is this very willingness to consider when, in advance, it is deemed morally good to terminate an innocent life or to violate some other moral absolute that shows the mainstream virtue ethical approaches to applied ethical questions to be most distant from Anscombe's recommendations, and in fact a partner in the consequentialism she decries.

Press, 1988). Unlike Foot, Hursthouse, Oakley, and other mainstream virtue ethicists, Pellegrino is not willing to divert from absolute prohibitions against killing, even in hard cases.

Chapter 3

ALL ANSCOMBE'S CHILDREN?

*The Varieties of Contemporary
Virtue Ethics*

> *If someone professes to be expounding Aristotle and talks in a modern fashion about "moral" such-and-such, he must be very imperceptive if he does not constantly feel like someone whose jaws have somehow got out of alignment: the teeth don't come together in a proper bite.*
>
> Anscombe, "Modern Moral Philosophy," 27

In pursuit of a clearer understanding of contemporary virtue ethics we have now considered the movement's place within contemporary moral philosophy as well as some features of Anscombe's essay that supply the motivation for its development. Some of the distinctive features of the movement have been touched on already, but a much more thorough consideration of those features is now called for. Therefore, we return again to the task of determining just what contemporary virtue ethics is, but now with an explicit focus on those features intrinsic to the movement itself.

There have been many attempts to describe just what contemporary virtue ethics is in the virtue ethical literature. Some of these are simply descriptive, at least for the most part, though a reader does find in them suggestions in the direction of support for or detraction from the movement.[1] Other attempts to define the movement have been made with the intention to criticize it, and one of the leading complaints found in such literature is that it is so difficult to determine what precisely virtue ethics is because there is so much variety among its adherents.[2] Others describe virtue ethics in order to lobby for their preferred angle within a movement to which they express adherence.[3] Some of these latter descriptions seem either unaware

---

1. Alasdair MacIntyre, "The Return to Virtue Ethics," in *The Twenty-Fifth Anniversary of Vatican II: A Look Back and a Look Ahead,* ed. Russell E. Smith (Braintree, Md.: Pope John Center, 1992): 239–49; Alasdair MacIntyre, "Virtue Ethics," in *Encyclopedia of Ethics,* ed. Lawrence C. Becker and Charlotte B. Becker (New York: Garland Publishers, 1992), 1276–82; Gregory E. Pence, "Recent Work on Virtue," *American Philosophical Quarterly* 21 (1984): 281–98; Daniel Statman, "Introduction to Virtue Ethics," in *Virtue Ethics: A Critical Reader,* ed. Daniel Statman (Washington, D.C.: Georgetown University Press, 1997), 1–41; Karen Stohr, "Contemporary Virtue Ethics," *Philosophy Compass* 1 (2006): 22–27; Gregory Trianosky, "What Is Virtue Ethics All About?" *American Philosophical Quarterly* 27 (1990): 335–44.

2. Conly, "Flourishing and the Failure of the Ethics of Virtue"; David Copp and David Sobel, "Morality and Virtue: An Assessment of Some Recent Work in Virtue Ethics," *Ethics* 114 (2004): 514–54; Julia Driver, "Virtue Theory," in *Contemporary Debates in Moral Theory,* ed. James Dreier (Oxford: Blackwell Publishing, 2006), 113–23; William Frankena, "Prichard and the Ethics of Virtue: Notes on a Footnote," *Monist* 54 (1970): 1–17; Robert B. Louden, "On Some Vices of Virtue Ethics," *American Philosophical Quarterly* 21 (1984): 227–36; Phillip Montague, "Virtue Ethics: A Qualified Success Story," *American Philosophical Quarterly* 29 (1992): 53–61; Nussbaum, "Virtue Ethics: A Misleading Category?"; Gerasimos X. Santas, "Does Aristotle Have a Virtue Ethics?" *Philosophical Inquiry* 15 (1993): 1–32; Jerome B. Schneewind, "The Misfortunes of Virtue," *Ethics* 101 (1990): 42–63; Simpson, "Contemporary Virtue Ethics and Aristotle."

3. Roger Crisp, "Modern Moral Philosophy and the Virtues," in *How Should One Live? Essays in the Virtues,* ed. Roger Crisp (Oxford: Clarendon Press, 1996): 1–18; Stephen M. Gardner, ed., *Virtue Ethics, Old and New* (Ithaca, N.Y.: Cornell University Press, 2005); Rosalind Hursthouse, "Are Virtues the Proper Starting Point for Morality?" in *Contemporary Debates in Moral Theory,* ed. James Dreier (Oxford: Blackwell Publishing, 2006), 99–112; Hursthouse, *On Virtue Ethics;* Hursthouse, "Virtue Ethics"; Christine McKinnon, *Character, Virtue Theories, and the Vices* (Peterborough, Calif.: Broadview Press, 1999); Stan van Hooft, *Understanding Virtue Ethics* (Chesham, U.K.: Acumen Publishing, 2006); Gary Watson, "The Primacy of Character," in *Identity, Character, and Morality: Essays in Moral Psychology,* ed. Owen Flanagan and Amélie O. Rorty (Cambridge, Mass.: MIT Press, 1990), 449–70.

of or insensitive to the many varieties of virtue ethics. Still others are more nuanced in their descriptions, pointing to fundamental oppositions in the movement and staking out a place for their own take on virtue ethics amid the contrasts.[4] One finds little unanimity regarding definitive features for virtue ethics within any of these classes of secondary literature. Permutations in definitions of the movement continue even in *The Cambridge Companion to Virtue Ethics,* where readers would, given the purpose of the Cambridge's "Companion" series, expect to find a fixed description of the movement.[5] The degree of variety of definitions of virtue ethics, competing approaches to it, and disagreements on its aims seem unprecedented in the history of philosophical movements. Is this enough to call into question the integrity of the movement and its claim to provide an alternative to other prominent approaches to moral philosophy?

Some observers have suggested as much. It is worth considering a second time Sarah Conly's efforts to summarize the different positions on virtue and the virtues already staked out in the literature at the relatively early time of her writing on the subject. Conly observes:

One's first impression on reviewing contemporary literature on virtue is that here, more than most places in philosophy, anything goes. Virtues may be learned like skills, or natural; unreflective desires (such as spontaneous promptings of affection) are considered virtues; introspection and

---

4. Annas, "Virtue Ethics"; Coope, "Modern Virtue Ethics"; Sean McAleer, "An Aristotelian Account of Virtue Ethics: An Essay in Moral Taxonomy," *Pacific Philosophical Quarterly* 88 (2007): 208–25; Amélie O. Rorty, "Virtues and Their Vicissitudes," *Midwest Studies in Philosophy* 13 (1988): 136–48; Michael Slote "Agent-Based Virtue Ethics," *Midwest Studies in Philosophy* 20 (1995): 83–101; Slote, *From Morality to Virtue;* Slote, *Morals from Motives;* David Solomon, "Keeping Virtue in Its Place: A Critique of Subordinating Strategies," in *Recovering Nature: Essays in Natural Philosophy, Ethics, and Metaphysics in Honor of Ralph McInerny,* ed. Thomas Hibbs and John O'Callaghan (Notre Dame, Ind.: University of Notre Dame Press, 1999), 83–104; Solomon, "Virtue Ethics: Radical or Routine?"; Rebecca L. Walker and Philip J. Ivanhoe, "Introduction," in *Working Virtue: Virtue Ethics and Contemporary Moral Problems* (Oxford: Oxford University Press, 2007), 1–40.

5. As noted already, the first and last chapters of the *CCVE,* by Daniel C. Russell and Christine Swanton, respectively, contain competing definitions of virtue ethics.

autonomy (presumably arrived at only through reflection) are considered as virtues. Virtue may or may not involve acting in accordance with rules one believes in. The virtuous person may or may not have an idea of the good. The desire to do what is right, as such, may be either the quintessence of or totally unrelated to virtue. And so forth.[6]

Conly argues that these differences are due primarily not to disagreements about virtue and the virtues, but to disagreements about what contemporary virtue ethics offers vis-à-vis the other dominant modern moral theories. The deeper disagreements that give rise to the secondary ones listed above arise from differences taken on three theses at the heart of debates within contemporary virtue ethics: "(1) that reason is means-end only, where ends are determined by some kind of desire; (2) that desires and emotions, and actions motivated by desires and emotions, can be morally evaluated as praiseworthy or blameworthy; (3) that states of character, somehow independent from actions, are central to moral evaluation."[7]

It is not the case that every virtue ethicist describes reason as means-end only, but it is the case that all take desire to be in some way fundamental to the ends we pursue. A qualification of the first thesis that includes the negation of the claim that reason is means-end only generally puts a thinker in the class Solomon designates as "radical," whereas an affirmation of that view of reason generally makes a virtue ethicist "routine." It is the case that all virtue ethicists adhere to the position that desires, emotions, and actions can be evaluated as praiseworthy or blameworthy. However, these two theses, taken singly or together, do not specify virtue ethics, for one finds them held by many moral philosophers who are not virtue ethicists. The third thesis, however, has generally been taken as sufficient to specify the movement.[8] Can we put forward then that the distinguishing mark of contemporary virtue ethics is some expression of Conly's third thesis?

---

6. Conly, "Flourishing and the Ethics of Virtue," 84.
7. Ibid.   8. Russell, *CCVE*, 2.

Perhaps. But, if that is the case, then there would seem a strange disconnection between the specifying mark of the contemporary virtue ethics movement and the Anscombean theses that gave it birth. Anscombe contends that the modern notion of "moral" is vacuous and that attempts to retain it are, in her word, "fishy." For many virtue ethicists, the return to aretaic language is made with the goal of avoiding Kantian or utilitarian moral vocabulary. If Anscombe's insight about the emptiness of modern moral vocabulary is taken as fundamental to the contemporary virtue ethics movement, how can a virtue ethicist speak of "*moral* evaluation" at all? Consider again the quote provided at the beginning of this chapter, "If someone professes to be expounding Aristotle and talks in a modern fashion about 'moral' such-and-such, he must be very imperceptive if he does not constantly feel like someone whose jaws have somehow got out of alignment: the teeth don't come together in a proper bite."[9] The evidence in the literature does reveal sensitivity to this concern of Anscombe's. If the evaluation of one's character entails applications of the contemporary sense of moral, then it would seem this concern with character is not a sufficient specifying difference for the movement. On the other hand, there are ways to incorporate a focus on character that do not rely upon the modern sense of moral. Is it only the case, then, that in some versions of contemporary virtue ethics the focus on character specifies the movement as distinct from modern moral philosophy? Alternatively, is there some other way to specify the movement? What might that be? Perhaps a different perspective on how to make sense of the movement is needed.

Identifying a Contemporary Virtue Ethicist

Virtue ethics is a movement in contemporary philosophical ethics that is not best understood by a common set of doctrines, principles,

---

9. Anscombe, "Modern Moral Philosophy," 27.

or commitments shared by each of its adherents because none can be found to serve as necessary and sufficient conditions for what makes a virtue ethicist a virtue ethicist. This is not to say, however, that something like Wittgenstein's notion of family resemblance could not be used to designate those belonging to the contemporary virtue ethicist family.[10] There are some common doctrines, principles, and commitments shared among some virtue ethicists, and other doctrines, principles, and commitments shared by others, but no common set between all of them that are distinctive of the movement as a whole. Such a family resemblance model does not imply that there may not be a few philosophical commitments shared by all virtue ethicists, but rather that, if some common commit-

---

10. Gregory Pence suggests this sort of model for thinking about the varieties of virtue ethics, and this at a stage in the movement's history that was considerably less complicated than it is now: "Some conclusions: a significant amount of material has been written about virtues, and they've become important topics in contemporary philosophy. Analysis of virtues will likely continue, but at a more sophisticated level. Some early claims about virtues appear to have been exaggerated. The arguments that *virtues* can replace *virtue* have not appeared (this problem is especially acute if justice is considered only as a virtue). Moreover, searching for a master virtue, or an essence of all virtues, appears quixotic. Differing historical origins, as well as differing reasons for valuing traits, preclude a common *eidos* for all virtues. At best, we have a family resemblance here" ("Recent Work on Virtue," *American Philosophical Quarterly* 21 (1984): 281–98, 294). Rebecca L. Walker and Philip J. Ivanhoe make a similar observation: "Although we cannot, and would argue that we should not, offer necessary and sufficient conditions for labeling a view 'virtue ethical,' there are significant generalities marking the family resemblances that virtue ethical views share with one another. In general, virtue ethical views assess human character as a primary mode of understanding the rightness or wrongness of actions and the goodness or badness of lives lived, view traits of character as stable dispositions to act and feel in contextually appropriate or inappropriate ways, and understand the virtues and vices as the primary mode of assessing character. As discussed above, we also accept that there is an important distinction to be made between views that incorporate accounts of virtue and those that are virtue ethical. Julia Driver has noted a distinction between virtue theory—giving an account of what virtues are—and virtue ethics—basing ethics on virtue evaluation (1998:111). We think a distinction like this is helpful in sorting out the difference between theories that merely incorporate an account of the virtues and theories that are virtue ethical. Consequentialist and deontological theories can include a virtue theoretical account while failing to be virtue ethical views" (*Working Virtue*, 4). It is notable that their list of "family resemblances" more or less corresponds to Conly's latter two theses.

ments were found, these would not necessarily be distinctively virtue ethical.

The metaphor of a family might be extended beyond its Wittgensteinian sense to describe the participants of the movement themselves. On the whole, contemporary virtue ethicists are an attractive family; they are concerned with living well, and they emphasize kindness, caring, and charity. More distant relations have taken an interest in their work—like the hoary-headed peripatetics and their younger cousins, the Thomists. These second cousins are often treated with respect by the nuclear family of virtue ethicists, but there is no replacing the bonds of the immediate family. Virtue ethics has its primary home in Oxbridge with its common mother, G. E. M. Anscombe; yet we have already observed that one finds a great philosophical distance between the grandmother of this movement and her children and grandchildren.

This extended family resemblance way of thinking about what contemporary virtue ethics is has its limitations, to be sure. Yet it does allow us at least to be in the right ballpark when it comes to noticing a virtue ethicist when we see one—a kind of "virtue ethics is as virtue ethics does" approach. It is not the case, however, that simply "looking" like a contemporary virtue ethicist—in the sense of being engaged in the sorts of activities that contemporary virtue ethicists tend to be engaged in—is enough.

We should consider a contemporary virtue ethicist also by way of self-declaration: a contemporary virtue ethicist is anyone who claims she is one. This condition, too, has its limitations. Consider, for example, somebody who plays basketball with other faculty members at lunch, but never played the game growing up. Do her current activities make her a basketball player? If another faculty member is fifty pounds overweight and hasn't picked up a basketball in years, but was a high school basketball standout, is he still a basketball player? The first person may not think of herself as a basketball player, while the second does think of himself as one, but a third party observer could certainly make the case that the first has more solid grounds for being designated a basketball player than the second. Similarly, calling oneself a virtue ethicist is necessary for being a virtue ethicist, but is not sufficient.

Here is a third condition in addition to looking like a virtue ethicist and declaring oneself one: such a person needs to be engaged in the practices of academic philosophy. There has been a renewed interest in virtue and the virtues by scholars in fields outside philosophy, for instance by educational theorists, sociologists, and social psychologists.[11] As encouraging as it is to see some interest in the virtues by those in these other fields, they are not especially attuned to the debates in modern moral philosophy within which contemporary virtue ethics positions itself. In a sense, they are doing what our parents did—telling us always to be kind, just, temperate, honest, and the like.[12] They seek to promote the development of good character using notions and terminology drawn from what Annas specifies as the default position of ethics, that of making sense of one's life as a whole by focusing on the development and exercise of traits of character, but they are not interlocutors in the current debates. To be sure, much is to be learned from them, but if we are to combine our three heuristics—family resemblance, self-declaration, and an academic philosopher, then we can exclude these peripheral researchers with an interest in the virtues from our considerations.

11. See for instance the online resources, initiated by Canadian primary and secondary school educational theorists, called the Virtues Project, at http://www.virtuesproject.com/index.php; the empirically based positive psychology anthology, Christopher Peterson and Martin E. P. Seligman, *Character Strengths and Virtues* (Oxford: Oxford University Press, 2004); Kwame Anthony Appiah's *Experiments in Ethics*, which seeks to engage nonphilosopher researchers in character and the virtues; and William Bennett's *The Book of Virtues: A Treasury of Great Moral Stories* (New York: Simon and Schuster, 1996).

12. It seems safe to assume that parents do not tell their young children to maximize their benefits or to formulate a categorical imperative. The fact that it sounds odd or amusing to imagine parents encouraging their children to reason like a modern moral philosopher indicates one of the intuitive reasons for the appeal of virtue ethics over modern moral theorizing; the former comes naturally whereas the latter has to be learned in school.

VARIETIES   89

We find it to be the case, then, that although we cannot find necessary and sufficient conditions on the level of propositions held by all virtue ethicists that bind this group together by a set of shared principles, we can nevertheless supply necessary and sufficient conditions for identifying a contemporary virtue ethicist: *a contemporary virtue ethicist is an academic philosopher who subscribes to some of the principles shared by some virtue ethicists and who self-identifies with this movement.* Applying these conditions is useful for narrowing the range of possible partners within the virtue ethics movement, but they achieve only limited goals of sorting out contemporary virtue ethicists from other identifiable adherents to dominant moral theories.

Classifying the Varieties of Contemporary Virtue Ethics

We have found a way to identify a contemporary virtue ethicist, but what sense can we make of the varieties of contemporary virtue ethics? Perhaps still another metaphor will be of use. Imagine a heap of clean clothes that has been amassed from piling up the yield from six loads of the washer/dryer cycle. What you find in it is a mess. There are several different ways in which you, the bewildered father of this family responsible for soiling the clothes in the first place, can organize this mess. One is to sort by color. All the reds go in one folded pile, all the blues in another, and so on. Another is to sort by articles of clothing—shirts here, pants there, and so on. Both these first two ways are not particularly helpful; that is, they will not get you much closer to returning the clothes to drawers. What you want is a method that will enable you to make piles of folded laundry, each of which represents one of the members of the family. That is the sort of method we should hope to find in order to classify the different varieties of contemporary virtue ethics. It recognizes that there are similarities that run through most of the piles (all piles have shirts, all have pants, some have jeans, most have white articles of clothing, etc.), but it focuses on the points of differentiation that correspond to the various people the clothes belong to. This way of sorting is made possible for our laundry-buried-father because each article of clothing has a history, and he can successfully trace that history (this shirt is worn by Jimmy; these pants, though they used to be worn by Maria, are now the possession of Helen; and so on). Though the example is of a mundane (but important!) activity, it points to the sorts of principles needed for producing a useful taxonomy of contemporary virtue ethics.

Most philosophers concerned with a taxonomy of contemporary virtue ethics begin with a significant distinction between classical and contemporary virtue ethics, and it will be instructive to consider this distinction, and how it is variously treated by two of the most prominent voices in the movement, before considering additional distinctions by means of which we can classify varieties of virtue ethics. We saw already that Annas considers virtue ethics the default form of ethical theory, with Kantianism and consequentialism upstart alternatives.[13] It is her specification of the classical and dominant virtue ethical approach that makes such a perspective on modern moral philosophy possible. This neatly turns the tables on the approaches that nowadays are treated as dominant. Rather than virtue ethicists feeling the need to justify their interests in the virtues and the role of virtue theory in ethics, Annas puts modern moral philosophy on the defensive, forcing it to provide the burden of proof that they have something new and important to offer.

Hursthouse also casts a wide net for virtue ethics, even wider than Annas's, so that it applies not just to classical theories and the recent resurgence of virtue ethical concerns, but to non-Western traditions as well.[14] Her encyclopedia entry provides a condensed but sweep-

---

13. Annas, "Virtue Ethics," 515.

14. This wide-open approach to including the varieties of virtue ethics is reflected in the collection of entries in the *Cambridge Companion to Virtue Ethics*, though it is not endorsed in each of the individual entries.

ing summary of her view of the field: "Virtue ethics' founding fathers are Plato and, more particularly Aristotle (its roots in Chinese philosophy are even more ancient) and it persisted as the dominant approach in Western moral philosophy until at least the Enlightenment. It suffered a momentary eclipse during the nineteenth century but re-emerged in the late 1950's in Anglo-American philosophy."[15] Hursthouse goes on to argue that dominant trends in modern moral philosophy have been enriched by the reemergence of virtue ethics, and also that Enlightenment thinkers themselves are now being shown to have been far more friendly to virtue ethics than originally thought. Kantians have been finding in Kant's *The Doctrine of Virtue* virtue ethical themes.[16] Utilitarians have begun developing virtue ethical arguments.[17] There have also been recent efforts to develop virtue ethical approaches from such ethical outliers as Hume,[18] and even Nietzsche.[19] Is it Hursthouse's strategy for defending virtue ethics as a movement to argue that we are all virtue ethicists now?

Yes and no. On the one hand, Hursthouse sees, I think, a strategic advantage in making the contemporary virtue ethics house a very large one indeed. On the other, she still wants to see contemporary virtue ethics, and naturally her own brand of it, to present some distinct advantages over other approaches. Even on this latter front, however,

15. Hursthouse, "Virtue Ethics," 1.
16. Marcia Baron, *Kantian Ethics Almost without Apology* (Ithaca, N.Y.: Cornell University Press, 1995); Sharad Deshpande, "Kant and the Revival of Virtue Ethics," in *Reason, Morality, and Beauty: Essays on the Philosophy of Immanuel Kant*, ed. Bindu Puri (Oxford: Oxford University Press, 2007), 11–25; Robert B. Louden, "Kant's Virtue Ethics," *Philosophy: The Journal of the Royal Institute of Philosophy* 61 (1986): 473–89.
17. Appiah, *Experiments in Ethics*; Julia Driver, *Uneasy Virtue* (New York: Cambridge University Press, 2001); Brad Hooker, *Ideal Code, Real World* (Oxford: Oxford University Press, 2000).
18. Slote, *Morals from Motives*; Jacqueline Taylor, "Virtue and the Evaluation of Character," in *The Blackwell Guide to Hume's Treatise*, ed. Saul Traiger (Malden, Mass.: Blackwell Publishers, 2006), 276–95; David Wiggins, "Natural and Artificial Virtues: A Vindication of Hume's Scheme," in *How Should One to Live? Essays on the Virtues*, ed. Roger Crisp (Oxford: Oxford University Press, 1996), 131–40.
19. Christine Swanton, *Virtue Ethics: A Pluralist View* (Oxford: Oxford University Press, 2003).

Hursthouse seeks to soften the lines of demarcation between different approaches to ethics. She argues in her central and celebrated work, *On Virtue Ethics,* how contemporary virtue ethics has been positively influenced by the central concerns of modern moral philosophy, and she anticipates an eventual harmonic blending of virtue ethics with modern moral philosophy:

> Indeed, I rather hope that future generations of moral philosophers, brought up on all three approaches [deontology, consequentialism, and virtue ethics], will lose interest in classifying themselves as following one approach rather than another; in which case all three labels might become of merely historical interest. But that is still over the horizon, for much of what those future generations could be taught under the label "virtue ethics" still needs to be provided.[20]

Working toward this singular moment, when all divisions between moral theorists shall be wiped away, and every distinction forgiven, emerges as one of the overarching themes of Hursthouse's important work.

Progress toward this goal of unifying deontology, consequentialism, and virtue ethics requires, in Hursthouse's case, seeing classical and contemporary virtue ethics as older and younger siblings of the same family: "But although modern virtue ethics does not have to take the form known as 'neo-Aristotelian,' almost any modern version still shows that its roots are in ancient Greek philosophy by the employment of three concepts derived from it. These are *arête* (excellence or virtue) *phronesis* (practical or moral wisdom) and *eudaimonia* (usually translated as happiness or flourishing)."[21] Certainly it is the case that all philosophical discussions of virtue, practical wisdom, and flourishing have their origins in ancient Greek philosophy. Hobbes, Locke, Rousseau, Hume, Kant, Mill, Nietzsche, and Rawls all discuss these notions, and they could not do so were it not for the contributions of Plato, and especially Aristotle.

20. Hursthouse, *On Virtue Ethics,* 5.
21. Hursthouse, "Virtue Ethics," 2.

However, do we in fact find the seeds by which unification of all moral theories can be achieved to be found within these virtue ethical notions noted by Hursthouse? What MacIntyre in *After Virtue* and *Whose Justice? Which Rationality?*, and Anscombe in "Modern Moral Philosophy," teach us is that these notions often mean very different things for these different thinkers, and that one of the central lessons to be taken from a careful history of philosophy is that much of the modern project in philosophy is to be understood by way of its deliberate rejection of the Aristotelian project—even if oftentimes it was only a caricature of the Aristotelian project that was being rejected.

It is Nietzsche, as MacIntyre takes pains to show us, who does the most to make this contrast between Aristotelian and anti-Aristotelian sorts of moral projects clear—even if he himself did not sufficiently take note of it with respect to the moderns he criticizes:

> But [Nietzsche's] interpretation of the history of morality makes it quite clear that the Aristotelian account of ethics and politics would have to rank for Nietzsche with all those degenerate disguises of the will to power which follow from the false turning taken by Socrates.... In a much stronger sense Nietzsche's moral philosophy is matched specifically against Aristotle's by virtue of the historical role which each plays. For ... it was because a moral tradition of which Aristotle's thought was the intellectual core was repudiated during the transitions of the fifteenth to seventeenth centuries that the Enlightenment project of discovering new rational secular foundations for morality had to be undertaken. And it was because that project failed, because the views advanced by its most intellectually powerful protagonists, and more especially by Kant, could not be sustained in the face of rational criticism that Nietzsche and all his existentialist and emotivist successors were able to mount their apparently successful critique of all previous morality.[22]

MacIntyre argues that Aristotelianism did not so much fail as it was simply cast aside. Modern moral philosophy arises to replace it—but

---

22. MacIntyre, *After Virtue*, 117.

it is shown to fail by means of Nietzsche's successful efforts at demonstrating all attempts at non-Aristotelian rational vindications of morality to be nothing but so many masks worn by a nonrational will. If MacIntyre is right, any effort, such as Hursthouse's, to harmonize Aristotelian ethical theory with the aims and concerns of modern moral philosophy are bound to fail for the same reasons Nietzsche gives for why all attempts to provide a coherent moral theory fail.

Annas has a far less irenic view of the unity between classical and contemporary virtue ethics than does Hursthouse, and in her hands classical virtue ethics serves as the standard by means of which to judge shortcomings in the contemporary:

> Virtue ethics is best approached by looking at the features of what I shall call the classical version of the tradition. Its theoretical structure is first clearly stated by Aristotle, but it is wrong to think of it as peculiarly Aristotelian, since it underlies all of ancient ethical theory (Annas, 1993, 1999). The classical version is our best entry-point into the subject, because we have a large amount of material that was developed and refined over hundreds of years by extensive debate and that contains resources for establishing the whole theoretical structure, and for understanding what in it is basic and what more parochial. Modern virtue ethical theories have not yet achieved such a critical mass of argument and theory, and most are as yet partial or fragmentary. As I will show, it is only when we have this whole picture in view that we can understand other theories that call themselves virtue ethics. So I shall first build up, cumulatively, a picture of the entire structure of classical virtue ethics, and then see how different versions of it result from ignoring or rejecting parts of that structure.[23]

Like Hursthouse, Annas designates practical wisdom, virtue, and flourishing as key terms in the classical approach. She adds to this both an emphasis on what she terms the "aspirational" dimension of classical virtue ethics—the view that at the heart of ethics is the desire to be better than we are, as well as some considerations on the

---

23. Annas, "Virtue Ethics," 515–16. Her self-references in the quotation are to *The Morality of Happiness* and *Platonic Ethics, Old and New* (Ithaca, N.Y.: Cornell University Press, 1999).

relationship between virtue ethics and metaphysics—arguing that classical virtue theory is often aligned with a type of naturalism, but in other corners with "otherworldly" metaphysical considerations in the Platonic, Jewish, and Christian traditions.[24]

The contemporary, and by her designation "reduced," versions of virtue ethics are specified by their departures from classical virtue ethics in at least one, but often in some combination, of the following ways: a weakened view of practical rationality, where practical reason is treated in a merely instrumentalist manner;[25] a narrowed view of human flourishing, which assumes flourishing to be defined in a way independent of the virtues, which results in an egoistic view of flourishing;[26] the rejection or ignoring of a final end, which results in the rejection of a unified rationale for the virtues;[27] and an excessive stress on the social embeddedness of the virtues, which denies the virtues their aspirational function—by which she means that if virtues are entirely circumscribed by their culturally derived connotations then there is no accounting for how virtues tend always to call us forth to become better than we hitherto thought possible.[28] What we really need to confront modern moral philosophy, one gathers from Annas's article, is contemporary virtue ethicists who take their orientation from the richer and unreduced approaches of the ancients:[29] "Contemporary virtue ethics with the ambitions of the classical theories, of which the most powerful example is that of Hursthouse, does in contemporary terms what the classical theories do in theirs."[30]

---

24. I think her assumption that Aristotelian naturalism does not open up to Platonic supernaturalism needs reconsideration.

25. Ibid., 528–29.

26. Ibid., 530.

27. Ibid., 530–31.

28. Ibid., 531–32.

29. In this and many other respects, Daniel C. Russell's efforts in *Practical Intelligence and the Virtues* shares much in common with Annas's approach to virtue ethics. Moreover, Russell's distinction between Hard and Soft Virtue Ethics (see esp. 66–70, 139–42, and 204–8, and the last two chapters) has significant overlap with Annas's distinction between reduced and unreduced virtue ethics, especially with respect to the role of *phronesis*.

30. Annas, "Virtue Ethics," 526–27. The context for this exhortatory observation is

Annas's method for distinguishing between unreduced and reduced virtue ethics is quite helpful, but her designation of Hursthouse as a representative of an unreduced virtue ethics is perplexing.[31] In addition to the consequentialist tendency we considered in the last chapter, and her optimism about unifying classical virtue ethics with deontology and consequentialism, Hursthouse is clearly working with a reduced view of human flourishing. In chapter 8 of *On Virtue Ethics*, "The Virtues Benefit Their Possessor," Hursthouse seeks to combine elements of a utilitarian view of flourishing, where typically flourishing is understood apart from the virtues, with a virtue-rich vocabulary. The chapter, like the whole of Hursthouse's book, merits close attention, but the point I seek to make here is that its argument places Hursthouse's effort within the class of reduced virtue ethics specified by Annas rather than in the unreduced. Hursthouse writes:

> The idea that morality is, provably from a neutral point of view, a form of enlightened self-interest has some currency. Hare supports it. David Gauthier supports it. Peter Singer seems to be a recent convert to it. It's around and it has its critics as well as its supporters. Its critics (apart from those who complain that it is improperly attempting to provide the wrong sorts of reasons for acting well) focus on ways in which various immoralists might disagree, and locate the source of disagreement in the different *values* (or desires or projects or ends) they suppose their immoralist to have. But the idea that we have to interpret the claim in terms of parameters that import the idea of *phronesis*—of an understanding of human nature and how human life works in a way that is not a matter of adverting to facts available from within a neutral point of view—is, as far as I know, quite unrecognized in the current literature.[32]

---

a discussion of the need for virtue ethicists to turn to the best contemporary science to enrich their understanding of human nature. But it expresses well the general thrust of her whole piece: we need to pursue virtue ethics like the classical theorists did.

31. Ibid., 532.
32. Hursthouse, *On Virtue Ethics*, 191.

To be sure, Hursthouse is not embracing an everyday variety of enlightened self-interest, but rather one that, as she says, "imports the idea of *phronesis*." It is not from a neutral point of view, but from a socially embedded and phronetic one, that the goal of *eudaimonia* as enlightened self-interest is to be defended on Hursthouse's view. Yet this approach seems to endorse a strategy by which we are to understand elements of Aristotelianism from within a utilitarian point of view, and not vice versa; and it is this that would seem to fit into Annas's description of a narrowed view of flourishing. Why not begin from an Aristotelian or Platonic or Stoic point of view and argue that acting virtuously is its own reward and that flourishing is constituted by virtuous activity? Why begin with a view of human flourishing not directly oriented from a view of virtuous activity and with the egoist overtones of utilitarianism in the first place? There are no doubt many reasons Hursthouse has, but one obvious one is that her tack advances the cause of unifying contemporary virtue ethics with the central aims and concerns of modern moral philosophy.

Despite differences in their respective applications of the distinction between classical and contemporary virtue ethics, both Annas's and Hursthouse's uses of the distinction encourage us to measure contemporary virtue ethics by way of its comparison with classical. Annas finds the contemporary to suffer by such comparison, whereas Hursthouse sees distinct advantages in the contemporary. Yet one of the shortcomings of the approach of thinking of virtue ethics as a unified movement with both old and new contingents is that it can obscure what is truly "new" about contemporary virtue ethics. On the face of things, the most immediately obvious new thing about contemporary virtue ethics is the use of the descriptor of what one is engaged in *as a virtue ethics*. Neither Plato, or Aristotle, or Epictetus, or Marcus Aurelius, or Augustine, or Aquinas ever self-identify as virtue ethicists. Perhaps the main reason why they did not self-identify in this fashion is that they did not have to bother with trying to distinguish themselves from modern moral philosophy.

Nevertheless, the self-conscious approach to stake out territory for themselves *as virtue ethicists* lends to the contemporary movement a shape the contours of which are determined more by what they seek to distinguish themselves from (modern moral philosophy) than by the approaches of Plato or Aristotle.

There are, however, other reasons why Plato, Aristotle, and the others do not call what they do a virtue ethics, and some of these point to the subtle but significant differences they, as opposed to contemporary theorists, attribute to the role of virtue in their ethics. For example, though classical thinkers give a certain pride of place to considerations of the virtues, they do not seek to reduce a whole moral theoretical apparatus to virtue ethical considerations. The classical lack of concern for deriving a morality from virtue notions in the manner of modern theorists, a lack Annas remarks on in *The Morality of Happiness*,[33] warrants regarding classical theorists as engaged in projects other than those found in the dominant contemporary virtue ethical literature such as is represented in the works of Hursthouse and Slote. What will be found on still further consideration of these and related issues is, to return to the laundry analogy, that what Annas and Hursthouse term "classical virtue ethics" is not to be found in the pile of contemporary laundry our father is poised to sort.

It seems that yet another new tack is required to make more significant headway in sorting out the varieties of contemporary virtue ethics. Martha Nussbaum applies the type of method needed to sort our heap of contemporary virtue ethical literature into relatively

---

33. "Ancient virtue theories, at any rate, do not aspire to be hierarchical and complete. In them, the notions of the agent's final end, of happiness and of the virtues are what can be called *primary*, as opposed to basic. These are the notions we start from; they set up the framework of the theory, and we introduce and understand the other notions in terms of them. They are thus primary for understanding; they establish what the theory is a theory of, and define the place to be given to other ethical notions, such as right action. However, they are not basic in the modern sense: other concepts are not derived from them, still less reduced to them" (Annas, *The Morality of Happiness*, 9).

VARIETIES 99

neat piles in "Virtue Ethics: A Misleading Category?"[34] This article is intended to fracture the façade constructed by those adherents to virtue ethics wishing to present the movement as a unified front. Strangely, considering Nussbaum's academic fame and her reputation as a defender of a Stoical approach to virtue ethics, the article has been remarked upon very little, not earning even so much as a mention in the bibliographies Hursthouse and Annas compiled for their encyclopedic and handbook contributions on virtue ethics.[35] Perhaps one reason for its being ignored is that if Nussbaum's analysis is correct, then it really is misleading to think of virtue ethics as a unified philosophical movement.

What are the dangers to the contemporary virtue ethics movement presented in Nussbaum's article? There are two foundational claims that Nussbaum makes about the contemporary virtue ethics movement. The first amounts to contending that the leading adherents of the movement have an insufficient grasp of the history of philosophy, and the second that the notion of a unified virtue ethics *movement* is incoherent.

Let us briefly consider first her rejection of what she considers a faulty historical narrative concerning the emergence of contemporary virtue ethics. This "confused story" she characterizes as follows:

---

34. Nussbaum, "Virtue Ethics: A Misleading Category?"
35. One exception is Sean McAleer's article, "An Aristotelian Account of Virtue Ethics." McAleer criticizes Nussbaum for an overly inclusive view of what constitutes a virtue ethical theory. His approach seems to fall squarely within the reductionistic boundaries decried by Annas: "An ethics is a virtue ethics just in case (1) it holds that virtue concepts are explanatorily more basic than deontic concepts, and that no other moral concepts are explanatorily more basic than virtue concepts and (2) it has a theory of virtue and the virtues" (216). Also, Christine Swanton provides a brief reply to Nussbaum in her concluding thoughts to *Virtue Ethics: A Pluralistic View*. A third mention of Nussbaum's article is to be found on 43, note 9, of Russell's *Practical Intelligence and the Virtues*. Although Russell agrees with many parts of Nussbaum's analysis, he disagrees with Nussbaum's conclusion that there is no substantial way to demarcate virtue ethics. See 66–70 of this same book for Russell's defense of Gary Watson's criteria for demarcating virtue ethics from other approaches.

We are turning from an ethics based on Enlightenment ideals of universality to an ethics based on tradition and particularity; from an ethics based on principle to an ethics based on virtue; from an ethics dedicated to the elaboration of systematic theories to an ethics suspicious of theory and respectful of the wisdom embodied in local practices; from an ethics based on the individual to an ethics based on affiliation and care; from an ahistoricial detached ethics to an ethics rooted in the particularity of historical communities.[36]

I do not think it the case that all those who consider themselves virtue ethicists subscribe to some version of this "confused story," but it cannot be denied that many do. One of Nussbaum's main concerns is to argue that a virtue ethical approach and universal claims to justice or equality are compatible, a concern she expresses even more forcefully in an earlier criticism of what she contends to be standard virtue ethical rejections of absolute ethical standards.[37]

This indicates Nussbaum's intention of harnessing some recent work on the virtues together with what she considers the best of Enlightenment moral philosophy. It turns out, then, that Nussbaum and Hursthouse have more in common than first meets the eye. Both see many promising features in the modern moral philosophical project, and both wish to see contemporary virtue ethics accommodated to modern moral philosophy and vice versa. The significant difference remains, however, with respect to whether or not contemporary virtue ethics offers a coherent and comprehensive moral theory.

The "confused story" takes its support, Nussbaum argues, "from the idea that there is such a thing as "virtue ethics," that this thing has a definite describable character and a certain degree of unity, and that it is a major alternative to both the Utilitarian and the Kan-

---

36. Nussbaum, "Virtue Ethics: A Misleading Category?" 163–64.
37. Martha C. Nussbaum, "Non-Relative Virtues: An Aristotelian Approach," *Midwest Studies in Philosophy* 13 (1998): 32–53. She designates Bernard Williams, Philippa Foot, and Alasdair MacIntyre to be the main relativistic offenders in this piece. She is certainly wrong about MacIntyre being a relativist in this sense.

tian traditions."[38] It is just this idea regarding virtue ethics that becomes the focus of her attacks for the rest of the article. Nussbaum recommends sorting virtue ethicists by their adherence to particular positions they take vis-à-vis dominant strains within modern moral philosophy. Before turning to the three categories of such positions she stakes out, it is important to her argument to note that she does recognize there to be overlapping concerns between the categories. The crucial claim with respect to these points of convergence between various virtue ethical positions is that they are too thin to constitute a coherent movement identifiable as virtue ethics.[39]

What is the common ground between the different categories of contemporary virtue ethics? Nussbaum designates three points:

A. Moral philosophy should be concerned with the agent, as well as with choice and action.
B. Moral philosophy should therefore concern itself with motive and intention, emotion and desire: in general, with the character of the inner moral life, and with settled patterns of motive, emotion, and reasoning that lead us to call someone a person of a certain sort (courageous, generous, moderate, just, etc.).
C. Moral philosophy should focus not only on isolated acts of choice, but also, and more importantly, on the whole course of the agent's moral life, its patterns of commitment, conduct, and also passion.[40]

The mistake, Nussbaum avers, made by contemporary virtue ethicists was in thinking that these three areas of concern are missing in Kant and the significant utilitarian thinkers, Mill and Sidgwick. Recent scholarship has shown, however, Kant and the utilitarians to have been much concerned with these areas comprising the common ground between virtue ethicists. The impression that they were not a matter of concern for modern moral philosophers was due to their being often ignored by interpreters of those thinkers on the one hand,

---

38. Nussbaum, "Virtue Ethics: A Misleading Category?" 164.
39. Ibid., 168.
40. Ibid., 170.

and on the other the accidental fact that most of the prominent early virtue ethicists were given extensive training in Ancient Greek ethics during their formative academic years.[41] To be sure, much good was done in emphasizing points A–C above, and perhaps it could not have been done were it not for the attention drawn to these areas by contemporary philosophers who noticed them in the ancients. Nevertheless, no great service is done if we continue to promote the misinterpretation that these areas were not of major concern for Kant and the fathers of utilitarianism.

This common ground, moreover, does not imply the following claims, which are often, Nussbaum contends, associated with partisans of virtue ethics: the rejection of moral theory; the rejection of universality in ethics; the rejection of the guidance of rules; and, that "we should rely less on reason and more on non-rational sources of guidance, such as emotion and desire (if we should construe them as non-rational), and habit, and tradition."[42] Both classical and modern thinkers promoted theory, sought universality in ethics, prescribed rules for moral conduct, and recognized a fundamental motivational role for reason.

The two categories into which different contemporary virtue ethicists fall are: anti-utilitarians and anti-Kantians, also designated by her as neo-Humeans. To be sure, Nussbaum is cognizant of the fact that these categories tend to simplify thinkers who are quite complex. Nevertheless, she contends that such categorization is helpful for allowing us to "make real progress in understanding where we are, and why."[43] Though she is right on both counts, in some cases her simplifications are more detrimental than beneficial.

41. "People like Wiggins, Williams, Murdoch, McDowell, and Foot were influenced in no small measure by the fact that they had done degrees in 'Greats' and/or regularly taught in that program, which devotes far more time to ancient Greek ethics than to Kantian ethics. On the American side, younger philosophers such as Sherman, Homiak, Richardson, and I were all beneficiaries of the exciting revival of Aristotelian studies lead by Gwilym Owen at Harvard and Gregory Vlastos at Princeton" (ibid., 170).

42. Ibid., 178; see her discussion of these points in 177–79.

43. Ibid., 169.

By "anti-Utilitarians" she means those virtue ethicists who are "friends of reason;" that is, they are those who "question [utilitarianism's] neglect of the plurality of goods; its narrowly technical conception of reason, which holds that reason can deliberate only about means and not about ends; and the non-cognitive conception of emotion and desire that has frequently been taken for granted in Utilitarian thought both in philosophy and, even more obviously, in economics."[44] These virtue ethicists emphasize the ways in which reason can educate our passions as well as our beliefs. She contends that they are not, for the most part, hostile to Kant, and seek to find some synthesis between Kant and Aristotle. Nussbaum places in this category Marcia Homiak, John McDowell, Iris Murdoch, Henry Richardson, Nancy Sherman, and herself.

Anti-Kantian and neo-Humean virtue ethicists are those who doubt the leading role that Kant gives to reason in governing human choice and put into question Kant's claims to universality in ethics.[45] They are not quite the mirror opposites of the anti-utilitarians because although they do seek a reduced role for reason, it is rather a turn to nonrational elements such as tradition and culture for moral guidance that interests them rather than the reduction of reason to a merely instrumental role.[46] They tend not to be admirers of Aristotle, tending instead to be more friendly to Hume. In this class of thinkers she places Annette Baier, Simon Blackburn, Philippa Foot, Bernard Williams, and Alasdair MacIntyre.

The fact that Nussbaum places Alasdair MacIntyre in a class with purportedly "other" nonadmirers of Aristotle and promoters of Hume is, frankly, unconscionable, and should not be passed over in silence. This classification reveals either an ignorance of MacIntyre's work over the last thirty years; a particular animus against MacIntyre

---

44. Ibid., 168; see for further specification of this class.
45. Ibid., 169.
46. Although Nussbaum does contend that this is a version of reason's enslavement to the passions, and so Humean, on 189.

inspired, perhaps, by Nussbaum's dissatisfaction with what she reprovingly refers to as "the increasingly conservative nature of his ethical thought;"[47] or, most likely, a combination of those two. Other thinkers placed by Nussbaum in this class have, no doubt, reasons to protest—Foot particularly, who severely criticizes Hume in "Hume on Moral Judgment,"[48] but none more than MacIntyre.

Although these two categories result only in a single division of our heap of contemporary virtue ethicists, Nussbaum contends that this is enough to rupture the notion of a unified movement that we can designate as virtue ethics: "This exposition has been too crude to capture many of the subtleties of each thinker's positions ... but even this crude account should at least have shown one thing: that the current tendency to teach there is any such unitary approach as 'virtue ethics' is a big mistake."[49] She concludes her essay with this reflection:

> I propose that we do away with the category of "virtue ethics" in teaching and writing. If we need to have some categories, let us speak of Neo-Humeans and Neo-Aristotelians, of anti-Utilitarians and anti-Kantians—and then, most important, let us get on with the serious work of characterizing the substantive views of each thinker about virtue, reason, desire, and emotion—and deciding what we ourselves want to say.[50]

This is a striking claim from a thinker many regard as a leading virtue ethicist, and yet the contemporary virtue ethics movement has taken almost no notice of it. In the following chapter Nussbaum's negative thesis regarding the status of contemporary virtue ethics will be examined in more detail. For our present purposes, we can

---

47. Ibid., 176.
48. In *Virtues and Vices*, 74–80. Foot also repudiates her more Humean slant in "Morality as a System of Hypothetical Imperatives," first published 1952 but also included in *Virtues and Vices*, in her more recent *Natural Goodness*, which appears two years after Nussbaum's article. Nussbaum notes that Foot would protest this purported Humean predilection, and yet, Nussbaum suggests, that is because of her slanted view of Hume (making of Foot not just a Humean, but a poor scholar), on 189, n. 49.
49. Nussbaum, "Virtue Ethics: A Misleading Category?" 200.
50. Ibid., 201.

look to Nussbaum at the very least for a number of useful distinctions for sorting different groups of contemporary virtue ethicists. Nussbaum's and Annas's categories for contemporary virtue ethicists are on the surface opposed. Nussbaum derives her categories from where different virtue ethicists stand with respect to major currents in modern moral philosophy, whereas Annas derives hers from the ways in which different thinkers promote a merely partial recovery of classical virtue ethics. But in other respects, they are looking at two different sides of the same coin. The very reasons motivating a merely partial recovery of classical virtue ethics resulting in what Annas dubs "reduced" versions of virtue ethics are those that have to do with various contemporary virtue ethicists' positions vis-à-vis major themes in modern moral philosophy. So, for instance, the antiutilitarians of Nussbaum's taxonomy, although not tending toward a reduced view of reason or an overemphasis on the social embeddedness of the virtues, do tend toward a narrowed view of human flourishing (category 2 of Annas's scheme) and a rejection of a final unifying end (category 3). Anti-Kantians, on Nussbaum's characterization, would seem to fall into all four categories of reduction, particularly strongly so with respect to an overemphasis on the social embeddedness of the virtues that entails a reduced view of reason that in turn entails a weakened role of reason for articulating ends.

What Nussbaum's characterization of contemporary virtue ethics fails to notice with sufficient clarity, and what Annas's acknowledges but does not always accurately apply, is what Hursthouse's view hopes to achieve: the accommodation of virtue ethics to dominant strands in modern moral philosophy. What we need is a further division pointing to the fissure between those contemporary virtue ethicists, or at least those considered by others to be virtue ethicists (again, MacIntyre, Foot, and Nussbaum all reject this mantle, and for good, but very different, reasons), who seek to accommodate their ethical thought to some version of the modern moral project, and those who do not.

David Solomon provides just such a distinction, utilized already in the introduction to this book, in his article that, like Nussbaum's, has not received as much attention as it deserves, "Virtue Ethics: Radical or Routine?"[51] His distinction between radical and routine provides a simple yet powerful tool for adjudicating where a thinker stands with respect to the question, all-important if in fact virtue ethics presents a "third way" to the dominant strains of Kantianism and utilitarianism in modern philosophy, of whether a particular virtue ethicist is or is not working to accommodate his or her theories to modern moral philosophy. It is not just some of the contemporary revivals of virtue theory that can be counted as radical, or even revolutionary, for Solomon thinks that Moore's *Principia Ethica*, the fifth chapter of Ayer's *Language, Truth and Logic*, and Rawls's *A Theory of Justice* can all be characterized as revolutionary with respect to Kantianism and utilitarianism.[52] I do not wish to enter here into a discussion of whether or not these three thinkers really are working outside the mainstream, or if they are rather seeking to harness other moral traditions to the dominant ones in modern moral philosophy. I want, instead, to return, now in more detail, to the way Solomon characterizes radical virtue ethics.[53]

Radical virtue ethicists, or those I have been calling unconventional or marginal, and Solomon has in mind principally Elizabeth Anscombe and Alasdair MacIntyre, are distinguishable in two main ways from their routine, or as I prefer mainstream or conventional, counterparts. On the one hand, the following ten features are prominent in their theorizing:

---

51. In *Intellectual Virtue: Perspectives from Ethics and Epistemology*, ed. Michael DePaul and Linda Zagzebski (Oxford: Clarendon Press, 2003), 57–80.

52. Ibid., 61–65.

53. There are some limitations to Solomon's distinction. One of these is that it does not sufficiently capture thinkers like Anscombe or MacIntyre, who are really neither unconventional nor conventional virtue ethicists, though perhaps "marginal" can be used in their cases because they are so often associated with the movement in some way. Another is that Solomon's project seems too hopeful about the prospects of righting a virtue

(1) a suspicion of rules and principles as sufficient guides to action
(2) a rejection of conscientiousness—in the sense of acting out of respect for the moral law—as the appropriate motivation state in the best human action
(3) a preference for concrete virtue terms as opposed to the more abstract "right" or "ought"
(4) a critique of modernity and especially Enlightenment models of practical rationality
(5) an emphasis on the importance of community
(6) a focus on the whole life as the primary object of moral evaluation
(7) an emphasis on the narrative structure of human life
(8) an emphasis on the centrality of contingently based special relationships with family and friends
(9) a suspicion of morality understood as a distinctive set of obligations and rights
(10) a special emphasis on thick moral education.[54]

Solomon argues that this list, even though partial and with the positions merely stated and not elaborated upon, is enough to show the rich diversity of interests that characterize unconventional virtue ethics, and its diversity points to the nonreductive features of this approach to moral theorizing. In fact, those friends of the virtues who seek to boil these features down to one or two distinguishing marks in order better to contrast virtue ethics with deontology or consequentialism reveal one of the distinguishing marks of embracing a conventional and accommodationist approach to the virtues.[55]

The second way in which unconventional virtue ethics is identifiable is by way of its reaction to the main objections leveled against

---

ethical ship that has been steered off course; I am less comfortable self-identifying as a virtue ethicist than Solomon seems to be.
54. Ibid., 64–65.
55. Ibid., 65.

virtue ethics. Solomon identifies these objections as internal—that is, objections arising from within moral philosophy as opposed to external objections of an epistemological, scientific, or metaphysical nature.[56] They are, in brief: "The action-guiding objection which claims that a virtue theory fails to give adequate guidance in situations of practical complexity"; "The self-centeredness objection that claims that ethics of virtue is insufficiently other-regarding"; and "The conscientiousness objection that claims that an ethics of virtue fails to do justice to the special kind of motivation peculiar to the moral."[57] The interesting thing to watch out for with respect to these objections is the extent to which a virtue ethicist feels the need to respond to them. For a mainstream virtue ethicist, these are significant objections to respond to, and they should, as they have, spend a great deal of intellectual energy making the case that virtue ethics can successfully overcome them. For an unconventional virtue ethicist, these objections are misdirected, for they employ criteria for judging the success of a moral theory that an unconventional virtue ethicist simply does not accept.

What the objections presuppose is that a successful moral theory must:

(a) Guide action in a particular kind of direct way. The theory itself must yield some devices that are directly and concretely motivating.
(b) Provide some conduit from self to other. Indeed, it is claimed that the problem of the ethical is how the agent can leap from egoism to altruism—or, even if the move from egoism to altruism is, as Bernard Williams says, 'a gentle slide' instead of a leap, how to accomplish that slide.
(c) Identify some distinctive motivational state appropriate to the realm of the moral. This motivational state must be qualitatively discontinuous with the normal motivational states in other non-moral practical cases.[58]

---

56. He explores them at much greater length in "Internal Objections to Virtue Ethics," *Midwest Studies in Philosophy* 13 (1988): 428–41.
57. Solomon, "Virtue Ethics: Radical or Routine?" 74.
58. Ibid., 74–75; footnote to Williams omitted.

Solomon contends that it is not as though unconventional virtue ethics does not think it important to address action guidance or ethical motivation, but rather that those concerns are addressed in radically different ways than they are in mainstream moral philosophy, virtue ethical or otherwise, and those concerns do not play the foundational role in unconventional virtue ethics that they do in modern moral theories.

The division between unconventional and conventional virtue ethics is then a division regarding what are taken to be the basic criteria by means of which a successful moral theory is to be judged. Mainstream virtue ethicists accept the criteria at the heart of the modern moral project, and marginal virtue ethicists do not. Mainstream virtue ethicists, represented most pronouncedly by Hursthouse and Slote, have a much more narrow area of focus in their attempts to defend virtue ethics—this is largely an internal affair regarding how best to achieve the aims of the modern moral project where the criteria for judgment are agreed upon, more or less, by all the major players.[59] Marginal virtue ethicists, like Anscombe, Foot, Geach, and MacIntyre, have a much broader range of concerns:

> They were concerned with certain larger questions both about the moral life and about the role of general philosophical thinking in that life. They thought there were certain deep difficulties in modern moral theory connected both to the history of modernity as well as to certain features of modern life. Modern moral philosophy was misleading not only in its answers, but also in its questions. It focused our attention on features of our practical life which are not central to the project of successful human living and it encouraged us to have certain ambitions for philosophical reflection or practice almost Promethean in their reach.... In this push for virtue theory, the focus was not on relatively technical questions of the

---

59. Just think of the dominant role Hursthouse gives to her V-rules, "P1. An action is right iff it is what a virtuous agent would characteristically (i.e. acting in character) do in the circumstances" (*On Virtue Ethics,* 28); or Michael Slote's aspirations to develop, "'"pure," agent-based virtue ethics in a more self-conscious and clear-cut manner" (*Morals from Motives,* 9).

ordering of normative and evaluative concepts, but on deeper questions about the nature and ambitions of modern ethics and its ability to satisfy our need for reflective guidance.[60]

This major divide between the unconventional and the conventional, between the broad and the narrow, between the general and the technical, between the deep and the shallow, goes a long way toward explaining the difficulties experienced by those seeking to understand contemporary virtue ethics as a unified movement. What it reveals is that it is in many respects a mischaracterization to regard contemporary virtue ethics as a unified movement, at least a unified movement according to the standard narrative of the movement one confronts in leading ethical handbooks and encyclopedia.

Solomon's distinction helps us understand why Foot is uncomfortable being labeled an adherent of virtue ethics, and why MacIntyre rejects the label altogether: their efforts have been anything but conformist. It also helps explain why so much of MacIntyre's post–*After Virtue* work is often ignored by mainstream virtue ethics, for in those works he extends his critique of the modern moral and political project; articulates an account of practical rationality that is neither Kantian, Humean, or utilitarian; develops an account of the rationality of tradition that flies in the face of Enlightenment aspirations; and forges a way to characterize what it is to be a human being that emphasizes our radical dependency on others and measures our flourishing by standards contrary to the aims of the individualism at the heart of the modern moral and political project. It is the dominant model of mainstream virtue ethics, which is responsible for the celebrated success of virtue ethics as a newly arrived "third way" in modern moral theory, and it is conventional or mainstreaming tendencies of this dominant contemporary virtue ethics that have led those Solomon deems radical virtue ethicists not to count themselves virtue ethicists at all.

60. Solomon, "Virtue Ethics: Radical or Routine?", 76–77

Taking Inventory

We have considered the work of several authors concerned to characterize varieties within the contemporary virtue ethics movement, and it will be of use to consider in this last section of the present chapter some ways in which they can be synthesized, and then in the next chapter how this synthesis can be further developed in some innovative ways. Classical virtue ethics—which come in Platonic, Aristotelian, and Stoical flavors, among others—can be divided from the bulk of contemporary virtue ethics. Contemporary virtue ethics can be measured, according to Annas, by the many ways in which it falls short of richer classical varieties—and by applying the standard of the four areas of reduction she specifies, we can make more fine-grained distinctions within reduced contemporary virtue ethics. We could also divide contemporary virtue ethics, on Nussbaum's telling, between anti-utilitarians on the one hand, and anti-Kantian neo-Humeans on the other. But these distinctions offered by Nussbaum fail to appreciate the deeper differences Solomon discovers between marginal contemporary virtue ethicists—who are virtue ethicists by others' descriptions if not their own—who are profoundly skeptical of the very criteria by means of which modern moral philosophy judges moral theories, but who nevertheless seek to revive premodern ethical concerns and criteria for judgment in a way made relevant within our contemporary context; and conventional contemporary virtue ethicists whose success in mainstreaming concern for the virtues has come at the cost of accommodating their theories to the presuppositions and criteria definitive of the modern moral project.

If these distinctions accurately cut across the virtue ethical terrain, it is worth repeating that it appears to be a great irony that mainstream virtue ethics has sprung from the unconventional ground first worked by Anscombe. After the initial break she made with fundamental features of the Humean, Kantian, and utilitarian projects, and her clarion call to desist from moral philosophizing until we have developed a suitable philosophical vocabulary for describing human life and action in a manner inspired by Aristotle, contemporary virtue ethicists have successively come to look more and more like their Humean, Kantian, and utilitarian counterparts.

The early phase of contemporary virtue ethics can be characterized by its acceptance of Anscombe's argument that the notion of the moral ought should be eliminated from modern moral philosophy because its Judeo-Christian foundation exists in only bastardized forms in deontology and consequentialism, which nevertheless pretend to speak with divine-like obligatory force. The later phases of contemporary virtue ethics fail to heed the Anscombean warning, and its adherents seek to cloak themselves in what to an Anscombean can only be described as illegitimate apparel. Kant, Hume, and Mill have been confirmed in their roles as the fathers of modern moral philosophy, even in mainstream contemporary virtue ethics, and even when described by quasi-Aristotelian terminology. What I think Anscombe would find most regrettable in this missed opportunity is the continued abandonment of those ethical absolutes that are at the heart of genuine moral education. Even worse, the consequentialism she so presciently exposed and sought to war against has come to be reshaped and reconfirmed by the very arsenal she sought to use against it, Aristotelianism.

Thus far, I have been resting much upon Anscombe's analyses, and extending her judgments in order to describe the state of mainstream virtue ethics. I will need to do more in order to substantiate the claims I have made, and particularly the claim that mainstream virtue ethics fails to be sufficiently Aristotelian. The question of whether or not the Aristotelian tools wielded by mainstream virtue ethics are truly or merely apparently Aristotelian will be directly examined in chapter 5. The question is more important than that of the right interpretation of Aristotle's ethics and action theory, for the vindication of Anscombe's hopes hinges in part on whether or not legitimately Aristotelian notions can be used to defend the consequentialism at the heart of the modern moral project. If it is not the case that mainstream virtue ethics has revived Aristotelian ethical inquiry, then, from Anscombe's perspective, there is no philosophical alternative, at least not yet, to the central aims of the modern moral project. If it is not the case that mainstream virtue ethics has revived Aristotelian ethical inquiry, then hope still remains to build a real alternative, along the lines that Anscombe has suggested, to modern moral philosophy. Before we pursue that examination, however, it is necessary to look more closely at mainstream virtue ethical attempts to package itself as an approach to moral philosophy that is simultaneously both partner and alternative to modern moral philosophy.

Chapter 4

CONTEMPORARY VIRTUE ETHICS AND ITS ASPIRATIONS

We must, as in all other cases, set the phenomena before us and, after first discussing the difficulties, go on to prove, if possible, the truth of all the reputable opinions about these affections or, failing this, of the greater number and the most authoritative; for if we resolve the difficulties and leave the reputable opinions undisturbed, we shall have proved the case sufficiently.

Aristotle, *NE* VI 1, 1145^{b}1–7

The differences between the variety of approaches to virtue theory and the virtues represented in contemporary virtue ethics and canvassed in the last chapter are, in many cases, deep and significant. These differences reveal, at least in some cases, competing sets of primary tasks for moral philosophy, competing strategies for addressing those primary tasks, and competing allegiances to core principles. There remains, however, at least some historical reason for regarding these competing approaches within the contemporary virtue ethics movement as unified insofar as they all take inspiration from Anscombe's watershed article. Even though some shapes taken

ASPIRATIONS 115

by that inspiration are very different from others, the common effort of reformulating a virtue-centered approach to ethics does provide some degree of unity to the movement. How deep does that unity go? This chapter takes up that question, and does so by giving special attention to the ways in which leading commentators on the virtue ethical movement have described the movement's aims, and then assessing the movement in terms of its claims to cohesiveness, coherence, and comprehensiveness.

Both opponents and adherents take as one of their fundamental assumptions about contemporary virtue ethics the view expressed at the beginning of Rosalind Hursthouse's online *Stanford Encyclopedia of Philosophy* entry:

> Virtue ethics is currently one of three major approaches in normative ethics. It may, initially, be identified as the one that emphasizes the virtues, or moral character, in contrast to the approach which emphasizes duties or rules (deontology) or that which emphasizes the consequences of actions (consequentialism). Suppose it is obvious that someone in need should be helped. A utilitarian will point to the fact that the consequences of doing so will maximize well-being, a deontologist to the fact that, in doing so the agent will be acting in accordance with a moral rule such as "Do unto others as you would be done by," and a virtue ethicist to the fact that helping the person would be charitable or benevolent.[1]

This provides a clear articulation of what can be called "the narrative of the big three." According to this storyline, virtue ethics, after much struggle, has reached a point of great success because it is no longer regarded as the product of the disaffected and nostalgic musings of modern moral philosophy's discontents, but a "powerful" moral theory in and of itself that has taken its rightful place beside the other two moral theories. What better proof is there of virtue ethics' power than its ability to tackle the fundamental question of normative ethics: why should I help someone in need of help? Deontologists and consequentialists each have their own distinctive answers to that

---

1. Hursthouse, "Virtue Ethics," 1.

question, and now, thanks to the work of Hursthouse and others, virtue ethicists have theirs. Not surprisingly, given its prevalence in contemporary political discourse, there are elements of a liberation narrative template at work in the narrative of the big three: initially a victim of neglect and scorn, virtue ethics rose up and infiltrated positions of philosophical authority and secured its place at the centers of academic power. This narrative rightfully emphasizes cause for admiration of the work of those who have labored in this effort, and it does so without insinuating triumphalism. The last chapter has anticipated some reasons for caution in endorsing this standard virtue ethics narrative, but justice requires we take it seriously and assume its accuracy unless there are sufficiently clear reasons to reject it.

Not every contemporary virtue ethicist would agree with Hursthouse that what makes virtue ethics distinctive is how it answers the questions of why we ought to perform a good action, but most do. Hursthouse herself counts her 1999 *On Virtue Ethics* as only the second book to deal with virtue ethics in a systematic manner, and at the heart of this work is her articulation and defense of virtue rules that provide guidance for right actions.[2] On the face of it, Hursthouse's claim to provide the second systematic book-length treatment of virtue ethics, with Michael Slote providing the first, is perplexing. Hursthouse is one of those who claim to be pursuing a neo-Aristotelian virtue ethics, and she endorses the view that there are both old and new versions of virtue ethics.[3] Would this not im-

2. "Although there are lots of articles, there is, as I write, only one book that explores virtue ethics systematically and at length, namely Michael Slote's *From Morality to Virtue* (1992). What I offer is another one, which addresses different issues, in different ways. My approach is more concerned with details, examples, and qualifications than Slote's, and, in being thereby less abstract, is more committed to exploring a particular version of virtue ethics" (Hursthouse, *On Virtue Ethics*, 5).

3. "The particular version of virtue ethics I detail and discuss in this book is of a more general kind known as 'neo-Aristotelian.' The general kind is 'neo' for at least the reason I noted above, that its proponents allow themselves to regard Aristotle as just plain wrong on slaves and women, and also because we do not restrict ourselves to Aristotle's list of virtues. (Charity or benevolence, for example, is not an Aristotelian virtue, but all virtue ethicists assume it is on the list now.) It is 'Aristotelian' in so far as

ply that Aristotle and his commentators were dealing with virtue ethics? Do they not provide book-length treatments of their ethical theories? Hursthouse's claim would seem to imply that Aristotle did not compose a systematic work on virtue ethics, which leaves one to wonder how she can regard him as a virtue ethicist. Notable, too, are the insinuated exclusions of the book-length works exploring virtue by MacIntyre, Nussbaum, Annas, Foot, Geach, and others in the contemporary period. In the last chapter it was seen that Hursthouse endorses a broad-tent approach to the movement, which includes in its expanse Plato, Aristotle, Augustine, Aquinas, Hume, Kant, Mill, Nietzsche, Geach, MacIntyre, Foot, and others.[4] With her claim to provide only the second book-length systematic treatment of virtue ethics we find on the other hand what must be a relatively narrow theory with really only two, at least at the time of her writing, representatives who had produced full-length treatments of the subject. What is to be made of these opposed positions on the scope of the movement? Whatever the reasons for it, the narrow approach to virtue ethics she advocates, the one to which she claims her book is but only the second systematic and significantly lengthy contribution, is an effort at proving that virtue ethics can in fact wrestle with the same problems worked upon by other leading figures in modern moral philosophy, and can provide just as good if not better solutions to them. The concern to make that case really does make her work, as well as Slote's, unlike the works of Geach and MacIntyre, not to mention Aquinas and Aristotle. At the same time, it is what makes her work paradigmatic of mainstream virtue ethics.

There is widespread agreement that Hursthouse provides contemporary virtue ethics with its distinctive brand.[5] Her *Stanford En-*

---

it aims to stick pretty close to his ethical writings wherever else it can" (Hursthouse, *On Virtue Ethics*, 8). See the discussion of charity in chapter 2.

4. This "broad tent" approach is outlined in the first four pages of her book, *On Virtue Ethics*.

5. Nicholas Everitt, in "Some Problems with Virtue Theory," *Philosophy* 82 (2007): 275-99, argues convincingly that Hursthouse can be treated as providing the touch-

cyclopedia of Philosophy entry, for instance, is the first item to arise if one searches for "virtue ethics" on Google.[6] It is Hursthouse's view, moreover, which seems to have shaped the characterization of virtue ethics in a recent and notable—because it is in an Oxford University Press handbook and made by a well-known ethicist, Russ Shafer-Landau—description:

> Virtue ethics is actually a form of ethical pluralism. Though there is a single ultimate standard—do what the virtuous person would do—there are many cases where this advice is too general to be of use. At such times we need a set of more specific moral rules. Virtue ethics can provide these, too. For each virtue there is a rule that tells us to act accordingly; for each vice, a rule that tells us to avoid it. So we will have a large set of moral rules—do what is honest; act loyally, display courage; deal justly with others; show wisdom; be temperate; avoid gluttony; refrain from infidelity; don't be timid, lazy, stingy, or careless; do not show hostility; free yourself from prejudice, etc.[7]

---

stone for virtue ethics. Everitt distinguishes between constitutive versus instrumental interpretations of the relationship Hursthouse envisions between the virtues, what we want, and flourishing; argues that her suggestions that the virtues are constitutive of flourishing fail, and fail by her own admission; and then argues for an instrumentalist interpretation of the relationship between virtues and flourishing that amounts to a sort of rule-consequentialism. Everitt argues that although it still retains some problems, Hursthouse's approach also has some merit. The consequentialist standards of rationality and flourishing that Everitt employs to make his case both expose some of the consequentialism in Hursthouse's own work and also reveal, though not remarked upon by Everitt, the gulf between consequentialist and classical accounts of rationality and flourishing.

6. As of July 26, 2013. The second item is the Wikipedia entry "virtue ethics," which heavily emphasizes Hursthouse's approach. The third is an entry by Nafsika Athanassoulis, "Virtue Ethics," in the *Internet Encyclopedia of Philosophy*, http://www.iep.utm.edu/virtue/. This entry places a heavy emphasis on an Aristotelian approach to virtue ethics, and designates three main types of virtue ethics: Eudaimonistic (for which Hursthouse is given as the main adherent, but we should certainly add Daniel C. Russell here, particularly in light of his work, *Happiness for Humans* [Oxford University Press, 2012]); Agent-Based, and non-eudaimonistic (for which Slote is the representative); and an Ethics of Care virtue ethics (of which Annette Baier is given as the prime example).

7. Russ Shafer-Landau, *The Fundamentals of Ethics* (Oxford: Oxford University Press, 2009), 241–42.

Shafer-Landau, like Hursthouse, characterizes the original perspective of virtue ethics to be in its focus on the character of the moral agent, unlike deontology and utilitarianism, which begin with a consideration of the moral act. Yet the test proposed by both Hursthouse and Shafer-Landau for virtue ethics' viability as a distinctive and substantial ethical theory is its ability (or lack thereof) to deal with considerations of action-guidance.

This same test is endorsed by Russell in *Practical Intelligence and the Virtues*. This remarkable book advances a strong defense of the role of practical wisdom, supplies an innovative approach to the challenge of situationism, advances an innovative defense of the unity of the virtues, and provides a rich defense of what Annas has characterized as an unreduced and classically based virtue ethics. Coupled with *Happiness for Humans*, we find in Russell a formidable defender of a comprehensive and classically grounded approach to the central questions of ethics. With respect to the question of what makes virtue ethics a unique ethical approach that can be demarcated from other ethical theories, however, his position is aligned with mainstream approaches to virtue ethics insofar as it provides, he argues, a unique account of right action. Russell derives his position on this from Gary Watson,[8] arguing: "What sets a virtue ethical account of right action apart from these other sorts of accounts is the fact that virtue ethics (a) makes the notion of a virtue prior to right action, in the sense that a virtue can be understood apart from a formula of right action, and (b) holds that right action cannot be fully understood apart from an account of the virtues."[9] Russell dubs Watson's conditions the "VE constraint," and argues that it is this constraint, rather than simply an emphasis on virtue or a serious regard for character, that makes virtue ethics a distinctive ethical theory. It is this constraint that, he argues, overcomes Nussbaum's misgivings about the unity and

---

8. Watson, "On the Primacy of Character."
9. Russell, *Practical Intelligence and the Virtues*, 66, footnote excluded.

substantial distinctiveness of virtue ethics.[10] He contends, moreover, that despite appearances, this constraint does not smuggle in a prior conception of right action, but rather that the very notion of right action, or conversely wrong action, depends upon the proper understanding of a virtue.[11]

It is Hursthouse herself who points to Slote as the other significant contributor to the movement to have produced a book-length systematic treatment of virtue ethics, and like Hursthouse, Slote is widely regarded as having given a distinctive shape to the contemporary virtue ethical paradigm. His approach departs from the eudaimonistic concerns we find in Hursthouse and seeks, rather, to be "pure"—in the sense of relying on no other considerations than the state of the agent.[12] It is this reliance that justifies the "agent-basing" label typically used to describe Slote's work. Like Hursthouse, he characterizes the distinctiveness of virtue ethics to be found in its focus on the character of the agent.[13] Unlike Hursthouse, Slote does not think it the primary task of virtue ethics to provide an account

---

10. Ibid., 67.

11. Ibid., 69–70, "the notion of virtue's priority to an account of right action must be understood as also including virtue's priority, not necessarily to the notion of good outcomes, but *to the notion that outcomes can bear on the rightness of action.*"

12. Roger Crisp applies this term as follows: "A pure virtue ethics, then, will suggest that the only reasons we ever have for acting or living in any way are grounded in the virtues. The fact that some way of life instantiates the virtues of justice, honesty, generosity, and so on constitutes the sole reason for pursuing it; and there is no reason to pursue any other kind of life.... More common than pure forms of virtue ethics are pluralistic views, according to which the virtues provide some very strong reasons, but other, non-virtue-based reasons are also present, including some perhaps that are consistent with utilitarianism and Kantianism" (*How Should One Live?* 7). Slote, though using "pure" in this sense, disagrees with Crisp's claim that "Aristotle can be interpreted as one of the few pure virtue ethicists" (ibid.).

13. "Virtue ethics makes primary use of aretaic terms in its ethical characterizations, and it treats deontic epithets as derivative from the aretaic or dispenses with them altogether. Thus an ethics of virtue thinks primarily in terms of what is noble or ignoble, admirable or deplorable, good or bad, rather than in terms of what is obligatory, permissible, or wrong, and together with the focus on the (inner character of the) agent, this comes close enough, I think, to marking off what is distinctive of and common to all forms of virtue ethics" (Slote, *Moral from Motives*, 4).

of practical rationality that is action-guiding.[14] Nevertheless, Slote does contend that it is indeed necessary for any successful theory to be able to address why we ought to be benevolent or charitable to others, and this concern is of such paramount importance as to justify dismissing as irrelevant any theories that do not have a way to explain why we ought to be charitable.[15]

In both Hursthouse and Slote, then, we find a background acceptance of those criteria specified by Solomon as distinctive of the modern moral project—that a successful moral theory must guide action in some direct way, provide a means by which a moral agent can move from egoism to altruism, and specify some distinctive motivational state that marks off moral from nonmoral sorts of actions.[16] That which, on the other hand, is distinctive between their respective approaches is the particular ways in which they seek to satisfy these criteria, and by doing such, make the case that their respective virtue ethical approaches provide a satisfactory alternative to what contemporary virtue ethics literature regularly refers to as the "rule-based approaches" of deontology or utilitarianism. Hence, we find in their combined efforts reasons to justify the narrative of the big three.

What Contemporary Virtue Ethics Promises

A central promise of contemporary virtue ethics is that it provides an alternative to those theories dominant in modern moral philosophy. We have been focusing on mainstream virtue ethics, but this promise is endorsed by marginal virtue ethicists as well. The difference between the two camps of virtue ethicists on this score has to do with the way the case is made. Marginal or unconventional virtue ethicists, to speak very broadly, seek an account of virtue and the virtues that has little chance of convincing those judging the suc-

14. Ibid., 193–96.
15. Ibid., vii–viii.
16. Solomon, "Virtue Ethics: Radical or Routine?" 74–75.

cess of a moral theory by the criteria entrenched in modern moral philosophy since unconventional virtue ethicists refuse to play by the same rules, and it is precisely those criteria they first put into question—albeit in a great many different ways. It is not with these efforts of the marginal virtue ethicists that we are concerned in this chapter, but rather with the more uniform efforts of the mainstream virtue ethicists.

Mainstream virtue ethicists work internally, in Solomon's sense, insofar as they seek to show that virtue ethics can better satisfy the generally accepted criteria employed in modern moral philosophy for determining the relative success of a moral theory; they are, so to speak, playing the same game as other contemporary moral philosophers.[17] Mainstream virtue ethicists seek to persuade other leaders in dominant corners of contemporary moral philosophy of the viability of virtue ethics by utilizing the generally agreed upon standards for judgment in assessing moral theories. One sign of mainstream virtue ethicists' success at these efforts is that they now represent what, in general, passes for contemporary virtue ethics. Still, many members of the two other major parties comprising modern moral philosophy, deontologists and consequentialists, often remain unconvinced, as do others.

If one is concerned to make the case that contemporary virtue ethics does not represent a viable alternative to deontology and utilitarianism, two general strategies can be employed. The first is to suggest, in line with marginal virtue ethical sentiments, that contemporary virtue ethics is playing the wrong game—that the criteria they use to judge the success of a moral theory are wrong, or at least superficial with respect to the deeper tasks of ethics. To really make such a case,

---

17. Russell illustrates this point by means of a Bollywood film, *Lagaan*, in which some villagers are compelled to play cricket against their British rulers in the hopes of avoiding an oppressive tax, and comments, "The situation is far less melodramatic for virtue ethicists, but in a sense their increasing efforts to offer theories of right action are not unlike being made to play someone else's game" (*Practical Intelligence and the Virtues*, 37).

one would have to lay out with care alternative criteria by means of which to judge the success of a moral theory, either drawing on the resources of moral traditions other than those constituting modern moral philosophy or working them up from scratch. The other way to argue that mainstream virtue ethics does not constitute a viable alternative to the dominant moral theories is to show that these contemporary virtue ethicists do not meet the standards represented by their own accepted criteria.

Arguments along this latter line have become commonplace objections to the contemporary virtue ethics movement, so much so that standard entries on virtue ethics make sure to include a section on "common objections" to the approach. These are worth reviewing. The most common of them is that virtue ethics does not provide sufficient guidance for action. The second most common is that a concern with the development of one's virtues is self-centered, and renders one unsuitably prepared to come to the aid of others in need. More recently, situationists have challenged the very notion of there being something like stable character traits, and this is often hailed as the situationist challenge. Other less common but significant objections include the charge of cultural relativity; the circularity problem of determining grounds by means of which a character trait can be claimed a virtue when virtues are taken as already epistemologically basic; and, the so-called conflict problem, where two or more virtues suggest different courses of action for resolving a moral conundrum.[18] We can add to this what Solomon dubs the "conscientiousness objection" in one article,[19] and the "contingency objection" in another,[20] which contends that virtue ethics does not sufficiently demarcate the special sort of motivation that marks moral actions from nonmoral actions, and fails thereby to insulate moral action from the wiles of luck.

---

18. Rosalind Hursthouse discusses these, in different order, in her 2004 entry, "Virtue Ethics," in the online *Stanford Encyclopedia of Philosophy*.
19. Solomon, "Virtue Ethics: Radical or Routine?" 74.
20. Solomon, "Internal Objections to Virtue Ethics," 433.

Hursthouse, Slote, and others have provided often ingenious replies to these objections, and their replies do not represent a uniformity of response. Hursthouse, for instance, argues extensively in *On Virtue Ethics* that virtue ethics provides action guidance through the application of V-rules; that V-rules provide a means to deal adequately with resolvable dilemmas, as well as provide the most nuanced way to deal with irresolvable and tragic dilemmas; that a naturalized account of human flourishing overcomes the charges of relativity and the justification problem; and that this account of flourishing is a moral, rather than scientific, concept, which address the conscientiousness objection. For his part, Slote, in *Morals from Motives*,[21] refuses to employ something like Hursthouse's V-rules, but nevertheless makes the case that the virtuous agent is the best equipped moral agent to deal with considerations about how best to act; he argues that rather than eudaimonism, a sentimentalism inspired by Hume and Martineau is the best safeguard against charges of relativity and the means by which to account for the conscientiousness objection; and he spends a great deal of time in this work, as he has in others, making the case that a sentimentalist and caring agent-based virtue ethics provides the means to strike the right balance between egoism and altruism.

Neither Hursthouse nor Slote have addressed the most recent of the objections, the situationist challenge.[22] Annas, however, does provide a pithy and useful response to situationism:

---

21. This later work represents, by Slote's own telling, a significant departure from his more Aristotelian inspired *From Morality to Virtue*, and I work primarily from it in describing Slote's positions to do justice to the approach he currently favors.

22. On situationism, see John M. Doris, "Persons, Situations and Virtue Ethics," *Nous* 32 (1998): 504–30; Doris extends this argument in *Lack of Character: Personality and Moral Behavior* (Cambridge: Cambridge University Press, 2002); Gilbert Harman, "Moral Philosophy Meets Social Psychology: Virtue Ethics and the Fundamental Attribution Error," *Proceedings of the Aristotelian Society* 99 (1999): 316–31. Kwame Anthony Appiah deals at length with the situationist challenge in his Millian inspired virtue ethical account, *Experiments in Ethics*.

However, these [situationist] studies assume a notion of disposition that is defined solely in terms of frequency of actions, where the actions in question are defined with no reference to the agent's own reasons for acting. For virtue ethics, however, a virtue is a disposition to act *for reasons,* and claims about frequency of action are irrelevant to this, until some plausible connection is established with the agent's reasons, something none of the situationists have done (Sreenivasan).[23]

Annas's response can stand, I think, for the sort of response that would be offered by Hursthouse and Slote,[24] though Slote's account of the reasons provided in a disposition to act falls short, on Annas's telling, of those provided in the more robust and classical virtue ethical account.[25]

In any event, the standard objections to virtue ethics, and the more or less standard responses by virtue ethicists to those objections, do not seem to be yielding further progress. Perhaps the realization of this motivates another strategy employed by some virtue ethicists, which is to argue that virtue ethics is no worse off than Kantianism or utilitarianism in handling those difficulties that are too often treated as problems unique to virtue ethics.[26] The opponents of virtue ethics contend in response that they *do so* do a better job of handling these difficult areas, whereas the virtue ethicists fail

---

23. Annas, "Virtue Ethics," 519. The reference is to Gopal Sreenivasan, "Errors about Errors: Virtue Theory and Trait Attribution," *Mind* 111 (2002): 47–68. Since Annas's entry, Sreenivasan has added to his criticisms of situationism with "Character and Consistency: Still More Errors," *Mind* 117 (2008): 603–12, and "The Situationist Critique of Virtue Ethics," chapter 13 of the *CCVE*, 290–314. Russell provides an innovative response to situationism in chapter 8 of *Practical Intelligence and the Virtues*, arguing, "not that virtue theorists should take heart *despite* what social psychology suggests, but should take heart *because of* what social psychology suggests. It is not just that virtue theory and social psychology can be consistent, but that they can actually go together rather *well*" (241).

24. Hursthouse, at least, indicates as much in "Virtue Ethics," 12, with her claim that situationists fail to account for the "multi-track" depth of traits of character, looking only at the level of action in response to a particular situation.

25. Annas, "Virtue Ethics," 529.

26. Solomon, "Internal Objections to Virtue Ethics," 433–41; Hursthouse, "Virtue Ethics," 9–10.

to do so.[27] The virtue ethicists reply again that the deontologists and utilitarians do not provide better answers, and that virtue ethics does more justice to our common intuitions about what ethics entails—a focus on character development. The literature on these points has begun to bear some resemblance to a carousel ride, where the same arguments whip around and around and around. Some point of entry into this cycle that is attentive to something other than just the standard objections to and responses from virtue ethics seems to be needed.

One such entry point appears when we pay closer attention to what is required for virtue ethicists to treat virtue ethics as a moral theory at all. Here the focus turns from a consideration of virtue ethics as an alternative moral theory to a consideration of whether virtue ethics is a moral theory at all. Two questions immediately arise from this change of focus: Does mainstream virtue ethics constitute a cohesive moral theory? Does mainstream virtue ethics constitute a comprehensive moral theory? It is, I think, the negative answers we find to these questions that points to a negative answer to a third question: Does mainstream virtue ethics present a coherent virtue theory?

Does Mainstream Virtue Ethics Constitute a Cohesive Moral Theory?

In turning, in this and the next sections to a consideration of the status of virtue ethics as a moral theory, it is important to note that the focus is not on virtue ethics as a *movement*. The term "movement" admits of more variety and is less concerned with hard boundaries

---

27. Most pointedly on this score, see David Copp and David Sobel, "Morality and Virtue." This essay reviews Hursthouse's *On Virtue Ethics*, Foot's *Natural Goodness*, and Slote's *Morals from Motives*, measures these works against the putative successes of deontology and consequentialism, and finds the virtue ethicists failing to measure up to those successes.

than is a moral theory. Virtue ethics is undeniably a unified movement, at least in respect to its shared history. The question in this section is whether this movement contains a cohesive moral theory.

Is the sheer variety of virtue ethical approaches, as Nussbaum suggests, enough to derive a negative answer to a question about whether virtue ethics represents a cohesive movement? Many supportive of the aims of mainstream virtue ethics are of course themselves well aware of the variety of approaches on offer, and a typical response is to count this in virtue ethics' favor. Karen Stohr, for instance, writes:

> The new variety among types of virtue ethics may seem to some to be a sign of its downfall as a cohesive moral theory. A category broad enough to incorporate not only Aristotle, but also Hume, Nietzsche, and the Stoics may indeed be too broad for many purposes. It thus could be argued that we should drop the category of "virtue ethics" in favor of more descriptive sub-categories, as is common with utilitarianism. That virtue ethics has evolved to the point of requiring sub-categories, however, is evidence of its internal richness.[28]

Stohr does not elaborate on why such variety is a sign of the richness of virtue ethics. One can certainly imagine cases where variety indicates vitality, but such is not always the case, and in any event the question here is whether the variety of virtue ethics preserves an underlying and significant core of similarity. Differences between Aristotle, Hume, Nietzsche, and the Stoics are deep and entrenched, and do not at all seem to be on the same level as the differences between subcategories of utilitarianism—all of which are inspired by Mill in one way or another. Why would the variety of virtue ethics not, contrariwise, point to the poverty of the term, suggesting the term cannot do the work it is employed to do? To be sure, Aristotle, Hume, and Nietzsche all employ virtue theories, but that hardly

---

28. Stohr, "Contemporary Virtue Ethics." Rebecca L. Walker and Philip J. Ivanhoe also note with approval the advantages of a variety of virtue ethical approaches of which no set of necessary and sufficient conditions can be given, in *Working Virtue*, 4.

implies that one can find within their radically different views on rationality, human nature, what a trait of character is, which character traits are to count as virtues, and the function of the virtues vis-à-vis flourishing, some common and underlying virtue ethic.

Christine Swanton takes up the case that, indeed, the variety of virtue ethical approaches is a sign of richness, and still more, that a stronger version of virtue ethics is to be found if these varieties are combined in a pluralistic virtue ethical approach. Like Stohr, Swanton counts diversity as one of the strengths of virtue ethics: "Although I prefer to get on with the job of developing a virtue ethics than in tarrying over questions of definition, the issue of definition of virtue ethics cannot be ignored.... 'Virtue ethics' resists precise definition, and rightly so."[29] It is somewhat surprising that Swanton expresses here some disappointment in needing to pursue the matter of defining virtue ethics. More surprisingly, she claims here that virtue ethics cannot, and should not, be defined. Why should it not be defined? She continues, "For as I mentioned, it is frequently observed that virtue ethics in its modern development is still in its infancy. It should not therefore be shackled by preconceived ideas about its progeniture and nature."[30] Yet, reluctantly, Swanton does yield to the demand for some definition of the movement she endorses: "However, this much at least can be said. In virtue ethics, the notion of virtue is central in the sense that conceptions of rightness, conceptions of the good life, conceptions of 'the moral point of view' and the appropriate demandingness of morality, cannot be understood without a conception of relevant virtues."[31] She provides a more elaborate defense of the work this concept-based definition of virtue ethics can do in her contribution to the *Cambridge Companion to Virtue Ethics*.[32] The key advantage of her concept-based approach to virtue ethics is that it avoids any narrowing of the field,

29. Swanton, *Virtue Ethics*, 5.   30. Ibid.
31. Ibid.
32. Swanton, "The Definition of Virtue Ethics," 315–38.

such as one finds in Russell's defense of Hard Virtue Ethics. By design, Swanton's definition tells us nothing about the priority, or lack thereof, with respect to these areas of concern that a conception of the relevant virtues is supposed to have. Are the virtue conceptions foundational? Explanatory? Grammatical? Derivative? Or that from which other notions are derived? A thinner thread for unifying virtue ethics cannot be found than that of the mere concept of virtue.

The emphasis on the "moral point of view" and conscientiousness, among many other aspects of her project, such as the extensive case for the effective action–guidingness of her virtue ethics, places Swanton squarely within the conventional virtue ethical camp. She argues, as is common among mainstream virtue ethicists, for the disunity of the virtues—which is largely responsible for the "pluralism" of her approach. What appears unique to her project is her attempt to combine an Aristotelian view of the virtues with what she considers Nietzschean "depth psychology."[33] One begins to see in her efforts on this score the effects of placing thinkers as diverse as Aristotle and Nietzsche side by side in a common moral project: they both tend to lose their defining characteristics. For instance, in an interpretation striking for what more typical interpretations of Nietzsche would consider an emasculating effect on his thought, Swanton reads Nietzsche as a proto-positive psychologist, bent on pursuing the aims of self-realization. This domestication of Nietzsche turns a fierce critic of modern theories of enlightened self-interest into a partner with them. There are many aspects of Swanton's unique approach to virtue ethics that merit careful attention, but her case fails to do justice to Nietzsche and his profoundly critical position regarding the central aims and methods of the modern moral project.

Hursthouse employs a *tu quoque* device for addressing concerns about the varieties of virtue ethics:

---

33. Swanton, *Virtue Ethics*, 11. See 56–95 for her efforts at utilizing Nietzsche's views for her account of the good life and the virtues.

Describing virtue ethics loosely as an approach which "emphasizes the virtues" will no longer serve to distinguish it. By the same token, of course, deontology and utilitarianism are no longer perspicuously identified by describing them as emphasizing rules or consequences in contrast to character. No one, as far as I know, is bothered by the fact that there are no longer satisfactory short answers to the questions "What is deontology?" and "What is utilitarianism?," but currently, at least some philosophers seem bothered by the fact that we virtue ethicists cannot come up with one to answer "What is virtue ethics?" The demand that virtue ethics, unlike the other two approaches, should be able to state its position succinctly, in terms both sufficiently broad (or disjunctive?) to get all virtue ethicists in and sufficiently tight to keep all deontologists and utilitarians out, seems a bit excessive. Why should anyone expect us, uniquely, to be able to do it?[34]

Is this an adequate response to the challenge of virtue ethics' opponents to provide a clear description of the project that demarcates it from others? The analogy with problems in the other two major moral theories seems not to hold. It is of course true that both deontology and utilitarianism are in need of more subtle treatment than the typical slogans attached to them warrant. Nevertheless, the slogans get one closer to those respective positions than do the typical slogans attached to virtue ethics, such as "emphasizes the virtues," "the primacy of character," "concern with being more than doing," and the like. Deontology and utilitarianism are more identifiable as moral theories than virtue ethics not simply because we are more accustomed to identifying them as moral theories, but because each has more clearly demarcated and so identifiable boundaries.

It was easier to identify and define virtue ethics when, in its early days, it was generally understood as a variety of neo-Aristotelianism. It is the historical legacy of deontology's attachment to Kant, and utilitarianism's attachment to Mill, that makes those varieties of deontology and utilitarianism that have departed from their founders still identifiable as types of deontology or utilitarianism. But the

---

34. Hursthouse, *On Virtue Ethics*, 4.

broad-tent approach to virtue ethics that both Hursthouse and Swanton endorse does not yield something similar. If Aristotle, Epictetus, Hume, and Nietzsche can each be regarded as yielding strands of virtue ethics, then the connecting fabric between them must be very thin indeed—too thin, in fact, to be considered a distinctive moral theory. What we have, instead, are neo-Aristotelian theories that emphasize a central role for the virtues (Hursthouse); neo-Stoic theories that emphasize a central role for the virtues (Annas, Nussbaum); neo-Humean theories that emphasize a central role for the virtues (Slote); neo-Nietzschean theories that emphasize a central role for the virtues (Swanton); and so on. Aristotelians, Stoics, Humeans, and Nietzscheans have a point when they contend that there is more "neo" than "Aristotelian," "Humean," "Nietzschean," and so on in these virtue ethical approaches. Conversely, those looking for some way to make sense of the diversity of virtue ethics have a point when they claim there is too much of Aristotle, or Hume, or Nietzsche in these different approaches to constitute a definitively cohesive moral theory.

Does, however, the "VE constraint" articulated by Russell provide a sufficient basis to demarcate virtue ethics from other moral theories, and so satisfy what is required for cohesiveness? There is much to recommend it, and it seems the only truly viable candidate for providing the basis upon which virtue ethics can be seen to be a substantially cohesive moral theory. If successful, then it would need to supply the means to include every virtue ethicist in its scope, where a virtue ethicist is defined by the parameters arrived at in the last chapter, where it was found that a contemporary virtue ethicist is an academic philosopher who subscribes to some of the principles shared by some virtue ethicists and who self-identifies with this movement. Swanton, Hursthouse, and Slote could all be included under the VE constraint. To the contrary of Russell's definition, however, Timothy Chappell argues powerfully in the *Cambridge Companion to Virtue Ethics* that the point of virtue ethics is not, and should not be, concerned with supplying an account of right action.[35] Engaging in those efforts is both, he argues, a departure from the classical foundations of virtue ethics and an abandonment of what ought to be of central concern to virtue ethicists. Chappell's view of virtue ethics, then, does not fit within the definitional scope provided by Russell. Russell, on the other hand, could hardly contend that Chappell is not in a position to provide a different definition of virtue ethics since Chappell's essay appears in a volume dedicated to the elucidation of virtue ethics by leading experts, and it is edited by Russell. Chappell provides a counterexample to the most viable means by which virtue ethics can be regarded as a cohesive moral theory, and that is enough to undermine the VE constraint as the basis for the demarcation of virtue ethics since its claim is to universality.

Does Mainstream Virtue Ethics Constitute a Comprehensive Moral Theory?

Let us now assume, contrary to what has just been concluded, but for the sake of further argument, that it does make sense to think of virtue ethics as a cohesive and unified moral theory, and let us take Hursthouse's understanding of virtue ethics as a model, and now ask whether the approach is comprehensive. By "comprehensive" is meant something like "able to be utilized in all areas of ethical reflection." The question is, then, can virtue ethics be used to pursue answers to all questions pertinent to philosophical ethics? Or, to put it negatively, is there any part of ethical reflection for which virtue ethics is irrelevant? An interesting exchange in *Utilitas* between Brad Hooker and Hursthouse provides a useful test case for answering these questions and determining whether virtue ethics is comprehensive.[36]

---

35. Chappell, *CCVE*, "Virtue Ethics in the Twentieth Century," 149–71, especially 150–52.

36. Brad Hooker, "The Collapse of Virtue Ethics," *Utilitas* 14 (2002): 22–40; Rosalind Hursthouse, "Virtue Ethics vs. Rule-Consequentialism: A Reply to Brad Hooker," *Utilitas* 14 (2002): 41–53.

ASPIRATIONS 133

Hooker seeks to show that virtue ethics is not as distinctive as it contends to be, that in fact it bears considerable resemblance to rule-consequentialism, but that on the points of disagreement between rule-consequentialism and virtue ethics, rule-consequentialism is to be preferred. To make his case, he focuses on what he takes to be Hursthouse's criterion of virtue, summarizing her position as follows:[37]

A human is virtuous if and only if her dispositions to act from reason, her emotions, and her desires are likely to promote

(i) her individual survival,
(ii) survival of the human species,
(iii) characteristic enjoyment and freedom from pain, and
(iv) good function of the social group

The implication of much of her discussion seems to be that any disposition that doesn't meet all the above criteria is to that extent "ethically defective," i.e., a vice.[38]

Hooker contends that Hursthouse sufficiently guards her first condition against egoism—though Hursthouse, rightly, responds that Hooker is wrong in the first place to see this as an issue between self and other-regarding virtues.[39] Hooker's focus is instead on the three "other-regarding" conditions.

It is on the question of the moral permissibility of homosexuality,[40] a permissibility that Hursthouse acknowledges, that Hooker seeks to put Hursthouse's criterion of virtue to the fire. He contends that there is no way both to admit the permissibility of homosexual acts in such a way as to regard them as virtuous and to retain the con-

---

37. His interpretation pertains to 198–201 of Hursthouse's *On Virtue Ethics*.
38. Hooker, "The Collapse of Virtue Ethics," 33.
39. Hursthouse, "Virtue Ethics vs. Rule-Consequentialism," 42–43.
40. Hooker and Hursthouse, in her reply, both speak of homosexuality, not homosexual acts. They both fail to make a distinction between homosexual orientation and homosexual acts. Yet it is not the orientation that is in ethical dispute, here or elsewhere, but rather the acts that can follow from it. The typical ethical objections to homosexuality are directed toward the acts (things over which one exercises control), not the orientation (over which one may or may not exercise some control).

dition of the survival of the species (criterion ii). Hooker contends:

> I think that, when we think about sex, the benefits we rightly focus on are (a) the role of sex in certain kinds of intimate personal relationships and (b) the sheer pleasure. Deep personal relationships and pleasure are two things that are especially good candidates for being fundamental components of well-being. There are others, such as important knowledge, achievement, and autonomy. Any activity that promotes any component of well-being is *pro tanto* desirable, whether or not it also promotes survival. The criterion of virtue should refer to the promotion of *well-being*, rather than to *survival*.[41]

The point of this line of reasoning for Hooker is to show why it is that virtue ethics "should evaluate dispositions with a view to the consequences for well-being generally (not just human well-being). But if virtue ethics does this, then virtue ethics seems to collapse into rule-consequentialism."[42] As much as one might disagree with Hooker's characterization regarding the ends of sex because of its exclusion of any reference to the natural procreative end of sex, and as strange as it is that the permissibility of homosexual acts is presented as a type of litmus test for the adequacy of a moral theory,[43] Hooker has an important point with respect to Hursthouse: Hursthouse would like to retain her criterion and pass this contemporary moral litmus test too, but it seems that she cannot.

Hursthouse's response to Hooker is particularly revealing for thinking about the comprehensiveness of virtue ethics. In it, Hursthouse reasserts her conviction that homosexual acts are permissible; in fact, doing so is of such importance to her that she tells her readers that if Hooker is right and her criterion had the consequence of forbidding homosexual acts, she "would feel compelled to abandon it forthwith."[44] The reason she thinks her position does not have this

---

41. Hooker, "The Collapse of Virtue Ethics," 37–38.
42. Ibid., 38.
43. Would Hooker reject consequentialism in the face of compelling arguments that permitting homosexual acts produces worse results than does forbidding them?
44. Hursthouse, "Virtue Ethics vs. Rule-Consequentialism," 44.

consequence is that homosexuality is not for her a character trait at all. She accuses Hooker of using too broad a notion of "disposition," one that cannot account for the difference between traits of character and practices: "Going in for homosexual activity, I said, is, like going in for solitude and celibacy, a *practice*, not a character trait, and it is only character traits that are up for assessment as virtues or vices."[45] It is significant that for Hursthouse the categories of virtue and vice are not to be applied in a consideration of practices per se, but rather are a matter of *how*, and *when*, and *why* one engages in such practices.

A still more significant issue for our considerations is Hursthouse's rejection of the label she sees Hooker as attempting to foist on her—that of a foundationalist. A foundationalist, on Hursthouse's understanding, is one who looks for some "unifying justificatory principle," and typically a nonnormative one, in order to ground one's moral claims. Hursthouse contends she is not doing that and that Hooker is wrong to see her criterion for virtue as suggesting that she is seeking to provide one. She replies, "In so far as I follow McDowell, I presuppose that all this unifying work has been done—in our acquired grasp of the concepts of the individual virtues—before we turn to the rather arcane philosophical task of considering whether those character traits that we standardly call 'the virtues' really are rightly so named."[46] Surely, she is on the right track in recognizing, with Aristotle it should be pointed out, that philosophical ethics begins only after one's moral education has reached a certain point of completion.

Nevertheless, it should be, and indeed is, a part of moral philosophy to attempt to persuade those who disagree with us on founda-

---

45. An exploration of the differences between Hursthouse's and MacIntyre's senses of "practice," and the relation of virtue to them, is worthwhile but not pursued here. See MacIntyre's *After Virtue*, 187, for his definition of practice, and 191 for his definition of virtue in relation to practices.

46. Hursthouse, "Virtue Ethics vs. Rule-Consequentialism," 51.

tional issues. That is, a comprehensive moral theory ought to provide us with some means for engaging in discussion those who disagree with us about what is to count as honest, or courageous, or just, or what have you. Hursthouse would seem to disagree with that claim when she contends that if faced with someone who really and truly believed that cruelty to animals was not wrong,

> I would have to try to change her ethical outlook before there was any point in our discussing whether compassion and courage are virtues. As described, her grasp of the concepts of *compassion* and *courage* is so different from mine that any "agreement" we reached would be merely verbal. But I would not try to change her ethical outlook with regard to animals by advancing some premise about the foundational value of the well-being of all living things.[47]

Although Hursthouse does not say what she means by "ethical outlook" in detail, we can glean that it is presupposed by philosophical discourse. It is also, it seems, impervious to alteration through philosophical discourse. However, it does seem to be a matter of deep convictions, and can be altered through some means. Hursthouse does not enlighten us with respect to how she would go about seeking to change it in a person who does not share her ethical outlook, but only that on the point of treatment of animals it cannot be altered by means of emphasizing the value of living things. It seems to be at a level of conviction that can be altered only by a sort of conversion to a new ethical outlook. But working toward such a conversion is not part of the task of virtue ethics. Virtue ethics is, she goes on to tell us, an explanatory rather than a justificatory enterprise, one in which we seek to discern how to fit certain significant notions together rather than one in which we seek to justify and defend our ethical positions.

She contends that this view of virtue ethics follows from the acceptance of Anscombe's and Geach's recognition that "good" is an attributive adjective, and that

---

47. Ibid.

the significance of the thesis in moral philosophy is that this grammatical feature of the word "good" (and its related terms) cannot undergo a miraculous change when we start doing ethics. What goes for "good cactus" and "good wolf" also goes for "good human being," and the adverb(s) "morally" or "ethically" added to "good human being" can do no more than restrict the aspects of human beings to be considered; it cannot change the grammar.[48]

There are good reasons to agree with the thesis that "good" is an attributive property. But one should, I think, disagree with Hursthouse's understanding of the limitations this imposes insofar as this grammatical understanding of "good" does point us to grounds by means of which we can contend with those who disagree with us over basic ethical notions. We do not need a deontologically charged notion of the moral good to describe a good human being in such a way as to derive a proposition such as "a human being who lacks any compassion for non-human animals fails as a good human being;" just as we do not need a miraculous notion of good to derive a proposition about a good carpenter such as "a carpenter who cannot frame walls with ninety-degree angles is not a good carpenter." An adequate understanding of entailments to the attributive use of good and its cognates can do far more work than Hursthouse grants. Can it give us a ground from which we could attempt to change somebody's ethical outlook? There are many reasons to think it can, though much depends on an interlocutor's willingness to engage in a discussion in good faith. That is, much depends on whether he or she assents to the proposition that "a human being who is unwilling to engage in critical reflection is not a good human being," and whether he or she lacks the vice of unwarranted stubbornness.

If we put her discussion of the limitations of virtue ethical discourse together with Hursthouse's deep-seated convictions regarding the moral legitimacy of homosexual acts, it seems that there is a disconnection between virtue ethics and deeper moral convictions.

---

48. Ibid., 52

It appears, then, that a prior conviction of what is included under the title of "moral legitimacy" underlies virtue ethical discourse. If this is the case, then Hursthouse herself seems to have used what she has described pejoratively as a miraculous sort of "good" when speaking of her own ethical outlook. How so? It is fundamental to Hursthouse's perspective that she considers forbiddance of homosexual acts to be morally illegitimate, and compassion for nonhuman animals to be morally legitimate. These *moral* convictions form aspects of the foundation of her ethical outlook, and those who disagree with her have different *moral* convictions composing different ethical outlooks. Between these two tiers of deep-seated moral convictions on the one hand, and virtue ethical discourse on the other hand, we find competing accounts of the entailments of good, with the first tier utilizing a morally pregnant sense of good and the second tier utilizing a thinly attributive sense of good. What this indicates, among other things, is that virtue ethics is not a comprehensive moral theory. How so?

Hursthouse's virtue ethics comes into play, by her admission, only when we seek to relate important ethical terms to each other. Virtue ethics is an explanatory, not a justificatory, enterprise. Yet Hursthouse is clearly working on these two levels in her reply to Hooker, as she is in her other works where she argues *from* the moral permissibility, provided the right qualifications are met, of abortion, of euthanasia, of suicide, and of other controversial actions. The first, again, is the level of her own deeply felt *moral* convictions about homosexuality, treatment of nonhuman animals, and a lot of other things. These convictions are so important to her that she tells us she would abandon important features of her virtue ethical theory should it be shown to overturn them. This, it seems plain, is indeed a type of moral philosophizing: her reasoning is being guided by her distinctively *moral* convictions. Those *moral* convictions provide the standard against which she measures her evaluative virtue ethical project. Yet, this is a type of moral philosophizing that she contends virtue ethics does not touch, for virtue ethics is only seeking to explain the relation between certain significant terms. If virtue ethics is merely descriptive, then Hursthouse is not a virtue ethicist when she is engaging in other acts of moral philosophizing. Thus, Hursthouse exposes in her reply to Hooker the incomprehensiveness of virtue ethics: the task of moral philosophy is, on the basis of Hursthouse's own descriptions, wider than the task of virtue ethics.

Does Mainstream Virtue Ethics Provide a Coherent Virtue Theory?

Recall the distinction, first emphasized by Driver and oft-repeated, between virtue ethics and virtue theory.[49] A virtue ethics is a moral theory that in some way or other evaluates other ethical notions from the vantage point of the virtues. A virtue theory is a theoretical explanation of virtue. Every virtue ethics includes a virtue theory, but not every virtue theory is part of a virtue ethics. A virtue theory must include some account of what virtue is, what makes a virtue a virtue, and what sort of work one expects virtue to do with respect to human action. Most virtue theories entail, as well, at least a partial tabulation of virtues.

A coherent virtue theory would enable us to identify a virtue when we see one, give a satisfying account of what makes that virtue a virtue, and be able to explain its function with respect to our lives. Does virtue ethics deploy a cohesive virtue theory? The incohesiveness and incomprehensiveness of mainstream virtue ethics would seem to make it impossible that we should find such a consistent and coherent virtue theory shared by all the various partisans to virtue ethics.

Conly's observation that in the contemporary literature on virtue, "anything goes," remains pertinent since her first making it.[50] Dis-

---

49. Driver, "The Virtues and Human Nature," 111–29, n. 1.
50. Conly, "Flourishing and the Ethics of Virtue," 84.

agreements abound concerning whether a virtue is a habit, disposition, passion, trait of character, or action. Different accounts of what makes a virtue a virtue follow the various patterns we would expect from different virtue ethicists taking their orientation from Plato, or Aristotle, or the Stoics, or Hume, or Kant, or Mill, or Nietzsche, or some creative combination of two or more of these thinkers, and with some of each of the virtue ethicist's own nuances thrown in for good measure.

There are also to be found disagreements over which habits, or dispositions, or traits of character, or passions, or actions are virtues and which are vices. Is universal beneficence a virtue? Hursthouse and Slote certainly think so. But it is unimaginable to think that Nietzsche would claim it to be one. Is autonomy a virtue? Kant would certainly think so, but not so Aristotle or Aquinas. What of justice? We find profoundly different perspectives on what justice is in the literature, with disagreements on whether or not it is a self or other-regarding virtue, whether it is a matter of fairness, whether it is a matter of merit, whether it is anything more than institutional and procedural. Temperance, too, comes in for a variety of treatments ranging from scorn to prudery. And practical wisdom runs the gamut from intuition, to instrumental reasoning, to reflection on ends, to reflection on the best means to achieve ends. Courage, alone, has come in for fairly stable treatment, though even for this widely admired virtue we find a variety of accounts.

Even more disagreement abounds regarding what the virtues are supposed to do in our lives. Do they make us flourish? Do they make us successful? Are they their own reward? Do they enable us to achieve mastery over ourselves? Do they enable us to master others? Or is it just common sense that we would acquire and exercise the virtues?

Of course it is the different philosophical traditions feeding into what has come to be known as the virtue ethics movement that makes for such variety in the theories of virtue informing contemporary virtue ethics. We can organize these different virtue theories that are part of the varieties of moral theories employed within the virtue ethics movement by brand, so to speak, with Aristotelian, Humean, Kantian, Nietzschean, and so on serving as qualifiers. But what really ought to interest us is what is behind these labels. There we find widely different accounts of human nature, of the ends of human life, and of the sort of standards by means of which we ought to judge a life as well-lived.

This brings us to what really seems to be the heart of the matter regarding the status of virtue ethics as a moral theory. We have, and will continue to have, profound and irreconcilable disagreements in moral philosophy, including virtue ethical moral philosophy, for as long as and to such extent that we have divergent positions about what Anscombe describes as an adequate philosophical psychology. Anscombe pointed us in the direction of Aristotle for a promising path by means of which we might address what this book contends are the foundational questions for moral philosophy: What is human nature? What is the purpose of human life? And by what means can we judge progress made toward achieving the goal of human life? Adequate answers to these questions would yield an adequate philosophical psychology. Before we can have a coherent virtue theory, we need these more basic questions answered.

Many contemporary virtue ethicists, especially in its early stages but still today,[51] embraced an Aristotelian, or more often neo-Aristotelian, approach. But they also began, and still continue, to make the case for the superiority of their approach by seeking to show how a modified Aristotelian account of the virtues can be utilized to solve

---

51. Russell's defense of Hard Virtue Ethics, and its companion, Hard Virtue Theory, in *Practical Intelligence and the Virtues* is the finest recent example of this sort of approach. His defense of Hard Virtue Theory, he acknowledges, goes against the grain of the current virtue ethical literature in its endorsement of a central role for *phronesis*, and he argues that virtue ethicists who do not embrace something like his Hard Virtue Theory are subject to a number of objections to which his Aristotelian approach to virtue theory is immune.

the pressing concerns of modern moral theory. In this respect Anscombe's warning that we must cease engaging in moral philosophy until we have developed the necessary Aristotelian-inspired philosophical psychology seems not to have been sufficiently heeded. Others, and MacIntyre is preeminent on this score with his extensive and systematic reenvisioning of Aristotelian ethics, stepped out of the current of modern moral philosophical concerns to reforge the fundamental tasks of ethics. As a result, unconventional virtue ethicists, and MacIntyre in particular, have been marginalized not just by modern moral philosophers, but by those mainstream virtue ethicists seeking to defend their own approaches by the accepted standards of the dominant moral project.

This chapter has attempted to demonstrate that although contemporary virtue ethics has a loose unity as a historical movement, it lacks a substantive unity of the sort that entails a cohesive, comprehensive, and coherent moral theory. Since much of the content of contemporary virtue ethics is informed by explicit recourse to Aristotle's ethics, one might well conclude that Aristotelian ethics is to blame for the lack of cohesiveness, comprehensiveness, and coherency of moral theory within the contemporary virtue ethics movement. Is that a valid inference? A more detailed account of the extent to which contemporary virtue ethics has been a successful revival of Aristotelian ethics needs to be pursued to answer this question.

Chapter 5

ARISTOTLE'S ETHICS AND CONTEMPORARY VIRTUE ETHICS

> *But it can be seen that philosophically there is a huge gap, at present unfillable as far as we are concerned, which needs to be filled by an account of human nature, human action, the type of characteristic a virtue is, and above all of human "flourishing." And it is the last concept that seems the most doubtful.*
>
> Anscombe, "Modern Moral Philosophy"

To what extent are the significant shortcomings with respect to a substantive moral theory within the mainstream virtue ethical movement attributable to shortcomings within Aristotle's ethics? If the mainstream variety of virtue ethics includes a genuine retrieval of Aristotelian ethics, then it would seem to be the case that these shortcomings are, at least in part, due to Aristotelian ethics. If it does not, then Aristotle's ethics, at least taken in their fullness, are not responsible for those difficulties, and the possibility is at least left open that a more thoroughgoing revival of Aristotelian ethics might still be made in such manner as to reground ethics along the lines suggested by Anscombe. Does mainstream contemporary virtue ethics represent a thoroughgoing retrieval of Aristotelian ethics?

That many contemporary virtue ethicists have claimed to have taken over an Aristotelian perspective is evident. Indeed, these claims are so widespread that some recent accounts of virtue ethics make a point to remind us that a virtue ethics need not be, despite appearances, Aristotelian. In her *Internet Encyclopedia of Philosophy* entry, "Virtue Ethics," Athanassoulis writes, "While some virtue ethics take inspiration from Plato's, the Stoics', Aquinas', Hume's and Nietzsche's accounts of virtue and ethics, Aristotelian conceptions of virtue ethics still dominate the field."[1] Annas also emphasizes the dominance of an Aristotelian account of the virtues within virtue ethics,[2] even though she herself argues for an approach to virtue ethics that takes more direct inspiration from the Stoics.[3]

Hursthouse emphasizes the dominance of Aristotle in virtue ethical literature while, as we have seen, also seeking to widen the tent to squeeze in other thinkers:

> It [the re-emergence of virtue ethics] has also generated [in addition to Kantian] virtue ethical readings of philosophers other than Plato and Aristotle, such as Martineau, Hume and Nietzsche, and thereby different forms of virtue ethics have developed.... But although modern virtue ethics does not have to take the form known as "neo-Aristotelian," almost any modern version still shows that its roots are in ancient Greek philosophy.[4]

Hursthouse's and other virtue ethical comments, taken together with the popular tendency to couple virtue ethics and Aristotelianism, prompt these questions: What does "Aristotelian" mean in the context of contemporary virtue ethics literature? What does the claim to adhere to Aristotelianism entail for one's moral philosophizing? Is a concern with virtue, practical wisdom, and some version of flourishing enough to constitute Aristotelianism? Just how extensively does

---

1. Athanassoulis, "Virtue Ethics."
2. Annas, "Virtue Ethics," 515.
3. Julia Annas, *The Morality of Happiness*; "My Station and Its Duties: Ideal and the Social Embeddedness of Virtue," *Proceedings of the Aristotelian Society*, new series 102 (2002): 109–23.
4. Hursthouse, "Virtue Ethics."

contemporary virtue ethics revive Aristotelian ethics? If contemporary virtue ethics is right to look to Aristotle as its most significant founder, does this mean that Aristotle is a virtue ethicist?

Hursthouse characterizes her own adherence to Aristotelianism as "neo-Aristotelianism" in *On Virtue Ethics*. Though it would be a mistake to conclude that all Aristotelian-leaning virtue ethicists would characterize themselves in the same way as does Hursthouse, it is safe to conclude that Hursthouse provides a paradigmatic description when she writes:

> The particular version of virtue ethics I detail and discuss in this book is of a more general kind known as "neo-Aristotelian." The general kind is "neo" for at least the reason I noted above, that its proponents allow themselves to regard Aristotle as just plain wrong on slaves and women, and also because we do not restrict ourselves to Aristotle's list of virtues. (Charity or benevolence, for example, is not an Aristotelian virtue, but all virtue ethicists assume it is on the list now.) It is "Aristotelian" in so far as it aims to stick pretty close to his ethical writings wherever else it can.[5]

The "neo" part of "neo-Aristotelian" is clearly a term of exclusion, the result of having excised those parts in Aristotle to which Hursthouse objects. Perhaps it is clear to some readers what exactly Hursthouse is excising, but it is not obvious from her text. It is notable that we do not learn from Hursthouse what exactly about those views of Aristotle on slaves and women she disagrees with are. Does she mean she disagrees with Aristotle's view in the *Politics* that slaves are capable of virtue, or his view in the *Nicomachean Ethics* that a free person can be a friend of a slave insofar as a slave is a human being? Should we presume that she means that she disagrees with Aristotle's claim that there is such a thing as natural slavery, or rather with Aristotle's implicit critique of the institution of slavery insofar as it allows for treating as tools those who are fit for self-rule? Are we to think, contrary to Aristotle, that friendship between a wife and her husband is not

---

5. Hursthouse, *On Virtue Ethics*, 8.

possible? Aristotle's views on slavery and woman are multifaceted, and yet they are treated by Hursthouse as one-dimensional. Certainly one ought to disagree wholeheartedly with Aristotle's claim that woman are, biologically speaking, incomplete men. But observation demands that one agree with Aristotle's claims that, on the whole, women tend to be less hairy than men, and smaller. Experience, moreover, teaches one that Aristotle is right that friendship between men and women is, indeed, both possible and mutually beneficial; but, for a host of reasons, one should strongly disagree with his claim that such friendships are always between unequals. The point is that some qualification would seem to be in order when one speaks of rejecting a complex thinker's "views on" a subject.

The sort of qualification Hursthouse most likely means to imply is that she disagrees with Aristotle's views on slaves and women *insofar* as his views conflict with what Hursthouse would characterizes as her ethical outlook, an outlook that is, one gathers from her judgments on particular points of ethical dispute, identifiable with a version of liberalism. Her employment of "neo" is intended, among other things, to clear the air, so to speak, so that one can make recourse to Aristotelian principles without being distracted by Aristotle's blindness with respect to the equal status of women and slaves. The "Aristotelian" in her "neo-Aristotelian" refers to those parts of Aristotle's works that Hursthouse considers worthwhile. The open-ended qualification that her account sticks close to Aristotle "wherever else it can," however, leaves some room for refinement. The assumption that Hursthouse follows Aristotle on everything but some of his views regarding women and slaves would be facile, for Hursthouse provides far more original argumentation than would follow from simply excising a few views of Aristotle and adopting the rest of his thought more or less *tout court*.

Hursthouse's concerns are not in fact primarily with making a detailed case for the particular ways in which her positions can be compared to Aristotle. In some regards, she is not particularly concerned with Aristotle at all, but rather with developing her distinctive approach to virtue ethics. But she is justly motivated to give Aristotle his due for the inspiration he provides, and toward this end she specifies the four main features of Aristotle's thought that she adopts from him, namely, a view that *eudaimonia* is an objective, and not merely subjective, notion; the view that a virtue is a trait of character that makes its possessor good; a sensitivity to the distinctions between mature rational action and desire on the one hand, and immature action and desire on the other; and a philosophical psychology that runs contrary to the prevailing dualist psychologies and that, among other things, recognizes that beliefs and desires are not antipodal.[6]

These specifications do much to flesh the skeleton of her claim that her position is Aristotelian. But we can, and should, ask again whether these four areas are sufficient to make one's ethics Aristotelian. The reasons why this question is important extend beyond an attempt simply to present an accurate tallying of similarities and differences between Aristotelian ethics and virtue ethics, or to seek to remove the Aristotelian mantle virtue ethicists may have wrapped themselves in for strategic reasons. Rather, what we need to determine is whether Aristotle's ethics is susceptible to the same flaws discerned within contemporary virtue ethics and discussed in the last chapter, and to do that, we need to see if we can disentangle Aristotle's ethics from contemporary virtue ethics.

Whose Virtue Ethics? Which Aristotelianism?

A number of difficulties beset an effort to clarify the relationship between Aristotle's ethics and contemporary virtue ethics, but two especially stand out. The first has to do with those difficulties entailed by the attempt to formulate a substantive and agreed-upon definition of what contemporary virtue ethics is.

---

6. Ibid., 8–16.

The importance of this issue has not gone unnoticed by several of the authors who have explicitly explored in some detail the relation between Aristotle's ethics and contemporary virtue ethics. Watson in "The Primacy of Character" and Trianosky in "What Is Virtue Ethics All About?" each make it their principal aim to specify what precisely virtue ethics is, and their reflections on the relationship between Aristotle and virtue ethics are made with the aim of clarifying virtue ethics.[7] Similarly Santas's article, "Does Aristotle Have a Virtue Ethics?" which has as its chief aim determining whether Aristotle has a virtue ethics, spends significant effort on the task of determining what virtue ethics is—leaving us with several ways to describe it.[8] Simpson's article on the relationship between contemporary virtue ethics and Aristotle, "Contemporary Virtue Ethics and Aristotle," is an exception to the rule of worrying over just how to define virtue ethics, adopting as definitive Pojman and Solomon's descriptions of virtue ethics.[9] Simpson thinks of virtue ethics in these terms: "According to virtue ethics, what is primary for ethics is ... the judgment of agents. The good person is the fundamental category for moral philosophy, and the good person is the person of good character, the person who possesses moral virtue."[10] Simpson's procedure enables him not to be distracted from his main task of pointing out what he considers the distinctive features of Aristotle's ethics, and to argue that central features of Aristotle's ethics turn out to be such as not to be acceptable to any virtue ethicist of whatever description. Yet it would seem that underlying his analysis is the assumption that contemporary virtue ethics as a whole identifies in some manner with Aristotelian ethics.

It is evident, however, that there are a variety of approaches within

---

7. Trianosky, "What Is Virtue Ethics All About?"; Watson, "The Primacy of Character."

8. Santas, "Does Aristotle Have a Virtue Ethics?"

9. Louis P. Pojman, *Ethics: Discovering Right and Wrong* (Belmont, Calif.: Wadsworth Publishing, 1990), 119–23; Solomon, "Internal Objections to Virtue Ethics." In this earlier essay, Solomon had not yet applied the radical/routine distinction that I make liberal use of in this book.

10. Simpson, "Contemporary Virtue Ethics and Aristotle," 503.

virtue ethics and that not all of them are Aristotelian. The last chapter arrived at the conclusion that virtue ethics does not represent a cohesive moral theory. How does one, then, contrast virtue ethics with Aristotle's ethics? It is not in fact on the whole of contemporary virtue ethics, but only on those varieties of mainstream virtue ethics that endorse Aristotelian ethics that we should focus to make a proper comparison. This specification, nevertheless, includes the majority of contemporary virtue ethical approaches.

There remains a second significant challenge to reflecting on the relationship between contemporary virtue ethics and Aristotle's ethics, namely, the interpretative difficulties of determining just what those main features of Aristotle's ethics are. On any number of issues central to Aristotle's ethics, we find a variety of interpretations regarding Aristotle's *Nicomachean* and *Eudemian Ethics*—not just from those philosophers seeking to contemporize Aristotle's ideas within moral philosophy, but also among those whose primary business it is to interpret Aristotle. To wit, one finds a variety of interpretations about how exactly to interpret Aristotle's function argument in *NE* I. 7, what the relation is between his definition of happiness in *NE* I. 13 and his account of the two sorts of happiness in X. 7–8, whether his account of happiness is logically prior to his derivation of the virtues or if he derives his conception of happiness from a given list of virtues, whether all of the moral virtues are equally susceptible to analysis according to the mean between passion and action, what exactly practical wisdom is, what the roles of the other intellectual virtues are vis-à-vis the rest of the ethics, whether and how to read the *Politics* as a continuation and culmination of Aristotle's reflections in the *Nicomachean Ethics*, whether one should regard the *Eudemian Ethics* or the *Nicomachean Ethics* as more or less definitive of Aristotle's mature thought, and others.[11]

---

11. There has been a vast amount of scholarship on the *Nicomachean Ethics* in the last 130 years. See Lockwood, "A Topical Bibliography of Scholarship on Aristotle's *Nicomachean Ethics*: 1880–2004."

The interpretative challenges notwithstanding, nobody can compare Aristotle's ethics with virtue ethics without making a number of claims about Aristotle's ethics. As a student of some of the thornier interpretative challenges in Aristotle's ethics and so well aware of some of the interpretative dangers, I do not pretend in this chapter to enter into the fray of scholarship on Aristotle's ethics with the intention of putting a persuasive and conclusive stamp on my own interpretation of the central features of Aristotle's ethics. That would be the task for a very different book, or several rather. What I *can* do here, however, is describe some of those main features of Aristotle's ethics that, even if subject to interpretative dispute, nevertheless provide points of contrast with what are taken to be the main Aristotelian-inspired efforts of contemporary virtue ethicists. The disadvantages of adopting this procedure of treating both contemporary virtue ethical literature that claims inheritance from Aristotle and Aristotle's ethics in general terms is that many of the fine-grained distinctions and controversies, as well as a running tally in the footnotes of where to look to chase out those distinctions and controversies further, are all pushed to the side. That is a significant loss. However, avoiding it would require something more than constructing a further stage of my argument regarding the contemporary virtue ethics movement. It is that next stage of my argument that I am concerned with, and directing our attention to the general contours of this map has the advantage of not becoming lost in the topological details. Moreover, just as you can take in more of a region as you "zoom out" from a Google map—doing so obscures details but does not jeopardize accuracy—so too the following reflections on the differences between the main features of Aristotle's ethics and the Aristotelian-like features of contemporary virtue ethicists provide us with a big-picture view, the details of which can be examined at some other point in time.

Contemporary Virtue Ethics and Aristotle

We have on the one hand contemporary virtue ethicists who claim inspiration from Aristotle, and on the other hand we have Aristotle's ethics. Whatever Aristotle is doing in his ethical writings, he is not pursuing the central concerns of what Anscombe characterizes as modern moral philosophy. It is the very lack of a concern in Aristotle's ethics with a special sense of "morality," and its attendant stresses on the moral "ought" and its cognates, that makes possible the contrast between it and modern moral philosophy. Yet we have come to see that the aims which are central to Hursthouse's project, as well as to the projects of other mainstream virtue ethicists, are the aims of modern moral philosophy. Indeed, mainstream virtue ethics justifies the very existence of the virtue ethics movement on the basis of its claims to handle the central concerns of modern moral philosophy better than, or at least as well as, those approaches responsible for generating modern moral philosophy; namely, deontology and consequentialism. The primacy of a concern for developing a scheme for rule-based action guidance and justificatory concerns directed toward a reductionistic account of distinctively moral principles, as well as the willingness to lay aside one's principles in order to achieve a desired consequence, which are in Anscombe's telling characteristic of the modern moral project, are simply lacking in Aristotle.[12] Any attempts to harness Aristotelian principles to those aims so foreign to his project are bound to yield an ethics that looks very different from Aristotle's.

The differences between the object, aim, and method of Aristotelian ethics and those theories that are part of modern moral philosophy indicate the most significant points of divergence between Aristotle's ethics and Aristotelian-inspired varieties of mainstream

---

12. This is not to suggest that Aristotle is unconcerned with action guidance, but rather that such a concern does not have the same place in his ethics as it has in modern moral philosophy.

contemporary virtue ethics. These differences, however, are not often stressed. Perhaps one reason for that is that stressing differences between Aristotelian ethics and mainstream virtue ethics would weaken the claim that virtue ethics is an alternative to the other dominant theories.

Another has to do with some ambiguities in the ways in which we tend to think about Aristotle and ethics. It is one thing to speak of Aristotle's ethics, and another to speak of Aristotelian ethics. The latter points to a tradition of moral enquiry that stretches well beyond Aristotle, a tradition that includes, for instance, Aquinas, whose Aristotelian credentials nobody doubts, but whose own ethical reflections include a closer attention to action guidance and the justification of moral principles than do Aristotle's. These features of Aquinas's Aristotelian ethics come in through his inheritances from additional traditions of moral inquiry, including influences from Cicero, Augustine, and the natural law tradition. So why is it that nobody doubts Aquinas's Aristotelian credentials, whereas Santas, Simpson, and others question the Aristotelian credentials of those virtue ethicists who claim inheritance from Aristotle? Could they not be thought to be stretching in their own unique ways the ethics of Aristotle to fit the concerns of modern moral philosophers in a way similar to—which is also to say very different from—how Aquinas stretched Aristotle?

I want to argue this is not the case, and for several reasons. Two of them have already been mentioned. Although Aquinas pays close attention to action guidance and the derivation of moral principles, he does not do so in a way that picks out a special sphere for "moral" human action that is distinct from other spheres of human action. For Aquinas, the realm of what we like to call "the moral" is exactly as wide as the realm of the deliberative, which is to say that any and every rational and so distinctively human action—that is, every action that proceeds from choice—is a moral action.[13] Aquinas also

---

13. *Summa theologiae*, I-II, *proemium*.

stands firm on absolute prohibitions against certain sorts of actions no matter the circumstances. Both of these principles are characteristic of Aristotle's ethics, and both are not uniformly endorsed by Aristotelian-inspired virtue ethicists. The wide scope of ethical consideration together with the refusal to reject the claims that moral absolutes make upon practical reflection yields the following two conditions, both of which are necessary to making an ethics Aristotelian:

(1) Aristotelian ethics finds incoherent the designation of a distinctive sphere of human action definable as "the moral."[14]
(2) Aristotelian ethics is nonconsequentialist, in the Anscombeian sense.[15]

It is precisely the range of concerns in Aristotle's ethics being as wide as the range of human action that makes Aristotle's ethics one that is concerned, like Plato's and so many other classical and medieval philosophers', with one's whole way of life. It is precisely the refusal to set aside one's absolutist principles about the conditionless forbiddance of actions such as adultery, theft, and murder, as well as feelings such as spite and envy, that, on Anscombe's score, makes Aristotle's ethics an ethics at all.

Though not sufficient conditions for defining the whole of Aristotelian ethics, these two are of primary concern with respect to the central differences between a distinctively modern moral phi-

---

14. Aristotle on the breadth of ethical reflection entailing all that touches the human being insofar as he is a deliberator: "Hence choice is either desiderative thought or intellectual desire, and such an origin of action is a man" (*NE* VI 2, 1139^{b}4-5, Ross translation, here as elsewhere).

15. Aristotle on the maintenance of moral absolutes: "But not every action or every passion admits of a mean; for some have names that already imply badness, e.g. spite, shamelessness, envy, and in the case of actions adultery, theft, murder; for all of these and suchlike things imply by their names that they are themselves bad, and not the excesses or deficiencies of them. It is not possible, then, ever to be right with regard to them; one must always be wrong. Nor does goodness or badness with regard to such things depend on committing adultery with the right woman, at the right time, and in the right way, but simply to do any of them is to go wrong" (*NE* II 6, 1107^{a}9-21).

losophy on the one hand, and on the other either Aristotle's own ethics or a sufficiently Aristotelian ethics. This provides us with a useful rule: if a variety of contemporary virtue ethics fails on either of these two conditions, it fails as an Aristotelian ethics.[16] This rule can be expanded to include other conditions if it can be shown that there are such. In the remainder of this section I will consider several other necessary features of Aristotle's ethics, and add to these considerations the claim that the failure to maintain any one of these additional conditions amounts to a failure as an ethics that can be considered as sufficiently Aristotelian.

(3) Aristotelian ethics insists on the paramount importance of contemplative wisdom.

A careful reading of the *Nicomachean Ethics* cannot fail to notice the several insistences Aristotle makes about the superiority of the philosophical activity of contemplative wisdom. From the perspective of much of contemporary ethics, this insistence appears strange. What is one to make of such a claim, especially if one thinks ethics is only supposed to reflect upon right or wrong actions? Activities, after all, are not always actions, and only some of them are candidates for what in some theories pass for "moral" actions.

There are many parts of both the *Nicomachean* and *Eudemian Ethics* that strike us as idiosyncratic and parochial. If we make it a point to ignore them, we run the risk of missing important features of Aristotle's ethics. For instance, Aristotle's employment of *to kalon* ("beauty and nobility" or "the fine") as a sort of aesthetical *cum* metaphysical standard for judging actions, or his insistence that courageous action can really be manifested only when death is imminent, can be considered as merely quaint features of his cultural

---

16. Some virtue ethicists might respond, and with justice, that they have no problem with being considered only distantly Aristotelian, and so are untouched by this line of criticism. This might be characterized as the "so what?" objection. I begin to answer it in the last part of this chapter, and continue to answer it throughout the next three chapters.

outlook that we have outgrown. Such an attitude, I would suggest, is chauvinistic, and blinds us not only to important concepts for interpreting Aristotle correctly but to resources for enriching our own ethical inquiries.[17] So too are Aristotle's exhortations to make ourselves, as much as possible, gods, often seen as the mere excrescences of a man who still occasionally feels the mesmeric pull of his former master, Plato. We are often encouraged by contemporary interpreters to turn quickly from these embarrassments and to direct our attention to what are considered more relevant passages on the definition of virtue or Aristotle's dialectical analysis of *akrasia*. But this prevents us from meeting Aristotle on his own terms, and instead we regard his works as mineshafts from which we wish only to grab a few of what we consider the more precious gems.

Such an attitude is particularly damaging when we fail to realize that for Aristotle the insistence that if we are to be fully happy, fully flourishing, we can only do so when engaging in contemplative wisdom is paramount. Indeed, that conclusion is rightly regarded as not just the summit of his ethical reflections, but an insight the defense of which justifies the work as a whole. This is why, though relatively few, those passages extolling the unsurpassable worth of contemplative activity are to be found at the most important junctures of his *Nicomachean Ethics:* he introduces the prospect of contemplative activity as most fitting to beings such as ourselves in his brief discussion of the "three lives;"[18] he concludes his analysis of the intellectual virtues stressing the supremacy of philosophical wisdom over practical—and this despite the indispensability of practical wisdom;[19] and he concludes—if we are to read, as I think we must, X.9 as a preamble to the *Politics*—his ten-book long discourse on the most fulfilling way to live by extolling the superiority of the life of

---

17. This is a point I seek to demonstrate in "Are You Man Enough? Aristotle and Courage," *International Philosophical Quarterly* 50 (2010): 431–45.
18. Aristotle, *NE* I 5, $1096^a 4$–5.
19. Aristotle, *NE* VI 13, $1145^a 7$–11.

contemplative activity, that is, the life in which one exercises contemplative wisdom.[20]

There is no getting around the fact, no matter what one makes of the inclusivist versus intellectualist controversy on the question of Aristotle's notion of happiness, that Aristotle thinks the fundamental task of a life maximally well-lived is to engage in the highest intellectual activity of philosophical contemplation. There are at least three reasons this goal is so often jettisoned by contemporary readers of Aristotle. First, it strikes our egalitarian-attuned ears as elitist. Second, a contemplator needs an object of contemplation. The ultimate contemplative object for Aristotle is the one self-sufficient god. This gives to Aristotle's naturalism a definite supernatural cast, and thus runs counter to many of the prevailing prejudices of our day. Finally, contemplation is not static, but rather dynamic. It is transformative. To know, for Aristotle, is to become the thing known.[21] To know god, then, in the manner necessary for contemplating him, is in some manner to become god. This is what Aristotle is referring to when he exhorts us to make of ourselves gods, so far as we can.[22]

Divinization, to put it mildly, is infrequently extolled as an overarching goal in the pages of contemporary moral philosophy. One does find it skirting around the margins, for there are still some Platonists, Aristotelians of the strict observance, and Thomists remaining in academic philosophy. Perhaps it is not surprising that the absence of a stress on divinization, or even on contemplative wisdom as a unifying goal for the whole of one's life, is missing, as well, in the literature of contemporary virtue ethics. Be that as it may, the ignoring of a goal so central to the Aristotelian project puts in jeopardy the claims of those contemporary virtue ethicists to be rehabilitating the Aristotelian project. A neo-Aristotelianism that fails to emphasize the importance of that virtuous activity which brings order to

20. Aristotle, *NE* X 7–8, 1177^{b}27–1178^{b}33.
21. Aristotle, *De Anima*, III 4, 429^{a}10–429^{b}9; 430^{a}3–5; 7, 431^{a}1, 431^{b}16–17.
22. Aristotle, *NE* X 7, 1177^{b}30–1178^{a}5.

the whole of Aristotle's ethics would seem not to be a sufficiently Aristotelian ethics.

(4) Aristotelian ethics insists happiness is the activity of virtue.

Most neo-Aristotelian contemporary virtue ethicists correctly point to the differences between Aristotle's understanding of *eudaimonia*—often translated as "flourishing," but still accurately translated as the more familiar "happiness"—and the different sense of happiness as treated in contemporary ethics, where Mill's utilitarian understanding of it has achieved dominance. Hursthouse puts the difference in terms of an objective Aristotelian notion as opposed to the subjective stress on contentment.[23] However, Simpson is right to point out that oftentimes the more robust and concrete Aristotelian notion is put to a very un-Aristotelian use in the writings of contemporary virtue ethicists: they seek to determine what is to count as a virtuous trait of character by means of arguing from happiness, whereas Aristotle defines happiness in terms of that which is constituted by the virtues. Simpson puts the point thus:

> According to virtue theorists, one is supposed to use the concept of flourishing to develop an account and justification of the virtues. Flourishing is the prior notion and the virtues are to be understood in terms of it. Aristotle does not argue to the virtues from some prior notion of flourishing, nor does he even attempt to do this. The virtues fall into the definition of *eudaimonia*, but *eudaimonia* does not fall into the definition of the virtues. *Eudaimonia* is defined as activity of soul along with virtue, while the virtues are defined as various habits of choice, lying in a mean relative to us, and determined by reason. What falls into the definition of a thing is prior to that thing and has to be understood before that thing can be understood. So the notion of virtue must be prior to the notion of *eudaimonia* and must be understood before *eudaimonia* can be understood.[24]

---

23. Hursthouse, *On Virtue Ethics*, 10; see Julia Annas, "Virtue and Eudaimonism," *Social Philosophy and Policy* 15 (1998): 37–55, for an extended treatment of some of the main differences.

24. Simpson, "Contemporary Virtue Ethics and Aristotle," 507.

One of the things Simpson's observation implies for Aristotelian ethics is that there must be some means by which we come to recognize what the virtues and vices respectively are that is epistemologically prior to the definition of happiness. Where do those judgments come from? Aristotle's answer is unsettling to many, since it both is elitist and, according to some commentators, opens the door to relativism: Aristotle argues that the judgments about what is virtuous or vicious, good or bad, just or unjust, and the like are the special possession of the noble few who are blessed with both gifted natures and solid educations. Aristotle is then frankly unconcerned with an issue that is, in many respects, of primary importance for contemporary ethicists.

One need not show the same reticence with respect to providing an account of what makes a virtue a virtue as Aristotle in order to provide a sufficiently Aristotelian ethics. But one does need to recognize the logical priority of the virtues to happiness—happiness is that which is constituted by virtuous activity. To attempt to define the virtues by happiness would necessarily be to engage in fallacious reasoning, or to be working with a very different notion of happiness than that which Aristotle provides. What we want, Aristotle tells us in both of his main ethical works, is an understanding of happiness; where we get that is through a careful examination of those virtues we are already acquainted with, even if we are not in possession of them.

It needs to be pointed out, however, that recognizing that a full-blown account of happiness is conceptually dependent on the virtues in Aristotelian ethics does not imply that all reflection on the good life for human beings is posterior to an account of the virtues. The ethically relevant virtues are those qualities of character that enable a human being to do the sorts of things that human nature makes them fit to do well. We need then, Aristotle recognizes, some account of human nature and its proper ends to make conceptual sense of the virtues. What is at issue here is not a vicious circle, but rather two levels of analysis: the first is a philosophically complete account of happiness that necessarily relies on a prior account of the virtues, and the second is a philosophical account of the virtues that relies on a prior account of the ends of human nature. We cannot make sense of happiness without the virtues; we cannot make sense of the virtues without an account of the ends of human nature. Because happiness is the ultimate answer to questions about the ends of human life, these two different levels of analysis are often treated as though they are just one.[25] But they are not, and care needs to be taken not to merge them.[26]

This brings us to a second important point of difference on this topic. Many contemporary virtue ethicists place great stress on the development of character. Virtue ethics, we are told, is about *being* a certain way, not *performing* certain actions.[27] The stress is harmless as far as it goes, for indeed, the happy life is not constituted by a string of performative actions understood as means in pursuit of some distinct reward such as we find described in varieties of utilitarianism. Yet happiness *is* a goal, and action does play a central role

---

25. MacIntyre seems sensitive to these two levels of analysis in *After Virtue*, and for this reason I think Simpson unfair in "Contemporary Virtue Ethics and Aristotle" to lump MacIntyre together with those who define the virtues in terms of happiness. Consider, for instance, this remark of MacIntyre's: "The virtues are precisely those qualities the possession of which will enable an individual to achieve *eudaimonia* and the lack of which will frustrate his movement toward that *telos*. But although it would not be incorrect to describe the exercise of virtues as a means to the end of achieving the good for man, that description is ambiguous.... For what constitutes the good for man is a complete human life lived at its best, and the exercise of the virtues is a necessary and central part of such a life, not a mere preparatory exercise to secure such a life. *We thus cannot characterize the good for man adequately without already having made reference to the virtues*" (*After Virtue*, 148–49, emphasis mine).

26. I return to this topic in chapter 7.

27. Or, as Daniel Statman puts it in his introduction to *Virtue Ethics: A Critical Reader*, "Only since the 1980s has the meaning of VE become more or less fixed. It now refers to a rather new (or renewed) approach to ethics, according to which *the basic judgments in ethics are judgments about character*. As Trianosky notes, this basic assumption embodies two main theses: 1. at least some judgments about the value of character traits are independent of judgments about the rightness or wrongness of actions; and 2. the notion virtue justifies that of right conduct" (7, emphasis his, endnotes deleted by me).

in its achievement; namely, the role of constituting happiness itself. It is this point, stressed throughout Aristotle's ethical texts, that makes nonsense of the oft-heard objection that Aristotle is inconsistent when he claims that virtue is worthy of pursuit for its own sake *and* is constitutive of happiness. We find something other than what has become customary means-end reasoning at work in Aristotle's ethics, and one of the most promising aspects of some contemporary virtue ethical literature has been to explore and seek to revive Aristotle's robust conception of practical reasoning.[28]

However, the stress on "being" rather than "doing" can tend toward a caricature of an ethics in which the virtues are of central importance, as well as obscure an essential and often overlooked point: Happiness is not a matter of possessing virtue, rather it is a matter of virtuous *activity*. Here is how Aristotle characterizes that contrast:

> With those who identify happiness with excellence or some one excellence our account is in harmony; for to excellence belongs activity in accordance with excellence. But it makes, perhaps, no small difference whether we place the chief good in possession or in use, in state or in activity. For the state may exist without producing any good result, as in a man who is asleep or in some other way quite inactive, but the activity cannot; for one who has the activity will of necessity be acting, and acting well. And as in the Olympic Games it is not the most beautiful and the strongest that are crowned but those who compete (for it is some of these that are victorious), so those who act rightly win the noble and good things in life.[29]

To be sure, one ought to strive to acquire, by repeated activity, imitation, and study the various virtues. But the mere development of a virtuous character does not constitute one's end if those virtues are not lived out in their proper activities. To have a virtue is to be

---

28. John McDowell, "Virtue and Reason," *Monist* 62 (1979): 331–50; Julia Annas, "Moral Knowledge as Practical Knowledge," in *Moral Knowledge*, ed. E. E. Paul, F. D. Miller, and J. Paul (Cambridge: Cambridge University Press, 2001), 236–56, and *Intelligent Virtue*; and Daniel C. Russell, *Practical Intelligence and the Virtues*.

29. *NE* I 8, 1098^{b}30–1099^{a}5.

disposed in a distinctive way toward certain activities, but it is the virtuous *activities* that constitute happiness, and, as has already been pointed out, the greatest of these activities is wisdom's activity of contemplation.

Aristotle's ethics, then, measures a successful life not in terms of the extent to which virtuous character has been developed, but in terms of the extent to which the person of a virtuous character acts and acts well. If a neo-Aristotelian virtue ethics presents as the ultimate goal of a well-lived life the having of virtue, it fails as an example of Aristotelian ethics.

(5) Aristotelian ethics insists that practical wisdom, not the practically wise person, directs the truly virtuous to right action.

Much is to be gained from looking to and imitating *ho phronimos*—a practically wise person who is a paragon of virtue. Aristotle, whose concern with ethical education is evident throughout the *Nicomachean Ethics* and that other work which is its sequel, the *Politics*, invites the *phronimos* even into his definition of moral virtue.[30] The point of doing so is a matter of presenting a standard by means of which the workings of reasoning rightly can be sufficiently understood. Both in the formative period of the development of our (hopefully) virtuous characters and in the theoretical exercise of pursuing a coherent and comprehensive virtue theory, the *phronimos* is indispensable.

One's goal however is not to be perpetually imitating one's particular collection of exemplars, but to become oneself a person of practical wisdom. Daniel Statman, commenting on one of the central themes of Santas's article,[31] remarks:

What is at stake here is how to understand Aristotle's *phronimos;* is the *phronimos* the standard for appropriate behavior so that an act is right because, and only because, the *phronimos* performs (or would perform)

---

30. *NE* II 6, 1106^{b}36–1107^{a}2.
31. Santas, "Does Aristotle Have a Virtue Ethics?"

it, or does the *phronimos* perform it because he perceives its independent value? ... Santas shows that according to Aristotle it is (practical) reason that determines whether some act should be done, and not virtue, which merely enables one to do the act reason selects. Hence, in the Aristotelian context, it cannot be the case that the value of acts derives from the value of traits of character.[32]

Santas is no doubt correct that it is an individual's own practical wisdom that determines a right course of action, a determination that is achieved neither by the mere possession of virtue nor by one's attempted imitation of a paradigm. However, I think that Statman's characterization of Santas's position goes too far in claiming that virtue "merely enables one to do the act reason selects." Right reason would not be able to select the right course of action were the reasoner not in possession of a virtuous character.

We need the moral excellences in order to establish the sort of perfected perceptive power that practical wisdom is. The virtues of character provide us with the *archai*, the first things of our reflections.[33] If one is temperate, one knows what sort of feelings and actions count as temperate and one is habitually inclined toward those sorts of feelings and actions. Because of this, the temperate person is spared the trouble of reasoning about whether to be temperate, for the choice to be temperate is compressed within the habit of temperance itself. Practical wisdom is needed to reason out *how* to feel or act temperately in this or that situation. There is no warehouse of rules that we can ship acts of reasoning out from when seeking to reason rightly, for the circumstances that face us are unrepeatable, as are we as the persons confronted with them. There are some very general rules of thumb that Aristotle indicates, like looking for the median and considering how the practically wise person would reason. These reference points provide some rough orientation, but do not provide detailed maps or a precise compass. There simply is no precise map.

32. Statman, "Introduction," in *Virtue Ethics: A Critical Reader*, 27.
33. *NE* I 4, 1095^{b}2–8

Every new action is, as Aristotle does not tire of reminding us, individual. The compass for one's own practical reflections is provided by one's virtues, and it is in the formation of those virtues that the practically wise person plays so pivotal a role, rather than in somehow providing the very stuff of one's practical reflections.

Some Aristotelian-leaning contemporary virtue ethicists appreciate these points about practical wisdom and develop sophisticated accounts of this intellectual virtue.[34] There has, nevertheless, been a tendency in the virtue ethical literature to overlook the special role of practical wisdom.[35] A neo-Aristotelian contemporary virtue ethics that seeks to determine one's course of actions from rules derived from one's view of the *phronimos*, and also fails to appreciate the full scope of practical wisdom's proper work, fails to be sufficiently Aristotelian.

(6) Aristotelian ethics insists it is impossible to exercise any virtue, with the exception of technical skill, wrongly.

Aristotle writes, "Every excellence both brings into good condition the thing of which it is the excellence and makes the work of that thing be done well; … Therefore, if this is true in every case, the

---

34. Hursthouse argues that V-rules are not dependent on a *phronimos* for their derivation (*On Virtue Ethics*, 80), and emphasizes the need for a virtuous agent to exercise his or her own practical wisdom in order to act virtuously (see especially *On Virtue Ethics*, 136). Russell's *Practical Intelligence and the Virtues* is especially notable for its rigorous defense of Aristotle's virtue of practical wisdom and its essential role in the happy life.

35. Russell argues extensively for the connection between practical wisdom and each of the virtues, as well as for the role of practical wisdom in action guidance. He acknowledges the tendency in virtue ethical literature to overlook the work of practical wisdom: "My view therefore stands in stark contrast to the trend toward increasing indifference to the notion of phronesis in recent thought about the virtues of character. Some virtue theorists argue that phronesis is important for some virtues, but certainly not all (Swanton 2003); others that while phronesis is part of the virtues, this requirement is soft enough that even the 'kindheartedness' of an 'imperceptive' person, fragmentary and deficient in phronesis, still counts as a virtue (Adams 2006, 187); others that phronesis and even deliberation are unnecessary if one's motives are virtuous in a 'balanced' way (Slote 2001); and yet others that the virtues require no particular underlying psychological attributes at all, much less phronesis (Driver 2001)" (*Practical Intelligence and the Virtues*, xi).

excellence of man also will be the state which makes a man good and which makes him do his own work well."[36] No neo-Aristotelian contemporary virtue ethicist doubts that virtue makes us good, and disposes us toward right action. The question here, however, is whether or not we can ever virtuously do the wrong thing—and by "wrong" I mean "ignoble, base, unjust or ugly." The position of Aristotle is that we cannot, which is an important part of the reason that he claims that we can never feel spite rightly, or commit murder or adultery rightly.[37] Note that he makes this claim without appealing to a deontological notion of right or wrong. The "rightly" here means "virtuously." There simply is not a notion of right or wrong that can separated off from "virtuously" or "viciously," and to argue for the possibility of virtuously performed wrong actions is to argue against the core of Aristotle's virtue theory.[38]

The point is brought home as well when Aristotle contends for the unity of the virtues by emphasizing the interconnectedness of practical wisdom with the moral (or ethical) virtues:

> It is clear, then, from what has been said, that it is not possible to be good in the strict sense without practical wisdom, nor practically wise without moral excellence. But in this way we may also refute the dialectical argument whereby it might be contended that the excellences exist in separation from each other; the same man, it might be said, is not best equipped by nature for all the excellences, so that he will have already acquired one when he has not yet acquired another. This is possible in respect of the natural excellences, but not in respect of those in respect of which a man is called without qualification good; for with the presence of the one quality, practical wisdom, will be given all the excellences.[39]

---

36. *NE* II 6, 1106^{a}15–18, 21–23.

37. Ibid., 1107^{a}9–26.

38. The defense of the position that virtues are, properly understood, traits of character that can never be misused is at the core of Platonic ethics as well. In fact, it is one of the touchstone differences in Plato's dialogues between sophistical and philosophical accounts of the virtues.

39. *NE* VI 13, 1144^{b}30–1145^{a}2.

Aristotle does provide some allowance in this passage for the uses of ordinary language with respect to the virtues when, for instance, one speaks of a courageous terrorist or a temperate thief. Yet these examples fail to draw on a full account of the virtues, an account that recognizes that courage or temperateness is not really so unless combined with practical wisdom. The truly virtuous, the practically wise one, can never "misuse" his or her virtues.[40] What appears, then, to be a misuse of a virtue can in fact only be the exercise of some counterfeit.

For these reasons, those neo-Aristotelian contemporary virtue ethicists who contend that virtues can be misused fail to have appreciated the reach of practical wisdom, which cannot be exercised excellently or poorly because it simply *is* an excellence,[41] when they claim that one can indeed be virtuously acting wrongly. To argue such is to have missed the extent of interrelation that exists between moral virtues and practical wisdom, a mistake that tends to breed as a further consequence flattened descriptions of moral virtues and truncated accounts of practical wisdom.

Hursthouse provides an interesting case on this issue. On the one hand, she recognizes that although in ordinary language people often use virtue terms to describe the ways in which certain wrong actions are done, these uses fail to appreciate the proper role of practical wisdom in truly virtuous actions.[42] On the other hand, in her attempt to skirt a fine line on the question of whether one can virtuously act wrongly in her chapter on irresolvable and tragic dilemmas—and to her credit she takes great care on this point, far more

---

40. Aristotle does allow that it can be possible for one to have the intellectual virtue of technical knowledge, because its product is distinct from the action that produces it, to misuse it (see *NE* VI 5, 1140^{b}4–6, 20–30). Although it is possible for one to misuse technical skill, it is impossible for a practically wise person, that is, a fully virtuous person, to do so.

41. Which is why Aristotle claims "there is no such thing as excellence in practical wisdom" (*NE* VI 5, 1140^{b}22).

42. See her discussion on 13–14 of *On Virtue Ethics*.

than many others of her persuasion who toss out the principle that one cannot misuse virtue with hardly any comment[43]—yet nevertheless she appears to cross it. She argues, on one side, that a virtuous agent is never forced to act viciously, but on the other that a virtuous agent may nevertheless be forced to *not* do well in her actions. Consider the following:

> However, if a genuinely tragic dilemma is what a virtuous agent emerges from, it will be the case that she emerges having done a terrible thing, the very sort of thing that the callous, dishonest, unjust, or in general vicious agent would characteristically do—killed someone, or let them die, betrayed a trust, violated someone's serious rights. And hence it will not be possible to say that she has acted *well*. What follows from this is not the impossibility of virtue but the possibility of some situations from which even a virtuous agent cannot emerge with her life unmarred.[44]

There is much subtlety in Hursthouse's discussion, and she does much to bring to the fore the genuine agony besetting those faced with extremely difficult choices. What concerns me here is her solution that a virtuous agent faced with what Hursthouse considers irresolvable (not merely apparent) and tragic (because nobody wins) dilemmas both does what in other circumstances would be considered vicious and yet continues to be a virtuous agent. It is not altogether clear whether Hursthouse imagines a suspension of one's virtue-acting apparatus at the moment of acting "not-well," or if such action springs *from* the virtuous agent acting in the only way available to her, and so acting virtuously. If the former, then we have an agent acting out of character, and motivated instead by

---

43. Gabrielle Taylor's following claim is a particularly striking example of a lack of care on this point, "The possessor of a countervailing virtue need not be a generous, charitable, or just person. But nor do they necessarily belong to that class sometimes labeled 'self-regarding' and sometimes 'executive' virtues, which an agent may exercise for either her own or someone else's benefit, so that person may possess all these virtues and yet be wholly self-interested and even wicked. Courage, prudence, patience, and self-control belong to this class."(*Deadly Vices* [Oxford: Clarendon Press, 2006], 126). According to Taylor, one can be wickedly courageous, prudent, patient, and self-controlled.

44. *On Virtue Ethics*, 74.

some contrary-to-virtue principles or appetites. If that is her position, it would weaken her claim that there really are irresolvable and tragic dilemmas *for the virtuous agent*. Her emphasis clearly lies in this chapter on there being such dilemmas for the virtuous agent, and so that leaves us with virtuous agents who must sometimes not do well *in the very exercise* of the virtues.

Acting as a virtuous agent is to act virtuously, and so, on Hursthouse's description of tragic situations quoted above, circumstances can produce a situation in which the virtuousness of an agent, say her honesty, can remain intact even as she violates a moral absolute such as lying or killing an innocent. Her life may be marred in some manner by this action, but her character not imperiled. The implication drawn from her treatment of tragic dilemmas is that, though such occasions are rare, a virtuous agent can violate someone's trust or kill them virtuously. Therefore, despite its nuances, Hursthouse's position serves as an example of the common tendency of contemporary virtue ethicists to speak of virtues as traits of character by means of which one can, on some occasions, do wrong. Anscombe, on the other hand, makes it clear that it would be better to die than to commit such deeds, and so stands with both Plato and Aristotle on this point.

(7) Aristotelian ethics does not, and cannot, endorse a selfless and generic benevolence.

The stress that contemporary virtue ethicists, neo-Aristotelian and otherwise, lay on altruistic notions of benevolence or charity has been remarked upon already in chapter 2, but more should be said about this trend in the context of the concern in this chapter with comparing Aristotelian ethics and neo-Aristotelian virtue ethics.

Hursthouse remarks, "Charity or benevolence, for example, is not an Aristotelian virtue, but *all* virtue ethicists assume it is on the list now."[45] Coope offers several pertinent remarks about this emphasis on charity. He notes, for instance, that Anscombe was alive when

---

45. *On Virtue Ethics*, 8; my emphasis.

Hursthouse wrote those words, and yet one finds no mention of charity in the index to volume 3 of her *Collected Papers*, the volume that includes her essays on ethics. Coope notes as well that charity as described by Aquinas seems not what either Hursthouse or Slote has in mind by the notion. Neither, for that matter, is the virtue of charity as described by Geach in *The Virtues* the virtue of charity referenced by Hursthouse or Slote.[46] Coope reminds as well of Nietzsche's impatience with attempts to employ features of Christian morality without Christian belief.[47]

There are few notions more central to Christian theology than charity. However, the charity extolled by neo-Aristotelian virtue ethicists is a thoroughly secularized notion—what Geach would call a "dubious" virtue. We have, with this secularized notion of charity or benevolence, a corollary to what Anscombe discovers about the moral ought—the continued life of a term that retains mesmeric force but lacks the foundation to justify its use.

Aristotle, of course, is no stranger to the importance of love, and indeed gives pride of place to the sort of love he calls friendship. Aquinas develops further Aristotle's notion of friendship and makes of it the very source and the summit of his whole ethics, arguing that it is God's friendship with us that makes possible all genuine virtue, and the deepening of that intimate friendship the very goal of a life

---

46. Coope quotes Geach on the subject: "If charity is love of God above all things in the world and of our neighbors for God's sake, charity is to be prized only if there is a God: otherwise it is a pathetic delusion like Don Quixote's love for Dulcinea. The word 'charity' bears other senses, but it is dubious whether in these senses charity is a virtue at all (Geach 1977: 17)" (Christopher Miles Coope, "Modern Virtue Ethics," 36). See Coope's full discussion of charity on 33–36.

47. Coope points us to this remark of Nietzsche from *The Twilight of the Idols*: "They [the English—he had in mind George Eliot in particular] have got rid of the Christian God, and now feel obliged to cling all the more firmly to Christian morality.... [But] when one gives up Christian belief one thereby deprives oneself of the right to Christian morality (Nietzsche 1968: 80)" (ibid., 36). Relevant here is Max Scheler's analysis of the pitfalls of a secularized version of Christian morality, while defending that morality against Nietzsche's attacks, in *Ressentiment*, trans. Lewis B. Coser and William W. Holdheim (Milwaukee, Wis.: Marquette University Press, 1998).

well lived.[48] But this is clearly not what the virtue ethicists are after. They want general benevolence, a virtue of secularized humanitarian concern, to serve as the master unifying virtue. In a word, they want a sort of universally applied altruism, not friendship.

Such a notion is hardly coherent, however, from an Aristotelian perspective that recognizes that all love for others must necessarily spring from self-love and that whether we are to think of love as an emotion or a virtue, it needs perceptible objects—that is, other persons we directly experience.[49] One does not really feel anything, not love, not benevolence, not hatred, for those one does not perceive. What we imagine to be an act of love for distant and unknown others is love for our necessarily vague imaginative creations—that is our ideas—of these others. These are points on which Aristotle is in agreement with Aquinas,[50] as well as with both the Old and New Testaments, where we are told in both Leviticus 19:18 and Matthew 22:39 that we are to love our neighbors *as ourselves*—thus establishing love for others on the love we have for ourselves. Our neighbors may be anyone we come into contact with, but we need to come into contact with them to perceive them as neighbors. We can, in other words, be ready to love any neighbor, but only can love particular neighbors.

---

48. *ST* II-II, qq.23–27.
49. *NE* IX 4, 166^{a}1–166^{b}29.
50. Aquinas argues in *ST* II-II, q.27 that God is to be loved not just first, but directly (a.4), wholly (a.5), and without measure (a.6). Aquinas is careful to show in qq.26–27, however, that this love does not stop with God, but extends to three other objects: ourselves, our neighbors, and our bodies, and in that order. The reasons that love for ourselves is prior to our love for our neighbors are both scriptural and philosophical. Both Leviticus 19:18 and Matthew 22:39 command us to love our neighbors as ourselves. The biblical mandate clearly holds up the love we have for ourselves as model for the love we ought to have for our friends. By way of extrabiblical reasons, Aquinas argues that man is a unity with himself, which is a state more powerful than being unified in fellowship with his friends, and this love (*amor*), which is not strictly speaking friendship (*amicitia*), because it is the expression of self-unity and not merely the union of community, provides the foundation upon which we incorporate our friends into our friendship for God. We see, then, that Aquinas affirms those same Aristotelian points of community and self-love as origins for friendship.

The secularized charity so popular today, both within contemporary virtue ethics as well as Rawlsianism, Kantianism, and utilitarianism, is not simply not recognized by Aristotle. The notion itself is incoherent from an Aristotelian perspective, as well as from the perspective of the Christian Aristotelianism of both Aquinas and Geach, who emphasize a very different notion of charity.

(8) Aristotelian ethics makes friendship thematically central.

The contemporary virtue ethical elevation of a secularized and dubious virtue of charity is at least partly responsible for one of the more surprising omissions in much of its literature, that of making friendship thematically central. Another reason, to which we will turn shortly, is an entrenched individualism. Whatever the reasons, upon a reading of the whole of Aristotle's *Nicomachean Ethics*, one cannot help but be struck by the fact that Aristotle devotes an entire one-fifth of his study to friendship—more than twice the space he devotes to justice, or to all five of the intellectual virtues. What is perhaps more surprising is the relatively little attention that friendship receives in contemporary retrievals of Aristotelian ethics. If we could at least begin to appreciate the significance that the topic of friendship holds for Aristotelian ethics we will be able to see, perhaps more clearly than on any other point, the divergence between Aristotelian ethics and contemporary moral philosophy.

It is not my contention that neo-Aristotelian virtue ethicists ignore friendship altogether. Gabrielle Taylor gives it some limited treatment,[51] Hursthouse recognizes that it is one of those features of moral philosophy that ought not to be ignored and mentions it without significant development in a number of places,[52] and Julia Annas has a couple of articles on the subject.[53] However, one simply does

---

51. Taylor, *Deadly Vices*, 130–32.
52. Hursthouse, *On Virtue Ethics*, 4; see index for the occasional references.
53. Julia Annas, "Self-Love in Aristotle," *Southern Journal of Philosophy*, supplement 27 (1988): 1–18; "Plato and Aristotle on Friendship and Altruism," *Mind* 86 (1977): 532–54.

not find anything close to the systematic treatment of friendship one would expect from those seeking to revive an Aristotelian ethics.[54]

Aristotle emphasizes friendship as an incalculable good the lack of which no one would desire. It makes life worth living, it plays a central role in helping us to further foster and nourish the virtues, and it prepares us for the deepest levels of the highest human activity, contemplation:

> If happiness lies in living and being active, and the good man's activity is virtuous and pleasant in itself, as we have said at the outset, and if a thing's being one's own is one of the attributes that make it pleasant, and if we can contemplate our neighbors better than ourselves and their actions better than our own, and if the actions of virtuous men who are their friends are pleasant to good men ... the blessed man will need friends of this sort, since he chooses to contemplate worthy actions and actions that are his own, and the actions of a good man who is his friend have both these qualities.[55]

The mutual contemplation of good friends is the fulfillment of a deep and natural desire, Aristotle contends,[56] for it involves the very essence of life.[57] Friends live out their lives, their human essence, in living together and philosophizing with one another:

---

54. One exception to this claim might be thought to be found in some works of Talbot Brewer—such as in his "Virtues We Can Share: Friendship in Aristotle's Ethical Theory," *Ethics* 115 (2005): 721–58; and in chapter 7, "Virtue and Other Selves," in his *The Retrieval of Ethics*. However, Brewer is highly critical of routine virtue ethical approaches, "as it has climbed to a position of prominence within Anglo-American philosophy departments, virtue ethics has retreated to an increasingly conventional conception of its central message" (*The Retrieval of Ethics*, 3). This retreat is due in part, he contends, to embarrassment about putting forward substantive claims about the good: "This liberal ethos makes itself felt in the contemporary academy under the guise of a prevailing sense of academic decorum. It is regarded as mildly embarrassing to forward substantive conceptions of the human good under the banner of philosophy" (ibid., 6–7). Brewer's goal in this ambitious work is described as follows: "The main concern of this book is not to explain the normalization of the initially radical philosophical movement launched by the works of Anscombe and MacIntyre, but to develop and extend some of the more radical themes sounded in these works" (ibid., 8). For these and other reasons, Brewer does not belong in the camp of mainstream neo-Aristotelian contemporary virtue ethicists.
55. *NE* IX 9, 1169^{b}31–1170^{a}3.
56. Ibid., 1170^{a}13–14.
57. "Now life is defined in the case of animals by the power of perception, in that of

And if as the virtuous man is to himself, he is to his friend also (for his friend is another self):—then as his own existence is desirable for each man, so, or almost so, is that of his friend. Now his existence was seen to be desirable because he perceived his own goodness, and such perception is pleasant in itself. He needs, therefore, to be conscious of the existence of his friend as well, and this will be realized in their living together and sharing in discussion and thought; for this is what living together would seem to mean in the case of man, and not, as in the case of cattle, feeding in the same place.[58]

Cattle feed at the same trough, but this does not make them friends; friends, too, of course, share meals together, but it is their conversation, mutual admiration, and shared virtuous characters that are distinctive of this best sort of human life.

Making friendship thematically central to one's ethics is not without its costs, and there is much that neo-Aristotelian virtue ethicists would be uncomfortable maintaining in order to make an Aristotelian account of friendship significantly central to their theories. One finds in the elements of Aristotle's theory referenced above elitism—only the truly virtuous can share their lives this way; an anthropology that connects a very broad conception of rationality with the very essence of human life—which puts Aristotle a very long way from both utilitarians and many varieties of naturalists; and a heavy emphasis on the climatic human activity of contemplation—something we have already remarked many virtue ethicists to be either uncomfortable with or simply unconcerned about. Holding these positions would certainly make one an oddity among contemporary moral philosophers, and it is perhaps the case that such a price is considered too high for many seeking a revival of Aristotelian virtue ethics to pay. The failure to make friendship thematically central combined with the excision of distinctively Aristotelian convictions regarding the rarity of those who can qualify for genuine friendship

---

man by the power of perception or thought; and a power is referred to the corresponding activity, which is the essential thing; therefore life seems to be essentially perceiving or thinking" (*NE* IX 9, 1170^{a}15–19).

58. *NE* IX 9, 1170^{b}5–13.

and the substance of the best activities of such friendship is, however, the greater price to pay, for it enervates our natural aspiration to live our communal lives to their fullest.

(9) Aristotelian ethics insists on the intelligibility and indispensable importance of the virtue of justice.

Friendship, Aristotle tells us, can be thought of as a perfection of justice.[59] Like friendship, justice looks to the good of others; but unlike friendship, justice does not entail intimacy. It is justice that ensures that we do well by others, whether or not we consider them our friends, and it this doing well by others that is brought to still greater perfection when intimacy is added to justice in friendship. Though not necessarily entailing intimacy, Aristotle does not hesitate to regale general justice—as opposed to its two particular types of "reciprocal justice" and "distributive justice"—as *arête men esti teleia*:

> And it is complete excellence in its fullest sense, because it is the actual exercise of complete excellence. It is complete because he who possesses it can exercise his excellence towards others too and not merely by himself; ... For this same reason justice, alone of the excellences, is thought to be another's good, because it is related to others; for it does what is advantageous to another, either a ruler or a partner.... Justice in this sense, then, is not part of excellence but excellence entire, nor is the contrary injustice a part of vice but vice entire.[60]

Justice is all the ethical virtues insofar as they are brought to the service of others. Its distinctive mark, vis-à-vis the other ethical virtues, is its other-relatedness. It is the spotlight on the common good, which is the shared good of all members of a community, that gives to justice its special brilliance: as good as it is to thrive as a single person, such flourishing pales in comparison to flourishing as a member of a community. The virtue of justice enables, and acting with justice is, that communal thriving.

---

59. *NE* VIII 1, 1155^{a}21–28.
60. *NE* V 1, 1129^{b}30–33, 1130^{a}3–5, 9–11.

Neo-Aristotelian contemporary virtue ethicists have struggled to find a significant place in their theories for justice. Santas, Simpson, and Coope all justly complain of this lack of attention. In Copp and Sobel's important survey of recent virtue ethics literature, there is, in fact, no mention of justice or injustice.[61] Hursthouse defends her demotion of justice in *On Virtue Ethics* with the following:

> In common with nearly all other existing virtue ethics literature, I take it as obvious that justice is a personal virtue, and am happy to use it as an occasional illustration, but I usually find any of the other virtues more hospitable to the detailed elaboration of points. But, in a book of this length, I do not regard this as a fault. I am writing about normative ethics, not political philosophy, and even when regarded solely as a personal virtue (if it can be), justice is so contested (and I would say) corrupted a topic that it would need a book on its own.[62]

Hursthouse's claim that a treatment of justice would require a work in political philosophy rather than normative ethics seems not to appreciate that Aristotelian ethics *is* political philosophy, though not the whole of political philosophy.[63]

Her claim that justice is a corrupted virtue requires further explanation, and there are several important points to note in the following continuation from the last quotation:

> I say "corrupted" because it has become all too common to allow a vague concept of justice and rights to encompass large areas of morality that virtue ethicists believe are better dealt with in terms of other, more concrete, virtues. According to virtue ethics—and in this book—what is wrong with lying, when it is wrong, is not that it is unjust ... but that it is *dishonest*, and dishonesty is a vice. What is wrong with killing, when it is wrong, may be not so much that it is unjust, violating the right to life, but frequently, that it is callous and contrary to the virtue of charity.[64]

---

61. Coope, "Modern Virtue Ethics," 41, referring to Copp and Sobel, "Morality and Virtue." It is the recent works of Hursthouse, Foot, and Slote that are examined in this piece.

62. Hursthouse, *On Virtue Ethics*, 5.

63. *NE* I 2, 1094^{a}25–1094^{b}13; X 9, 1179^{a}33–35, 1181^{b}12–15.

64. Hursthouse, *On Virtue Ethics*, 6.

This is a particularly significant passage insofar as several of the fundamental assumptions of mainstream virtue ethics are revealed in it. Consider: First, Hursthouse complains that justice is vague, and not a concrete virtue. What exactly does she mean by that? What, in particular, does she mean by "concrete"? Are not all of the virtues vague to a certain extent, given the imprecision of the subject, ethics? Justice seems to have been unfairly marginalized. Second, Hursthouse speaks of "according to virtue ethics" as though there is a set doctrine, called "virtue ethics," that doctrinally holds that lying is not an offense against justice, but only against honesty. Let us recall that Anscombe emphasizes the importance of justice in several of her works, including "Modern Moral Philosophy"; Geach gives it a robust chapter in *The Virtues;* and MacIntyre not only gives it serious attention in *After Virtue,* but wrote his next book on the subject, *Whose Justice? Which Rationality?* Perhaps Hursthouse is happy to have broken company with MacIntyre, but she dedicates *On Virtue Ethics* to Anscombe. Anscombe does in fact consider lying to be a sin against justice. Hursthouse is therefore either displaying an insensitivity to the perspectives of other virtue ethicists or working with a narrow definition of virtue ethics. Third, notice the two "when it is wrong" qualifications—these make it clear that for Hursthouse neither lying nor killing is always wrong. These should serve as reminders that Hursthouse does not endorse conditionless moral absolutes, and because of that falls into the form of consequentialism that Anscombe denounces. Fourth, it is, on her view, charity, not justice, that makes killing wrong. Why Hursthouse does not consider killing to be a violation of justice does not receive an explanation. Perhaps one of the main difficulties with justice for Hursthouse is that it is not so readily codifiable by a V-rule; if so, this should serve as a reason to reassess whether V-rules do all the work they are intended to, rather than a reason to diminish the role of justice. In any event, on Hursthouse's understanding justice is no longer, as Aristotle claims it to be, the whole of the ethical virtue. This is evident by her claims that it is dishonesty and not injustice that makes lying wrong and that killing is a violation not of justice but of charity.

The separation of political philosophy from "normative ethics" is no doubt a significant part of the story of why justice is downplayed and truncated by Hursthouse and other mainstream virtue ethicists who look to her work as a paradigm. Another important part of that story is the treatment justice has received in modern moral philosophy, in its Humean (an unnatural virtue), utilitarian (a maximizing procedure), Kantian (a universal requirement), and Rawlsian (a procedural affair that secures fairness) varieties. On the one hand, to the extent that mainstream virtue ethicists embrace essential features of these other theories of justice, the distinctively Aristotelian notion of justice as a virtue suffers a loss in its meaning and its power. On the other hand, contemporary virtue ethics, in its desire to distinguish itself from its moral philosophical competitors, has replaced the classical understanding of the virtue of justice with a new version of the virtue of charity. This new virtue of secular charity does much of what justice used to do for Aristotelians. Hursthouse confirms that replacement of justice with charity when, continuing the last quote, she writes: "From the perspective of virtue ethics, one can say that it is 'absolutely required' that one does not 'pass by on the other side' when one sees a wounded stranger lying by the roadside, but the requirement comes from charity rather than justice."[65] One would think that an Aristotelian would want to say that the good Samaritan is indeed just, for he does what is required by his other-regarding virtue. If he is an especially good Samaritan, he will do this not only from justice, but from that perfected justice that is friendship—and that Aquinas calls charity. But Hursthouse seeks to oppose justice and charity, and for that there is no precedent in the Aristotelian tradition.

---

65. Ibid.

(10) Aristotelian ethics insists that to be human is to be communal.

Why are justice and friendship so prized by Aristotle? Why does Aristotle see his ethics as a contribution to political theory? Why does Aristotle see us fully flourishing only in communion with others—in the shared reflective life of genuine friendship, and optimally in contemplative union with God? At the core of his ethical *cum* political philosophy is the conviction that to be human is to be a communal being: "Surely it is strange, too, to make the blessed man a solitary; for no one would choose to possess all good things on condition of being alone, since man is a political creature and one whose nature is to live with others."[66] By "political creature" Aristotle, of course, means that the human being is a creature meant to live in a polis, a city, a community.[67] "Meant to live" may not put this strongly enough; a being is human only to the extent that he or she exists in community. Beyond the community lie brutes on the one side, and gods on the other.

The mark of the human being is the ability to speak, which is the ability to deliberate with others about how to live together, an ability that can be fostered by and then reach its perfected state only in a community:

> Now, that man is more of a political animal than bees or any other gregarious animals is evident. Nature, as we often say, makes nothing in vain, and man is the only animal who has the gift of speech.... The power of speech is intended to set forth the expedient and inexpedient, and therefore likewise the just and the unjust. And it is a characteristic of man that he alone has any sense of good and evil, of just and unjust, and the like, and the association of living beings who this sense makes a family and a state.[68]

---

66. *NE* IX 9, 1169^{b}17–19.
67. *Politics* I 1, 1252^{a}1–2: "Every state is a community of some kind, and every community is established with a view to some good" (B. Jowett's translation from the Princeton Collected Works, here as elsewhere).
68. *Politics* I 2, 1253^{a}8–10, 14–18.

The power to speak not only implies the power to think, and vice versa. Contra Hobbes, Rousseau, and their modern heirs of so many different guises, there is no such thing as a truly isolated and rational human being:

> But he who is unable to live in society, or who has no need because he is sufficient for himself, must be either a beast or a god: he is no part of a state. A social instinct is implanted in all men by nature, and yet he who first founded the state was the greatest of benefactors. For man, when perfected, is the best of animals, but, when separated from law and justice, he is the worst of all: since armed injustice is the more dangerous, and he is equipped at birth with arms, meant to be used by intelligence and excellence, which he may use for the worst ends. That is why, if he has not excellence, he is the most unholy and the most savage of animals, and the most full of lust and gluttony. But justice is the bond of men in states.[69]

Communities come in different shapes and sizes, and the states formed by collections of communities can be more or less conducive to fostering a common life of virtue. This is why Aristotle makes it his task to explore what sort of way of living our political, that is to say, our human, lives is most conducive to living a flourishing life. The *Nicomachean Ethics* explores happiness, and explains it as the activity of virtue; the *Politics* explores the conditions needed to foster the virtuous life.

It is worth pointing out that while the Aristotelian perspective on the human being's communal nature is revolutionary with respect to individualistic strains that have remained dominant since the seventeenth century, this perspective is not as bizarre as it is sometimes supposed to be. Nothing mystical is meant by it. It is entirely other than the sorts of New Age ecological or mystical or sociological efforts at dissolving personal identity. It is, rather, a frankly biological and ruddy sort of notion that begins with recognizing that we come into this world only thanks to our radical dependency on parents, and can begin to acquire the sorts of skills needed to thrive as indi-

---

69. Ibid., 1253^{a}28–38.

viduals only because of the constant nurture and support of others. It recognizes that we can thrive only to the extent that we have taken in those lessons taught by our dependency on others, and it seeks to do justice to the social dimensions of our personalities. We are not naturally feral creatures, but rather beings born into families whose adult lives must be responsive to the involuntarily acquired obligations to those who nurtured us, and to the voluntarily acquired obligations we develop over the course of our lives, if we are to thrive in any relevantly human sense.

Neo-Aristotelian virtue ethicists have shown what appears to be an inability to appreciate the perspective of Aristotelian ethics on this issue of our political natures. They, like the majority of moral philosophers working today, begin with the notion of a human being as an independently acting human agent. The oddity of this, of course, is that such a beginning is a fiction, and a dangerous one at that, for it blinds our theorizing to what we otherwise all know to be at the center of our lives: our profound dependency on our own particular network of family, friends, coworkers, collaborators, and others. There are some exceptions to this inattention to the issue of our political natures, such as with Lawrence Blum, who explores some of the links between virtue and community.[70] But even in his refreshingly explorative articles what we seem to find are attempts to connect individual human beings to communal concerns—rather than seeing that it is precisely one's community that renders one an individual human being in the first place. This latter point is of course a theme explored by MacIntyre in *Dependent Rational Animals,* but MacIntyre's book, to which we will return shortly, is the work of an Aristotelian, not a neo-Aristotelian contemporary virtue ethicist.

70. See, for examples, Lawrence Blum, "Compassion," in *Explaining Emotions,* ed. Amélie O. Rorty (Berkeley: University of California Press, 1980): 507–18; "Moral Exemplars: Reflections on Schindler, the Trocmes, and Others," *Midwest Studies in Philosophy* 13 (1988): 196–221; "Community and Virtue," in *How Should One Live?* ed. Roger Crisp (Oxford: Oxford University Press, 1996): 231–50.

The modern, individualistic-rational-moral-agent perspective continues to reign supreme in modern moral philosophy. There are some Aristotelians of various stripes who have battled against this dominant anthropology, but no neo-Aristotelian mainstream contemporary virtue ethicists who have made the communal dimensions of Aristotle's anthropology central to their project. At most we find rational individuals groping for community, efforts that fail to recognize the absolutely radical features of our communal being, as well as fail to satisfy a necessary requirement for making one's ethics sufficiently Aristotelian.

Aristotle's Ethics Is Not a Virtue Ethics

The range of concerns articulated above and evidenced as central in Aristotelian ethics is largely ignored across the variety of the works of neo-Aristotelian virtue ethicists, and some of the most important features of Aristotelian ethics are dismissed altogether. Insufficient attention given to any one of those areas of importance surveyed above is enough to render a theory dubiously, if still at all, Aristotelian. Because of their central importance for Aristotelian ethics, completely ignoring any one of these areas constitutes a failure to be an Aristotelian ethicist in a sufficiently relevant sense. It is the case that most neo-Aristotelian virtue ethicists of the mainstream variety ignore or obscure many of these areas of importance in Aristotelian ethics. What one finds, instead, is, at least for the most part, a largely nominal rather than substantive Aristotelianism.

If neo-Aristotelian contemporary virtue ethicists are not substantively Aristotelian, is it nevertheless possible that Aristotle is a virtue ethicist? It seems not. We simply do not find any of the dominant strains of mainstream virtue ethics represented in Aristotle's approach. To be sure, Aristotle is attentive to the central role of virtue in our lives, and provides a powerful virtue theory. But that hardly makes his ethics an ethics of virtue. Questions pertaining to character loom large in Aristotelian ethics, but they are not the starting point, the *archē*, from which spins the whole of his theory. Neither is he concerned with what Hursthouse calls the justificatory problem, the effort to defend what he designates as virtues to be virtues by means of some more primitive notions. Nor do we find the special motivational concern so distinctive of contemporary normative theory evidenced in his writings, but rather an all-encompassing concern with human actions and their common and ultimate end as such. Aristotle's writings, moreover, are elitist to such an extent that all he has to say to those who have not been well brought up is that they will have nothing to learn from his writings. The unvirtuously reared are better served by taking direction from their legislators than by worrying themselves with questions of theory and casuistry. It is ultimately to the perspective of a well-honed practical reason, a reason marked by practical wisdom, that we are urged to turn for action guidance, rather than to a set of rules derived from inquiries into ethical exemplars.

Finally, the ultimate stress of Aristotelian ethics is placed not on the acquisition of a virtuous character, but on virtuous activity. The best of such activities is only possible with friends, and in the presence of the living God. Aristotle's ethics is an ethics of virtue not where character is of primary importance and action is derived from reflections on character, but where the development of character is put at the service of the human being's practical and speculative activities—those activities that constitute our secondary and primary happinesses respectively. One does not find Aristotle primarily concerned with the methodologies and queries at the heart of modern moral philosophy, but with a much vaster, deeper, and richer set of concerns.

A Way Forward

That much of professedly Aristotelian contemporary virtue ethics fails to be substantively Aristotelian does not, in and of itself, amount to a dire criticism of virtue ethics. It is a criticism, to be sure, but one could easily maneuver out of it by saying something to the effect of, "OK, so maybe my virtue ethics is not sufficiently Aristotelian. So what? I'll just describe it some other way. My central claims, however, remain untouched. For who's to say that Aristotle, or what you presumptively call a 'substantively Aristotelian ethics,' provides the benchmark for good moral philosophy? Stop arguing from authority." My response is that I am not arguing from authority—which is not to say that I think arguments from legitimate authority invalid. They often are valid, provided there is mutual acceptance of a given authority. And, frankly, those virtue ethicists claiming to provide an Aristotelian-inspired virtue ethics seem to make this claim precisely in order to lend the support of Aristotle's authority to their arguments. So, it does in fact seem that one of their supporting premises has been removed.

Nevertheless, I accept the charge that an argument from authority will not suffice. What it is essential to see here is that if purportedly Aristotelian virtue ethicists fail to be substantially Aristotelian, and—as I think we have also found—there are fatal flaws of incohesiveness, incoherence, and incomprehensiveness at the heart of the contemporary virtue ethics movement's efforts to provide an alternative moral theory, then Aristotle's ethics, or some more substantively Aristotelian extension of it, remains immune from those fatal flaws. This of course is not yet tantamount to being able to claim that Aristotle's ethics is without fatal flaws, but it does imply that whether or not there are such flaws has yet to be determined. The fate of Aristotle's ethics does not stand or fall with the fate of contemporary virtue ethics.

Chapter 6

ANTHROPOLOGY IN ARISTOTELIAN ETHICS

Every Virtue Needs a Home

Now if the function of man is an activity of soul in accordance with, or not without, rational principle ... human good turns out to be activity of soul in conformity with excellence, and if there are more than one excellence, in conformity with the best and most complete.

Aristotle, *NE* I.7, 1098ª7–8, 16–18.

A significant turning point in this book's argumentation has been reached. Evidence has been produced in order to show that the movement to which Anscombe's watershed piece, "Modern Moral Philosophy," gave life has in many respects betrayed the recommendations of its mother. Instead of the cessation of ethics-as-usual until a comprehensive and coherent philosophical psychology has been produced,[1] we have seen the proliferation of rule-based ethics both

---

1. "But meanwhile—is it not clear that there are several concepts that need investigating simply as part of the philosophy of psychology and—as I should recommend—*banishing ethics totally* from our minds? Namely—to begin with: 'action,' 'intention,' 'pleasure,' 'wanting.' More will probably turn up if we start with these. Eventually it

in what has come to be called virtue ethics and in the other fields of modern moral philosophy. After the initial period of virtue ethical writings, which spent a great deal of time exploring the weaknesses of salient trends in modern moral philosophy, what have grown in dominance since the early 1990s are varieties of virtue ethics united in their shared acceptance of the basic presuppositions of modern moral philosophy—what Solomon calls routine virtue ethics. This mainstreaming of contemporary virtue ethics has led to the development of strategies that, if at all, are often Aristotelian in name but lack a resuscitation of Aristotelian ethics on the order that Anscombe envisaged. This has yielded a mainstream approach to virtue ethics that bears little resemblance to its unconventional older siblings and that does not prove itself to be a cohesive, comprehensive, and coherent moral theory.

But if, as I think is the case, Anscombe's analysis of modern moral philosophy is both incisive and true, at least on balance if not in every detail; and if, as I think is the case, Anscombe's call to begin thinking along the lines sketched out by Aristotle in some significant fashion presents a promising alternative to those problems endemic to modern moral philosophy; and if, finally, the failures of contemporary virtue ethics to, on the one hand, adequately take in the problems Anscombe points out in the modern moral project, and on the other, make recourse to Aristotelian ethics in a sufficiently substantive manner, does not signal the failure of Aristotelian ethics or the illegitimacy of Anscombe's encouragements toward its resuscitation; then, there is indeed still room to hope to build the sort of approach to moral theorizing that Anscombe calls for. In short, Anscombe's suggestion to make recourse to Aristotelian ethics remains a live option.

But where does one begin to make the case that such a recourse is in fact both possible and a promising salve to what ails modern

---

might be possible to advance to considering the concept of a virtue; with which, I suppose, we should be beginning some sort of a study of ethics" (Anscombe, "Modern Moral Philosophy," 40).

moral philosophy, including that subset of it that goes by the name of contemporary virtue ethics? Anscombe has already indicated the direction in which to turn with her admonition that what we need is an adequate philosophical psychology. An adequate philosophical psychology demands, among other things, focused attention to be given to those classes of questions I already specified in chapter 1 as foundational to any moral philosophy: What is human nature? What is the purpose of human life? By means of what standards do we assess progress made in pursuing the purpose of human life?

One way to describe the advantages of Aristotelian ethics is by observing that it is precisely in this tradition of ethics that one finds these questions at the heart of its inquiries. I have already argued that every moral philosophy utilizes answers to these questions, whether tacitly or explicitly. Aristotelian ethics has the distinction of giving significant attention to these questions in such fashion as to make answers to them explicit in its project. Since, then, these foundational questions are put under the light of philosophical scrutiny, this at least gives Aristotelian ethics a significantly better chance of finding thoughtful and correct answers to them. But more than that, the answers given to these questions in Aristotelian ethics are, at the risk of sounding presumptuous, correct, by which I mean they accord with the world, with the nature of human life, with human rationality and action; that is to say, I think the answers offered in the Aristotelian tradition to these questions are, at least for the most part, true.

The following three chapters are an attempt to sketch some arguments in defense of this claim. What follows is all too brief, schematic, and tentative to be regarded as anything close to a comprehensive defense of Aristotelian ethics. Yet in the space remaining, a beginning can nevertheless be made. My aim in what remains of this book is to provide not a complete vindication but rather a modest defense of Aristotelian ethics by laying out some of the salient features of an Aristotelian answer to the fundamental questions of ethics with an eye to those issues that are important to rounding out my critical evaluation of the contemporary virtue ethics movement. If I succeed, then an approach that bears many resemblances to contemporary virtue ethics, but that does not suffer from those weaknesses in the movement I have investigated above, can at the very least be regarded as a promising field for further philosophical investigation.

The effort to discover answers to the foundational questions of ethics is intended as a contribution to the development of what Anscombe has characterized as a philosophical psychology. Such a psychology should be a unified achievement, for its subject is a unity, but this is a unity composed of various parts. We want to understand in Aristotelian ethics, ultimately, what life is all about with an eye to making sense of how we are best to live it. A human being is a unified whole, but knowing *what* sort of unified thing a human being is does not yield on its own an account of the whole of human life. To achieve that we need to understand the nature of human action; we need as well an account that links fundamental human inclinations with their teleologically described objects; we further need an account that enables us to collect the many actions performed by any human being under one description—which is a task at which MacIntyre has proved most helpful through his application of the notion of narrative to make sense of the unity of human life; and finally, we need a description of human rationality that does justice to our abilities to reflect upon our ends, to organize our lives around those reflected-upon ends, and to ascertain and apply principles of action by means of which we can guide ourselves toward our proper ends.

What these tasks suggest, among other things, is that though the three questions I have specified are each distinct, answering any one of them reveals its dependency on the others. They are interrelated questions. And, though I will reflect on some aspects of Aristotelian answers to each one of them separately, these separate reflections each import Aristotelian answers to the others, and all three converge on what is—in a manner that continues to be open to new insights, clarifications, stresses, and other modifications—a unified account of human life.

Virtues Are Perfections of Human Beings

Virtue, Aristotle tells us, relying on the connection between virtue (*arête*) and function (*ergon*) forged by Plato,[2] is that which enables whatever has a function to perform its function well.[3] "Virtue" is a term wide enough to be mundane. When knives cut well, eyes see well, and hands grasp well, it is so because they are virtuous. There are virtues that pertain, then, to human beings that have no direct (but certainly an indirect) role in human action: our senses, physical appearance, and health are all susceptible to descriptions in which virtue or vice (that which impairs proper functioning) is operative. How does this more general account of virtue and vice come to carry its specific meaning in ethical discourse?

"Virtue" and "vice" become key terms in ethical and political philosophy insofar as they come to be used as primary categorical designations for characterizing human activity, and it is human activity that is the subject of ethical and political philosophy. Such designations do not imply that every human action is either virtuous or vicious—for some could be, for example, continent, and others incontinent—but it does imply that every human action can be judged as being more or less virtuous, more or less vicious. Such designations, moreover, imply in any account of human activity a primary focus on the manner in which the actions were completed—the knowledge, passions, motivations, choices, and in general the state of the actors, rather than focusing exclusively on the type of action that was completed. This narrowing of the terms' connotations to the subject of human activity is still too broad for modern moral philosophy.

---

2. Plato, *Republic* I, 352d–354a.
3. Aristotle, *NE* I 7, 1098^{a}10–12.

The virtues and vices Aristotle explores in his ethical and political philosophy include what seem irrelevant to the aims and concerns of modern moral philosophy—virtues like technical knowledge, intuitive understanding, demonstrative science, and philosophical wisdom are at the heart of Aristotle's ethics, but seem not to fit into contemporary descriptions of the contents of ethical theorizing where the term "moral" attached to virtue or vice is used to narrow the term's reach to a restricted subset of human actions, and often with a primary or even exclusive focus on the type of action completed rather than on the manner in which it was completed.

One test to determine whether one's appreciation of virtue and vice terms as used in moral and political philosophy owes more to Aristotle than to modern moral philosophy is the following: if it strikes one's ear as strange to hear scientific knowledge and technological skill described as virtues—not merely as qualities that involve other virtues like temperance in order to avoid distractions in the acquisition of technical skill or assiduity in study in order to acquire scientific knowledge, but rather as themselves virtues—then one can take that as some measure of the hold modern moral philosophy has on one's way of regarding human activities. The notion that there are human feelings, actions, choices, and habits that are irrelevant to moral philosophical inquiry is foreign to Aristotle.[4]

What enables Aristotle to produce a catalogue of those virtues and vices pertinent to ethical and political inquiry is not simply the connection between function, functioning well, and virtue, and not at all a regard for some sort of special motivation that separates out moral human action from nonmoral human action, but his view of rationality. Aristotle's account of rationality is narrow enough to

---

4. As Pierre Hadot has repeatedly shown, the contemporary view of moral philosophy (and philosophy in general) is truncated compared not just to Aristotle, but to ancient philosophy as a whole. See especially Hadot's *Philosophy as a Way of Life: Spiritual Exercises from Socrates to Foucault,* ed. Arnold I. Davidson, trans. Michael Chase (Oxford: Blackwell Publishing, 1995); and *What Is Ancient Philosophy?* trans. Michael Chase (Cambridge, Mass.: Harvard University Press, 2002).

pick out that which is distinctively human in the logical sense of our specifying principle of difference from the common genus we share with all other animals, and sufficiently broad to include the full range of powers that spring directly from reason as well as those over which reason exercises some degree of governance. Each of these powers has its own particular work to do, its own particular function; and when functioning well, each of these powers is enabled to do so by the virtue perfective of it.

Because human beings are rational, those powers we possess that are either powers of rationality itself or powers over which rationality exerts some influence are not in and of themselves determinate toward their proper acts. That is to say, these rational powers have each their own distinctive function, but they do not function well automatically. Rationality implies, among other things, indeterminacy.[5] This is why Aquinas, following Aristotle, explains:

> Virtue denotes a certain perfection of a power. Now a thing's perfection is considered chiefly in regard to its end. But the end of power is act. Wherefore power is said to be perfect, according as it is determinate to its act. Now there are some powers which of themselves are determinate to their acts; for instance, the active natural powers. And therefore these natural powers are in themselves called virtues. But the rational powers, which are proper to man, are not determinate to one particular action, but are inclined indifferently to many: and they are determinate to acts by means of habits, as is clear from what we have said above (Q. 49, A. 4). Therefore human virtues are habits.[6]

The virtues that are of special focus in Aristotelian ethics are those that bring indeterminate rational powers and powers that share in

---

5. "[I]n soul and in the rational part of the soul, clearly some potentialities will be non-rational and some will be accompanied by reason.... And each of those which are accompanied by reason is alike capable of contrary effects, but one non-rational power produces one effect; e.g. the hot is capable only of heating, but the medical art can produce both disease and health" (*Metaphysics* IX 2, 1046^{b}1–2, 5–7; following Ross's translation in *The Complete Works of Aristotle*, here as elsewhere).

6. Aquinas, *Summa theologiae* I-II, q. 55, a. 1, *respondeo*; here, and elsewhere, I am making use of the Dominican Fathers translation of the *ST*.

rationality to perfection by enabling those powers to achieve their ends—that is, to perform their distinctive function well. Habits are what coordinate rational powers within persons and direct them toward determinate actions. Those habits that direct human beings toward ends that are perfective of them are called virtues.

It is possible to describe the structural features of a virtue in such a way as to forget its homey basis. We can search, as Plato does so well, for the structural essence of each virtue. What is justice? What is courage? What is piety? Plato leads us through analyses of these virtues in various dialogues, and what he seems to be looking for is something along the lines of necessary and sufficient conditions that satisfy the demands of universal definition. These efforts, worthwhile as they are, can have the effect of leading us to forget that these perfections are not substantial entities themselves. They are not free-floating goods that we come to make real in ourselves in some fashion; they are, rather, always perfective habits of rational beings, of ourselves (hopefully), and of those whom we admire. But of course it is Plato himself who first forges the union of function and virtue, and we should be wary of overly idealized—in the manner of treating each virtue as most real only when an Idea—interpretations of Platonic ethics. With Aristotle, such idealized interpretations are impossible for metaphysical—because of Aristotle's trenchant attacks on Plato's theory of Ideas for its failure to distinguish adequately between being in the mode of the intellect and being in the mode of reality—as well as for anthropological reasons.

Skeletal View of Human Beings

What then, are these powers of human beings that have just been mentioned? Aristotle, urging at least a general study of the soul on his students,[7] provides a schema by means of which we can begin to

---

7. *NE* I 13, 1102^{a}16–25.

enumerate them: his division of the soul. Of course *De Anima* is the work to turn to for the more complete science of the soul in Aristotle's corpus, but so thorough an examination is not necessary for the purposes of ethical and political inquiry. It is enough, Aristotle tells us at the end Book I of the *Nicomachean Ethics*, to observe the following points: the soul, that principle by means of which we are vivified, has both rational and irrational powers. The irrational element of the soul is responsible for what Aristotle describes as the vegetative activities of the soul, those directed toward nutrition, growth, and nurture of offspring. This part of the soul is not directly subject to the operations of reason: reason cannot touch the operations of digestion, for instance—though of course we can and should reason about what we offer to the power of digestion.

Another division of the soul has both irrational and rational qualities. This is that class of powers of the soul responsible for local movement, the appetitive or desiring powers, what Aquinas will call the passions. In the incontinent, the passions rebel against reason, in the continent they obey, and in the virtuous they speak with reason's own voice.[8] Reason combined with passion points to a manner in which reason, as well, is twofold in its basic operations. One basic power of the rational element of the soul is concerned with governance of passions, productions, and actions. The other is reason in the strict sense and in itself (*to men kuriōs kai en autō*), and it is the various perfections of reason under this description that can properly be called intellectual virtues (*tēs arête dianoētikēs*).[9] These latter are given special attention in Book VI of the *NE*. Insofar as passions and actions bear the stamp of rational persuasion in a habituated manner they are moral or ethical virtues (*tēs arêtes ethikēs*), and these are investigated especially in Books II–V.

One of the hallmarks of Aristotelian ethics is the insistence that

---

8. Ibid., 1102^{b}27–28.
9. *NE* II 1, 1103^{a}14–19.

the passions are educable. To be sure, they can be, and often are, rebellious. But they need not be; and one can either establish a kind of master-slave control over them—which Aristotle explores in Book VII of the *NE*, or, optimally, bring them to perfection through the acquisition of particular ethical virtues. This is possible only because passions are not opposed to beliefs as they so often are in contemporary accounts of the passions,[10] nor are they themselves simply beliefs such as we find in Stoic thought. Rather:

> The passions [or emotions] are those things [Roberts inserts "feelings" here] that so change men as to affect their judgments [or beliefs], and that are also attended by pain or pleasure. Such are anger, pity, fear and the like, with their opposites. We must arrange what we have to say about each of them under three heads. Take, for instance, the emotion of anger: here we must discover what the state of mind of angry people is, who the people are with whom they get angry, and on what ground they get angry with them.[11]

Passions or emotions are changes—I hesitate to call them feelings because of the opacity of that term—within a person,[12] but changes of such a sort that they not only affect judgment, but are themselves expressive of judgments. This is clear in the manner by which Aristotle proposes to study the passions. What we find in any passion is a three-part structure: the "state of mind" the person is in—such as "I'm feeling angry"; the object of the passion—"at Tim"; and, the reason for the elicitation of the passion—"because he insulted me." Passions affect judgments insofar as they dispose us to respond in

---

10. See Talbot Brewer's discussion of the "three dogmas of desire" for a discussion of currently dominant theories of desires, beliefs, and propositional attitudes, in *The Retrieval of Ethics*, 12–36.

11. Aristotle, *Rhetoric* II 1, 1378^{a}21–26, following W. Rhys Roberts's translation in *The Complete Works of Aristotle*. Emendations based on Ross's OCT edition, 1378^{a}19–23.

12. I am not making a distinction between "passion" and "emotion" here, though such a distinction may be appropriate in some contexts. See the introduction to Robert Miner's *Thomas Aquinas on the Passions: A Study of Summa Theologiae, 1a2ae 22–48*, (Cambridge: Cambridge University Press, 2009) for a discussion of the relevant history of the terminology.

some way or other to those objects that incite them. If I am angry at Tim, I seek—if I am courageous and just—proper recourse to correct the wrong he did me. If I am attracted to Jessica, who is not my wife, I seek—if I am temperate and chaste—to ensure that I treat her with dignity and respect and guard myself against dwelling on her in such a fashion that my attraction could turn romantic.

It has long been noted that readers must turn to Aristotle's *Rhetoric* to find an expansion of the compressed treatment of the passions we find in his political and ethical writings. Aquinas on the other hand is more systematic than Aristotle on this score insofar as Aquinas develops a detailed and nuanced treatment of the passions within the overall structure of his ethical inquiry,[13] for Aquinas prefaces his work on the virtues and the natural law with twenty-five dense and nuanced questions on the passions.[14] What he argues there, among other things, is that the passions are each modifications of one of two basic appetites of a human being, the concupiscible, by means of which we are attracted to things and persons, and the irascible, by means of which we are protective of those things and persons we love. Love and hate are both basic appetites, but love is the more basic of the two:

---

13. Research on Aquinas's work on the passions has been accelerating lately. Notable contributions include Robert Miner's *Thomas Aquinas on the Passions*, cited above; Diana Fritz-Cates, *Aquinas on the Emotions: A Religious-Ethical Inquiry* (Washington, D.C.: Georgetown University Press, 2009); and Nicholas E. Lombardo, OP, *The Logic of Desire: Aquinas on Emotion* (Washington, D.C.: The Catholic University of America Press, 2010).

14. Aquinas's treatment of the passions is too often ignored in accounts of his moral philosophy. After treating happiness in the first five questions of the first part of the second part of his *Summa theologiae*, he provides an account of the structure of our rational and voluntary nature in questions 6–17, then treats good and evil actions as such in questions 18–21, provides his account of the passions in questions 22–48, then treats habits in questions 49–54, then virtue and the virtues in questions 55–70, then vice and sin in questions 71–89, and finally the law in questions 90–108. Though this treatment takes place within the overall context of a theological investigation, it pertains to investigations of human nature, action, and perfection that do not rely on theological dogma for their principles. His treatment of the theological virtues, and the effect they have on our nature and on the virtues that bring that nature to perfection, takes place throughout the second part of the second part of the *ST*.

Love consists in a certain agreement of the lover with the object loved, while hatred consists in a certain disagreement or dissonance. Now we should consider in each thing, what agrees with it, before that which disagrees: since a thing disagrees with another, through destroying or hindering that which agrees with it. Consequently love must needs precede hatred; and nothing is hated, save through being contrary to a suitable thing which is loved. And hence it is that every hatred is caused by love.[15]

Love in its broadest sense is primarily that by means of which we feel an affinity, a kinship, an attraction toward completion by means of union with some other thing or person. Hate in its most general sense is an experienced disinclination for or revulsion at whatever comes between ourselves and what we love.

The ethical virtues pertain to passions as those traits of character that make them determinate toward their proper ends—that we feel a passion at the right time, toward the right person, in the right manner, and so on. They pertain to action by disposing us toward those acts that accord with right reason: "Every excellence both brings into good condition the thing of which it is the excellence and makes the work of that thing be done well."[16] Whether we think of the virtues and vices as traits of character or as dispositions toward actions, we see that each one of them needs, so to speak, a home. Such a home, as I intend the metaphor here, is, like your home, a place for both resting and springing forth with new initiative; it is a place occupied by a few regular dwellers as well as a place of interactive hospitality with outsiders. Within the person, one finds each virtue to represent a degree of stability as a distinctive coordination of powers, but also to be subject to modification by means of new experiences achieved through self-reflection and repeated actions. It is each virtue's share in reason, the common governor of a self now conceived as an organized collection of homes, a polis, that enables the intentionality of habitual activities—whether they be virtue- or vicious-directed ac-

---

15. *ST* I-II, q.29, a.1, *respondeo*.
16. *NE* II 6, 1106^{a}15–17.

tions, or actions that fall somewhere in between—and modifications to those habits themselves.

The intellectual virtues, though unlike the ethical virtues insofar as they are not habits that share a home with the passions, nevertheless are perfections of some power of the person and bear structural similarities to the ethical virtues. Their neighborhood, so to speak, is the intellect, and each occupies a particular home—each one of which is distinguished by its distinctive intellectual function. Like the ethical virtues, the intellectual virtues dispose us toward certain sorts of acts—technical skill toward making things, practical wisdom toward acting well, intuitive understanding toward grasping first principles, demonstrative science toward articulable knowledge, and wisdom toward contemplation.

Aristotle specifies eleven ethical virtues and five intellectual. To extend my metaphor, this means that there are sixteen different homes within the person-as-polis. Does this mean there are only eleven basic ways in which our passions can be habituated well, and five basic operations of the mind? I think there are reasons to think that indeed Aristotle took himself to be providing an exhaustive list of those virtues pertinent to ethical and political inquiry, at least with respect to their paradigm cases. Aquinas, however, demonstrates that an Aristotelian can work with a much larger collection of virtues. This expansion is not achieved, however, by loosening the definition of virtue. In fact, we find in Aquinas a tighter treatment of virtue, an initial paring down of the list of the virtues, and more precise descriptions of the virtues than we do in Aristotle. Each of the ethical virtues, Aquinas argues, is subsumable under temperance, or justice, or courage; the intellectual virtues, as in the works of Aristotle and yet more rigorously for Aquinas, are divided between the practical and speculative operations they enable. Such subsumptions, rather like the pruning of a fruit tree, enable a more abundant harvest.

Aquinas and Aristotle both build their moral philosophy on an action theory that sees every act as an actualization of an underlying potency. It is this relation between act and potency that justifies divisions between different sorts of virtues (and vices). They follow the trail, so to speak, that activities leave behind, making their way back to the points of operational generation, inferring potencies from the activities that are manifested. The same sort of inference is applied to the human being considered as a whole. Aristotle stresses a view of the human being as a source of action, "for good action is an end, and desire aims at this. Hence choice is either desiderative thought or intellectual desire, and such an origin of action is a man."[17] Though a human being has diverse powers, it is as a unity that he or she acts. That unity is made manifest in our actions, a point to which common language bears witness. It is not my mouth that eats, but me. It is true that it is my arm that swings the hammer, but I am the one hammering. It is true that I think with my intellect, but it is I who am thinking. As a unified whole I am the *archē* of these actions, rather than merely those powers of mine that are most proximately involved in their accomplishment.

Aquinas eloquently weaves together into one garment Aristotelian-inspired reflections on the interplay between potency and act on the level of particular activities of a human being with the view of the human being as a unified principle of action, and both of these with an account of the human being as an actualized, organized, intelligent biological being:

Nothing acts except so far as it is in act; wherefore a thing acts by that whereby it is in act. Now it is clear that the first thing by which the body lives is the soul. As life appears through various operations in different degrees of living things, that whereby we primarily perform each of all these vital actions is the soul. For the soul is the primary principle of our nourishment, sensation and local movement; and likewise of our understanding. Therefore this principle by which we primarily understand, whether it be called the intellect or the intellectual soul, is the form of the body. This is the demonstration used by Aristotle (*De Anima* ii.2).[18]

---

17. *NE* VI 2, 1139^{b}3–5.
18. *ST* I, q.76, a.1, *respondeo*.

We are "in act" by our soul, and our soul is named by its highest function, its rational power.[19] The life principle is defined but not exhausted by its rational principle, for "intellectual soul" superimplies all lower powers of soul we find in living things. To deny this, both Aristotle and Aquinas urge, is to deny that it is I myself who thinks, or who sleeps, or who is typing these words. That which common language bears witness to with respect to human beings as principles of action is explainable only if in fact the actors are unified beings. We act in the diverse ways that we do because we are the embodiments of a unifying principle that sustains our biological integrity and grants our abilities.

The basic methodological principle guiding an Aristotelian skeletal view of human beings is relatively simple: every activity is the actualization of a potentiality.[20] One corollary to this principle is that there are no uncaused activities. To deny this is tantamount to denying that version of the principle of sufficient reason which claims that there is an explanation for all phenomena (which is not to imply that we can discern or sufficiently comprehend all explanations). It is this principle applied to the human being that reveals one of the more attractive features of an Aristotelian schema of the self: Human beings perform unified rational actions, and so there must be an actual potential for rationality that is the agentive source of rational actions. Our rational activities are sometimes directed at things that are always what they are, or are so for the most part, and so there must be a speculative power within human rationality. Our rational activities are also sometimes directed at things that can be altered

19. *NE* I 7, 1098^{a}7–8.
20. This principle is at the basis of Aristotle's investigations of any sort of motion whatsoever, and is explained at length in *Physics* III, where motion, understood in the widest sense to mean change of any kind, is defined as such: "thus the fulfillment [or actualization] of what is potentially, as such, is motion—e.g. the fulfillment of what is alterable, as alterable, is alteration; of what is increasable and its opposite, decreasable (there is no common name for both), increase and decrease; of what can come to be and pass away, coming to be and passing away; of what can be carried along, locomotion" (*Physics* III 1, 201^{a}10–14).

through additional actions, both things we make and things we do, and so there must be a practical power within human rationality. Human actions exhibit attraction toward some things and persons, and so there must be a basic power by means of which these attractions are enabled, the concupiscible appetite. Human actions exhibit varieties of revulsion directed at some things and persons, and so there must be another basic appetite that enables these acts of jealous protection concerning our loves, the irascible appetite. Through such actions as imitating those we admire, reflecting on what we ought to love or hate and how we ought to act out that love and hate, and practicing the sorts of actions we hope someday to perform with less effort, we recognize that our appetites are in a variety of ways persuadable by reason. Multilayered patterns of behavior—each pattern involving one or more power of rationality, passion, and other physical factors—are developed over the course of a lifetime, beginning with the formation we receive as children, the exemplars we are led to or choose to admire, the decisions we make, the thoughts we think, and the actions we perform. These patterns of actions compose our character, the various elements of which are more or less virtuous or vicious. The virtues are those qualities that bring our diverse action-bearing powers to perfection, enabling them to perform those actions and engage in those activities that are most perfective of the beings we are.

Understanding the virtues as traits of character, each of which has a home, so to speak, within the whole of the human being, is just one part of the story. Much more needs to be said, however, about what entitles one to claim that virtues bring powers to perfection. Before we turn to further teleological considerations, there is both a concern about and an important contribution to the anthropology undergirding Aristotle's treatment of those virtues pertinent to ethical and political inquiry that should be addressed.

Dependent Rational Animals

Both the concern and the contribution arise from a thinker who is generally regarded, and for very good reason, to be one of the most, if not *the* most, significant moral philosophers of our time. He is often regarded as a major contributor to contemporary virtue ethics,[21] but the contrasts between his own inquiries and contemporary virtue ethics—especially contemporary virtue ethics of the dominant and conventional variety—provide a good point of departure for understanding why Alasdair MacIntyre dissociates his own efforts from those of the contemporary virtue ethics movement. If anything, MacIntyre prefers to describe himself as an Aristotelian Thomist. It is strange, then, since it is the opposite of MacIntyre's own declarations of his adherences, that one does not find in the literature challenges to the claim that MacIntyre is a virtue ethicist, but there are a number of challenges in print to his claim to being an Aristotelian on the one hand,[22] and a Thomist on the other.[23] Generally, the doubts about his Aristotelian and Thomist *bona fides* arise from criticisms to the effect that his historical and tradition-constituted perspective prevents him

---

21. Even Hursthouse, whose version of virtue ethics has little affinity with MacIntyre's inquiries, credits him as one of the few who helped put virtue ethics on the map; see Hursthouse, *On Virtue Ethics*, 3. Nussbaum expresses a similar view about MacIntyre's importance for virtue ethics in both "Non-Relative Virtues," and "Virtue Ethics: A Misleading Category?"

22. Nussbaum regards herself as an Aristotelian, and MacIntyre as an un-Aristotelian relativist virtue ethicist in "Non-Relative Virtues," and as a (peculiar sort of) Humean virtue ethicist in "Virtue Ethics: A Misleading Category?"

23. Janet Coleman, "MacIntyre and Aquinas," in *After MacIntyre: Critical Perspectives on the Work of Alasdair MacIntyre*, ed. John Horton and Susan Mendus (Notre Dame, Ind.: University of Notre Dame Press, 1994), 65–90; John Haldane, "MacIntyre's Thomist Revival: What Next?" ibid., 91–107; and Robert P. George, "Moral Particularism, Thomism, and Traditions," *Review of Metaphysics* 42 (1989): 593–605. MacIntyre replies briefly to Coleman and Haldane in "A Partial Response to My Critics," in *After MacIntyre: Critical Perspectives on the Work of Alasdair MacIntyre*, 283–304. Christopher Stephen Lutz defends MacIntyre against all three essayists in the fourth chapter of his *Tradition in the Ethics of Alasdair MacIntyre: Relativism, Thomism, and Philosophy* (Lanham, Md.: Lexington Books, 2004).

from making truth claims, or at least unacceptably limit the strength of his truth claims. MacIntyre's little-remarked-upon Aquinas Lecture, *First Principles, Final Ends, and Contemporary Philosophical Issues*, puts, as far as I am concerned, those criticisms to rest.[24] In these inter-Aristotelian-Thomist disputes, much turns on a sufficiently subtle reading of the purposes to which MacIntyre puts his notion of rationality as tradition constituted and constituting.

As an unintended tribute to his intellectual honesty, it is MacIntyre himself who generates one of the most significant criticisms of his celebrated work, *After Virtue*, in a later retrospective. That to which his self-criticism is directed concerns that portion in *After Virtue* in which MacIntyre explicitly rejects what he calls Aristotle's "metaphysical biology," as well as the manner in which he plants on the field he has cleared his own practice-centered account of the virtues, taking care to distinguish it from Aristotle's "biologically teleological account."[25]

Many questions arise from MacIntyre's rejection of Aristotle's biological foundations in *After Virtue* regarding what MacIntyre thinks Aristotle's position to be and why he thinks its rejection is warranted, and not all of those questions are resolved in MacIntyre's retrospective remarks. To begin with, the reasons for MacIntyre's rejection of Aristotle are not given, nor does MacIntyre explain what exactly is to be entailed by "metaphysical" or "biology" in this rejection. Indeed, the very terms MacIntyre employs in his rejection are ambiguous: "Metaphysical biology" is, from an Aristotelian perspective, an oxymoron. Biology is part of physics, which is second philosophy, and the principles derived from second nature become essential to car-

---

24. Alasdair MacIntyre, *First Principles, Final Ends, and Contemporary Philosophical Issues* (Milwaukee, Wis.: Marquette University Press, 1990). See also "Moral Relativism, Truth, and Justification," first published in *Moral Truth and Moral Tradition: Essays in Honor of Peter Geach and Elizabeth Anscombe*, ed. Luke Gormally (Dublin: Four Courts Press, 1994), 6–24, and reprinted as the third chapter of the first volume of *Selected Essays: The Tasks of Philosophy* (Cambridge: Cambridge University Press, 2006).

25. *After Virtue*, 196–97.

rying forth the study of first causes and principles, first philosophy, or what Aristotle's heirs (but not Aristotle himself) call metaphysics. In any event, does MacIntyre mean only to reject many of the details of Aristotle's biology, such as the mistaken claims about how generation takes place, the incomplete status of women, the means by which blood is circulated, and the like—all of which have been refuted already by scientific developments? Or did he mean as well to reject the basic principles Aristotle employs in his biological studies, such as that biological unity in an organism is achieved by means of a principle of life and that an organism's formal cause implies a final cause? Is it those principles he means by "metaphysical"? It is not clear.

Though these questions about precisely what MacIntyre sought to reject about Aristotle's "metaphysical biology" are never explicitly answered, in his later writings MacIntyre does employ Aristotelian notions of the soul, as well as formal and final causality, in a manner that emphasizes his acceptance of them as necessary principles for generating a coherent account of the virtues. For example, he writes:

> I remarked earlier that for an Aristotelian, whether Thomist or otherwise, what is good or best for anyone or anything is so in virtue of its being of a certain kind, with its own essential nature and that which peculiarly belongs to the flourishing of beings of that kind.... Take away the notion of essential nature, take away the corresponding notion of what is good and best for members of a specific kind who share such a nature, and the Aristotelian scheme of the self which is to achieve good, of good, and of pleasure necessarily collapses. There remains only the individual self with its pleasures and pains. So metaphysical nominalism sets constraints upon how the moral life can be conceived. And, conversely, certain types of conceptions of the moral life exclude such nominalism.[26]

Without recognizing the unity of the self that is achieved by means of the rational principle of soul—that which gives to each of us our essential nature—it is impossible to build a coherent account of the self and those goods perfective of the self. Whatever MacIntyre

---

26. MacIntyre, *Three Rival Versions of Moral Enquiry*, 138.

means by rejecting Aristotle's metaphysical biology in *After Virtue*, he clearly accepts some of the physical cum metaphysical features of Aristotelian anthropology by 1990.

This observation prepares us in some ways, then, for the complaint MacIntyre makes of his earlier comments regarding Aristotle's metaphysical biology in a still later work:

> In *After Virtue* I had attempted to give an account of the place of the virtues, understood as Aristotle had understood them, within social practices, the lives of individuals and the lives of communities, while making that account independent of what I called Aristotle's "metaphysical biology." Although there is indeed good reason to repudiate important elements in Aristotle's biology, I now judge that I was in error in supposing an ethics independent of biology to be possible ... and this for two distinct, but related reasons. The first is that no account of the goods, rules and virtues that are definitive of our moral life can be adequate that does not explain—or at least point us towards an explanation—how that form of life is possible for beings who are biologically constituted as we are, by providing us with an account of our development towards and into that form of life. That development has as its starting point our initial animal condition. Secondly, a failure to understand that condition and the light thrown upon it by a comparison between humans and members of other intelligent animal species will obscure crucial features of that development.[27]

This remarkable admission and redirection introduces a work that breaks new ground both in MacIntyre's ongoing project and in moral philosophy generally.

To be sure, the Aristotelian tradition, unlike modern luminaries such as Hume, Kant, and Mill, has always been comfortable in acknowledging our animality. Our animal nature is something not to fight against or fly from or subjugate, but rather to educate. The principal means of that education is the development of the virtues. With *Dependent Rational Animals*, however, MacIntyre dwells on a num-

---

27. MacIntyre, *Dependent Rational Animals: Why Human Beings Need the Virtues*, Paul Carus Lecture Series 20 (Chicago: Open Court, 1999), x.

ber of the features of our animality that have been little remarked upon, even within the Aristotelian tradition. What MacIntyre brings to our attention is our shared lot of vulnerability, disability, and dependency.

For extended periods of our adult life, if we are so fortunate as not to be handicapped in some significant way, we can fancy ourselves as independent, autonomous agents. Such autonomy, of course, is a fiction—think of your reliance on emotional support from your friends, on stocked grocery stores, on the electric company, and gasoline stations for starters; nevertheless, it is a fiction that we often indulge in. It takes no great stretch of the mind to recognize that we came to be only through the conjugal activity of our parents, we were nurtured in our mothers' wombs, and spent our first years in diapers, suckling at our mothers' breasts and slurping processed foods from spoons held to our mouths. We learned to walk, talk, read, and calculate through our radical dependency on parents, other family members, and teachers. Those early marks of dependency remain formative parts of the narrative of our lives, and the expectation of similar sorts of dependency in our old age is part of the anticipatory arc of the same narrative. We begin and end in the hands of others, those (hopefully) who love us. And this recognition of our dependency undergirds (or at least ought to) the sort of help we are ready to offer others.

We are not, then, merely rational animals. We are dependent rational animals. The virtues of what MacIntyre calls "acknowledged dependency" form the basis of how we come to flourish as the dependent rational animals we are. The virtue that is at the structural root of the virtues of acknowledged dependency is, as Aquinas had already stressed,[28] *misericordia*, which is that part of the virtue of charity that entails "grief or sorrow over someone else's distress, just insofar as one understands the other's distress as one's own."[29] It is

---

28. *ST* II-II, q.30, a.3.

this virtue that provides the unifying thread tying together all members of a community, recognizing in each a brother, a sister, a neighbor: "But to recognize another as brother or friend is to recognize one's relationship to them as being of the same kind as one's relationship to other members of one's own community. So to direct the virtue of *misericordia* towards others is to extend one's communal relationships so as to include those others within those relationships."[30] Aristotle remarks on the importance of recognizing our communal selves, but it took Aquinas, reflecting as he does on charity as the efficient cause of all the virtues, to put real flesh on Aristotle's observation. It has taken, in turn, MacIntyre to bring to light the importance of this virtue and those others that proceed from our acknowledged dependency in a manner that takes special note of the features we share with other intelligent and social animals.

To be sure, we should be concerned about those features of Aristotle's biology that are false or exaggerated. But Aristotle was certainly right to stress the importance of a biological account of our nature with respect to making sense of the virtues. We learn from Aristotle, as from other important figures in the Aristotelian tradition, both the necessity of an account of our shared essential nature that makes sense of those goods we ought to be directed toward, and that that essential nature is no mere logical matter by means of which we can derive the appropriate conclusions about our ends, but in fact the flesh and blood reality of our shared life of mutual dependency.

29. MacIntyre, *Dependent Rational Animals*, 125.
30. Ibid., 125–26.

Chapter 7

TELEOLOGY IN ARISTOTELIAN ETHICS

Every Virtue Needs a Goal

> Now excellent actions are noble and done for the sake of the noble.
>
> Aristotle, *NE* IV.1, 1120^{a}23.

❊

Whether talking about a part of a substance, or a substance as a whole, grasping a thing's *telos* proves essential to making sense of what sort of thing it is. This insight is employed to explain how each virtue is a perfection of some power or some coordination of powers and passions of a person, and contributes to the character of the whole person. Whatever the field of inquiry, Aristotle's principle that we can know a thing only by knowing what it is for is heuristically primary. This formula implies, among other things, that the formal cause (or explanation) of anything is logically dependent on our understanding of its final cause (or explanation). Insights about the goods or ends of human life inevitably inform discussions of human nature, and this remains true whether one is an Aristotelian naturalist, or a physicalist, or a dualist, or any variety of other doctrinal adherent on questions pertaining to what we are. The same sort of logical connection holds when we focus on virtue: we are able to name a certain trait of character a virtue because of what it enables us to do; and, in the Aristotelian tradition of ethics, what a virtue enables one to do is to act well, that is to say, to do those things that are good. "Good," then, in an Aristotelian context, takes on the nature of the end, of completing something, of bringing to perfection some particular power, a network of powers, or indeed an entire life.

"Teleology" is often used in contemporary philosophical literature to mean something other than an Aristotelian-inspired reflection on human good, something more along the lines of a trained focus on the results of actions rather than on actions as their own ends. "Teleology" in this utilitarian and consequentialist sense is not the focus of this chapter. This is not to suggest that reflection on consequences has no place in Aristotelian ethics, but that a consideration of consequences lacks in Aristotelian ethics the utilitarian embrace of consequences as definitive in decision-making procedures. Much confusion has been caused by the consequentialist appropriation of the semantics of ends, but the bad consequences from this can be avoided if one takes care not to read Mill into Aristotle.

Theorizing about the ends of human life demands more than querying whether there is some overarching end to human life, and if so what it might be, but must include reflection on individual virtues as ends on the one hand and means to further ends on the other. The holistic line of analysis about human ends plays off of the particular, and vice versa, and so the two weave together to form a synoptic whole. I begin with some thoughts about the holistic line of analysis.

Thinking about the Ends of Life

There are challenges peculiar to our age regarding the manner in which we take up questions concerning the ends of life. Some of those challenges are uncovered when one considers how rarely the following question is posed in philosophical discussions: What is the purpose of life? To many this question has the ring of a caricature of a philosophical question, rather than the sort of question a serious philosopher would ask in earnest. Why is that? Socrates certainly asks it in sincerity, whereas many of his current heirs cannot. At least part of the reason for our discomfort with the question as well as the reflections on substantive goods it prompts is what Talbot Brewer describes as a "prevailing sense of academic decorum." Brewer continues:

> It is regarded as mildly embarrassing to forward substantive conceptions of the human good under the banner of philosophy—embarrassing not merely to the philosopher forwarding the conception but to the field as a whole. Good taste, along with a sound grip on what could and what could not possibly form the subject of a genuine academic expertise, requires that one stay clear of the topic of the good life, or restrict oneself to one-size-fits-all theories that do not disqualify any particular cultural tradition as a possible avenue to the good life.[1]

Brewer has, I think, put his finger on two important points in this passage, and taken together they ought to lead us to see that it is our typical academic reaction to this question, rather than the question itself, that should strike us as odd. Recognizing that takes a sort of self-reflection of the naively-playful-able-to-laugh-at-oneself Socratic variety that is in at least as short supply now as it was in Socrates's day.

The first point Brewer stresses is that it is impossible to answer a question about the meaning or purpose of our lives in anything approaching an adequate manner without providing a robust or thick account of the good. Such accounts put their adherents at odds with a sentiment prevailing not just in philosophy, but in academic culture in general, that it is bad taste to offer a position on so fundamental a matter. To be sure, disagreements on important matters still abound in academia, but they are often confined within surprisingly solid walls that tend to skirt the deepest matters of metaphysical significance. Just as good manners might lead one to avoid

---

1. Brewer, *The Retrieval of Ethics*, 6–7.

raising controversial issues of politics or religion over Thanksgiving dinner, academic good taste has come to consider the raising of metaphysical questions touching on the overarching meaning of human life to be inappropriate for the classroom or journal article.

This sentiment of academic decorum seems to be accompanied with the conviction that efforts to propose robust concepts of the good life for human beings commit someone to several dubious propositions: supposing there to be some best way, in general, to live; supposing it can be described; and suggesting that those who are not pursuing it are failing, to put it bluntly, as humans. There is, it must be admitted, something uncomfortable about arguing over such important matters, and they do tend to reveal deep fissures between interlocutors. As a result, philosophers have in the modern period tended to stick to thin, if any, accounts of the good life for human beings. There are, of course, exceptions to this rule, but I am here trying to lend support to the observation that Brewer has made, an observation that strikes me as more or less correct and that helps to explain why Anscombe, Geach, MacIntyre, and others proposing a radical reappraisal of moral philosophy remain marginal figures.

Brewer's second observation touches on the natural desire of professional philosophers to be accepted within the academic ranks. Academic philosophy has, like so many other disciplines, splintered into many specializations. This is in part the expected result of graduate school training that teaches young philosophers to focus on a narrow batch of topics of current interest in the journals, and at the same time to avoid devoting too much time to the grand questions characteristic of philosophy's early and middle years. We learn to collaborate as fellow researchers on well-circumscribed problems and to build our discipline like natural scientists build theirs. It is this sort of narrow focus that is rewarded with publications in top journals. Measured against the scope of traditional philosophy, however, contemporary specialization in philosophy is unusual.

Traditional philosophy understood itself as a way of life that endeavors to grasp a view of the whole—an aspirational zenith whose remnant is still paid tribute to by the fact that mathematicians, biologists, classicists, historians, and sociologists all receive doctorates in philosophy. Asking about the meaning of our lives is the sort of question that demands a wide scope, one that does not present itself in bite-size pieces, but rather one that requires openness to a variety of other disciplines and that nevertheless seeks a unifying answer. It is the philosopher's task to strive for that synthetic achievement. Unless one has spent a great deal of time studying classical and medieval authors, an activity nowadays sometimes derided as merely engaging in the history of philosophy rather than philosophy proper, one would likely not have been introduced to the speculative activities nurtured in the philosophical tradition as the necessary propaedeutic to sustained reflection on the good of one's life as a whole. That does not mean that contemporary philosophers avoid such reflection altogether, but just that reflections on life's purpose and the methods that have been cultivated to sustain it are not part of the systematic efforts of current philosophical practices. The result of this is that a typical contemporary philosopher thinking about one's life as a whole is not necessarily in a better position to sustain such an inquiry than his or her non-philosophically trained peers, and may even be in a worse position than they. Both are in need of drawing on resources that have not been essential to their training.

In her own way, Anscombe draws attention to discontinuities between classical and modern philosophical preoccupations and practices in "Modern Moral Philosophy," as well as other essays of hers.[2] Attention to the division between ancients and moderns can be found as well in both the novels and philosophical writings of Iris Murdoch, in MacIntyre's writings especially since the first publica-

---

2. In particular, see Anscombe's "Authority in Morals," chapter 5; and her even more pointed defense of a thick account of the good in "Morality," chapter 13 of *Faith in a Hard Ground: Essays on Religion, Philosophy and Ethics,* ed. Mary Geach and Luke Gormally (Charlottesville, Va.: Imprint Academic, 2008).

tion of *After Virtue*,³ and throughout the oeuvre of Pierre Hadot. In fact, a recognition of the need to break out of narrow contemporary patterns of philosophical reflection and to renew an approach to philosophy that is suited to sustained reflection on the purpose of life is the heart of the impetus behind the early days of the virtue ethical movement. One can discern echoes of this motivating insight in, for instance, Foot's *Natural Goodness* and part 3 of Hursthouse's *On Virtue Ethics*, but these works, while raising the classical question, avoid recourse to classical religious and metaphysical strategies for addressing the purpose of life.

For Anscombe and MacIntyre both, the answers to this question, or at least the means by which we can pursue answers to this question, are to be found in a tradition that is, broadly speaking, Aristotelian. Speaking more narrowly, theirs is an Aristotelianism that is filtered through a mixture of Judeo-Christian religious and ethical thought, Augustinian and neo-Platonic theology, and that sort of Aristotelian philosophy which goes by the name of Thomism. Such a confluence of influences on a contemporary thinker is not as rare as its description might suggest. The challenge for these thinkers is to address this wide philosophical question about the meaning of our lives in a fashion that both incorporates the answers of the best minds of the Aristotelian tradition and makes the case for the relevance of those tradition-bound answers to philosophers, professional or otherwise, who are concerned with the question today and who may not embrace the same tradition of Thomistic-Aristotelianism.

---

3. MacIntyre's "The Ends of Life, the Ends of Philosophical Writing," chapter 7 of *The Tasks of Philosophy, Selected Essays*, vol. 1 (Cambridge: Cambridge University Press, 2006), addresses these points with special focus on philosophical writing. MacIntyre's *God, Philosophy, Universities: A Selective History of the Catholic Philosophical Tradition* (Lanham, Md.: Rowman and Littlefield, 2009), addresses these points through a sustained reflection on philosophical inquires and tradition within the institution of the university.

The Good Life for Man

MacIntyre's first and still best known attempt to meet this challenge comes in *After Virtue*, a work that predates his explicit embrace of Thomism but represents his first explicitly Aristotelian book-length project. He argues in this work that "the New Testament's account of the virtues" and Aristotle's account have the "same logical and conceptual structure," even if they do not share the same content:

> A virtue is, as with Aristotle, a quality the exercise of which leads to the achievement of the human *telos*. The good for man [in the New Testament's account of the virtues] is of course a supernatural and not only a natural good, but supernature redeems and completes nature. Moreover the relationship of virtues as means to the end which is human incorporation in the divine kingdom of the age to come is internal and not external, just as it is in Aristotle. It is of course this parallelism which allows Aquinas to synthesize Aristotle and the New Testament. A key feature of this parallelism is the way in which the concept of *the good life for man* is prior to the concept of a virtue in just the way in which on the Homeric account the concept of a social role was prior. Once again it is the way in which the former concept is applied which determines how the latter is to be applied. In both cases the concept of a virtue is a secondary concept.[4]

The link that MacIntyre draws here between human nature, its completion, and the role that virtue plays is especially to be noted. Seen from the perspective of reflections on the ends of human nature, the virtues are *means*—not means in the sense of external goods to be achieved in route to some final payoff, but rather themselves internal goods or ends that are constitutive of the ultimate and complete human end. The same structural relationship between human nature, ends, and virtue applies whether or not one thinks human nature perfectible within one continuous natural lifetime—as Aristotle is often interpreted as arguing[5]—or only in an activity achieved through a supernatural completion of human nature.

---

4. MacIntyre, *After Virtue*, 2nd ed., 184–85.
5. I think the evidence we have from Aristotle is inconclusive as to whether he thinks

The point was made in chapter 5 that it is one thing to define the ultimate human *telos* in terms of the virtues, and another to define the ethically relevant virtues as those qualities of our character that enable us to achieve the ends appropriate to our nature. I argue there that one of the distinctive features of Aristotelian ethics is that virtue serves as a logically and generationally prior concept to the full-blown account of happiness. Despite some appearances to the contrary, I think MacIntyre's approach in *After Virtue* embraces this feature of Aristotelian ethics since MacIntyre argues that the attempt to provide a philosophically complete account of human happiness is a feature of the larger set of reflections on human goods. MacIntyre makes plain, and by doing so seconds in his own way Anscombe's call for a more adequate philosophical psychology, that *before* we can have an adequate account of virtue, significant progress needs to be made in reflecting on human nature in a manner that includes reflections on its ends.

There are of course a great many ends of human nature, by which I mean the ends or goals of any variety of activities that involve at least some minimal degree of rational reflection. The virtues are those qualities that enable us not simply to perform those activities, or to engage in those practices, but to do so well. Whatever happiness or flourishing is, it is something more than the sorts of reflections on those human ends that form the stuff of our active lives, and must imply, among other things, a still further extension of the reflective life whereby we synthesize the many goals of our lives into a comprehensive whole. We can make sense of happiness only insofar as we have made sense of the virtues, for happiness is the activity of the rational principle of soul in accordance with virtue; but we

---

our natural lives are extendable and perfectible, at least in part, via some supernatural divine-like activity. It should be noted, however, that we have less than half of Aristotle's literary output, and that most of Aristotle's neo-Platonic and Islamist commentators interpreted him as a patent supernaturalist on the question of the soul's immortality and its ability to achieve perfection in an afterlife.

can make sense of the virtues only insofar as we have reflected on the proximate ends of human nature and how best those ends are to be realized.

Several lines of analysis have a tendency to be conflated in discussions of Aristotelian ethics: reflection on human nature and those ends proper to beings who are dependent rational animals; reflection on the virtues as those habituated and learned traits of character that enable us to achieve the proximate ends of human nature; reflection on happiness as the overarching good of a whole human life that is intelligible only because of its dependence on an understanding of the virtues. To define virtues as means to the achievement of proximate human ends is not to define virtue by means of happiness.[6]

Much of MacIntyre's treatment of the virtues focuses on this second line of analysis, and particularly on how those proximate ends of human nature manifest themselves as our proper ends. It is in this line of analysis that the special attention he gives to "practice" is to be understood. A practice is "any coherent and complex form of socially established cooperative human activity through which goods internal to that form of activity are realized in the course of trying to achieve those standards of excellence which are appropriate to, and partially definitive of, that form of activity, with the result that human powers to achieve excellence, and human conceptions of the ends and goods involved, are systematically extended."[7] Practices do not represent our ends, but rather are the activities in which our proximate ends are realizable. This does not imply that one can exercise a virtue only within a practice,[8] but does imply that it is practices that make virtues intelligible. The value of practices is not exhausted by their role in providing the means by which virtue can be acquired

---

6. And Simpson is wrong to accuse MacIntyre of doing just that in his "Contemporary Virtue Ethics and Aristotle."

7. MacIntyre, *After Virtue*, 187.

8. See MacIntyre's first caveat, ibid., 187.

and exercised through achieving the goods internal to them, but it is from this that their value primarily derives. Practices are, then, in a certain sense, the socially embedded vehicles by means of which the virtues are carried.

Practices themselves, however, are not self-supporting. They interweave with the narratives of our individual and collective lives, are typically housed within institutions (with which they often find themselves at odds), and can be sustained only by "tradition"—another term to which MacIntyre gave his own peculiar stamp in his account of the virtues:

> A living tradition then is an historically extended, socially embodied argument, and argument precisely in part about the goods which constitute that tradition. Within a tradition the pursuit of goods extends through generations, sometimes through many generations. Hence the individual's search for his or her good is generally and characteristically conducted within a context defined by those traditions of which the individual's life is a part, and this is true both of those goods which are internal to practices and of the goods of a single life.[9]

With his notions of practice, tradition, and his account of the narrative unity of human life, MacIntyre fills one of the lacunae present in Aristotle's own account of the virtues: namely, the designation of certain habits as virtues without sufficient justification or even description of what makes them virtues. What makes the Aristotelian virtues virtues at all, MacIntyre teaches us, is that they are the traits of character that enable us to achieve the goods internal to practices, which are in turn made intelligible by the traditions that support them. So virtues are understood to be virtues to the extent that by means of them we can achieve the human goods, the human goods are made intelligible by the very practices by means of which they can be attained, and those practices are at one and the same time preserved and rendered intelligible by the traditions to which they belong.

9. Ibid., 222.

MacIntyre is concerned, as well, to address the question having to do with the overarching good of a whole human life, and here his account of the narrative unity of life is particularly relevant, for "the unity of a human life is the unity of a narrative quest."[10] Such an understanding of a human life recognizes that we can make sense of the beings we are only insofar as we have some conception of what we are for. However, this is a quest in which clarity about what it is exactly that we are questing for is yet (and ever) in need of fuller explanation. The virtues seen in this light are those qualities needed to sustain us on this quest: "The virtues therefore are to be understood as those dispositions which will not only sustain practices and enable us to achieve the goods internal to practices, but which also sustain us in the relevant kind of quest for the good, by enabling us to overcome the harms, dangers, temptations and distractions which we encounter, and which will furnish us with increasing self-knowledge and increasing knowledge of the good."[11] In sustaining us in this fashion, the virtues can be seen as goods internal to our life conceived as a whole, a life best understood as an extended Socratic exercise in self-reflection; "the good life for man is the life spent in seeking for the good life for man, and the virtues necessary for the seeking are those which will enable us to understand what more and what else the good life for man is."[12] Is this a sufficiently "thick" account of the good life for man?

MacIntyre himself thickens this account in his later writings, but his *After Virtue* answer to the question of what is the purpose of human life is, I think, provisionally adequate. A few more observations about an Aristotelian reflection on the good life for man are still in order, but not before some remarks on the peculiar role that the virtues have as both means and ends.

---

10. Ibid., 219.
11. Ibid.
12. Ibid.

Virtues as Ends, Virtues as Means

One of the points of difference between Aristotelian ethics and contemporary virtue ethics I emphasized in chapter 5 is that for Aristotle, the exhortative stress is on virtuous *activity* rather than on the mere acquisition of the virtues and the building of a just and noble character.[13] Perhaps Aristotle is partly responsible for why this point is so often overlooked, for he does indeed accentuate the value of the acquisition of the virtues for their own sake. This is so because the acquisition of any virtue is the perfection of some power of a person, and so the achievement of some good internal to the life of that person. Virtues are then ends, and they are also means. The dual role of virtues as ends and means is elucidated, perhaps most clearly, in Aristotle's discussion of the utility of both practical and philosophical wisdom. Even if no further good followed from these virtues, Aristotle argues that we ought to strive to acquire them: "Now first let us say that in themselves these states must be worthy of choice because they are the excellences of the two parts of the soul respectively, even if neither of them produces anything."[14] Judged on their own terms, practical wisdom, philosophical wisdom, and each of the other ethically relevant virtues is worth having, for each contributes in its distinctive way to the perfection of the person. It is also the case, however, that each of these virtues is conducive to some further good: "Secondly, they do produce something, not as

---

13. Talbot Brewer strikes a similar note as he writes: "It is Aristotle's view, after all, that the highest human good lies in sustained activity—and in particular, the life of activity that constitutes *eudaimonia*—and not in passive experiences nor in achieved states of character. While Aristotle is routinely called a virtue ethicist, he did not ground value in the virtues of character themselves, but rather in the intrinsically valuable activity that flows from the virtues under minimally propitious conditions. Given this, we must resurrect a broadly Aristotelian notion of intrinsically value activity if we are to grasp the nature and value of Aristotelian virtues, and by extension the sort of alternative that Aristotelianism can offer to Kantian and utilitarian moral theories" (*The Retrieval of Ethics*, 92).

14. Aristotle, *NE* VI 12, 1144^{a}1–3.

the art of medicine produces health, however, but as health produces health; so does wisdom produce happiness; for being a part of excellence entire, by being possessed and by actualizing itself it makes a man happy."[15] Aristotle goes on to argue that philosophical wisdom contributes more to the primary happiness of the person than do the other virtues,[16] but the special status of one virtue does not hinder the same logic evidenced in the last quotation being applied to each of the other virtues.[17] Every virtue is not only a perfection of a particular power of a person, but a contributor to that overarching good that is a fully flourishing life.[18]

15. Ibid., 1144^{a}4–6.
16. "But the activity of intellect, which is contemplative ... will be the complete happiness of man, if it be allowed a complete term of life (for none of the attributes of happiness is *in*complete)" (*NE* X 7, 1177^{b}17–18, 24–25).
17. "But in a secondary degree the life in accordance with the other kind of excellence is happy; for the activities in accordance with this befit our human estate. Just and brave acts, and other excellent acts, we do in relation to each other, observing what is proper to each with regard to contracts and services all manner of actions and with regard to passions; and all of these seem to be human. Some of them seem even to arise from the body, and excellence of character to be in many ways bound up with the passions. Practical wisdom, too, is linked to excellence of character, and this to practical wisdom, since the principles of practical wisdom are in accordance with the moral excellences and rightness in the moral excellences is in accordance with practical wisdom. Being connected with the passions also, the moral excellences must belong to our composite nature; and the excellences of our composite nature are human; so therefore, are the life and the happiness which correspond to these" (*NE* X 8, 1178^{a}9–22).
18. The last two footnotes quote texts at the center of a controversy about whether Aristotle's notion of happiness is intellectualist/dominant (being found in one best sort of activity) or inclusivist (comprising all virtuous activities). An incomplete list of some of the principal players in this debate includes the following: W. F. R. Hardie, "The Final Good in Aristotle's Ethics," *Philosophy* 40 (1965): 277–95; J. L. Ackrill, "Aristotle on Eudaimonia," in *Essays on Aristotle's Ethics*, ed. A. Rorty (Berkeley: University of California Press, 1980): 15–33; John Cooper, *Reason and Human Good in Aristotle* (Cambridge, Mass.: Harvard University Press, 1975); Anthony Kenny, *The Aristotelian Ethics* (Oxford: Clarendon Press, 1978); Stephen L. Clark, *Aristotle's Man* (Oxford: Oxford University Press, 1984); John Cooper, "Contemplation and Happiness: A Reconsideration," *Synthese* 72 (1987): 187–216; Richard Kraut, *Aristotle on the Human Good* (Princeton, N.J.: Princeton University Press, 1989); Anthony Kenny, *Aristotle on the Perfect Life* (Oxford: Oxford University Press, 1992); and Jeffrey S. Purinton, "Aristotle's Definition of Happiness (*NE* I, 7, 1098a16–18)," *Oxford Studies in Ancient Philosophy* 16 (1998): 259–97.

There is indeed a sense in which the having of a virtue represents a kind of stasis, a standing-readiness-for-focused-action, if you will. Yet even perceived from this angle, where we are looking at each virtue in "the now," there is a depth of activity packaged into each virtue: a history of repeated actions that have formed it and that make its past, and the active anticipation of how best to exercise it that makes its future. Virtues are, so to speak, active states, and their telic orientation toward virtuous activity is what makes them intelligible *as* virtues. Aristotle stresses time and again the importance of this forward-lookingness of the virtues, for their purpose is measured by the degree to which they contribute to activities that are completive of our lives.

The very frequency of Aristotle's insistence on the possession of virtue for virtuous *activity* bears witness to his appreciation for our human tendency to overlook just such a point. We, like Aristotle's contemporaries, tend to measure accomplishment by the possession of desired objects. A day of hard work earns a good night of sleep. A stressful period deserves a vacation. A wise investment strategy earns us a nice home. The rewards we commonly hold out for ourselves are the very opposite of activities; what we really want is rest (just ask the parents of young children). There is a potential lotus eater in all of us, and it especially yearns to be fed during times of intense activity. Why on earth would someone think our happiness lies in still more activity?

Aristotle's view of life and its purpose runs against this everyday way of thinking about success, but the contrast between Aristotle's position and this everyday attitude is only apparently paradoxical. What Aristotle brings to light are other common judgments we make about having and acting. What desired good, possessed merely to possess it, does not lead to disappointment? To be sure, a good movie affords us some rest, but what makes it good is the degree to which it leads us to see some features of reality in a new light. To be sure, we want to own a good home, but what makes it valuable is its attractiveness to friends and family members who will want to visit us in it. To be sure, we want a good night of sleep, but its value is measured by its making us even more able to accomplish those tasks laid before us the next day. We want to possess goods, unless we are vicious misers, so as to *enjoy* them. Life is activity, and acting well is living well. To want the cessation of all activity is a denial of life, a perverse celebration of despair, and directs us toward the nadir of flourishing. Aimlessness, undirected anxiousness, and a lack of focused energy are some of the symptoms of those unhappy souls we call depressed. The purpose-driven types, those who are on a quest to live the good life and who are sustained in that quest by the appropriate virtues, are the ones who seem, both to themselves and to others, to be flourishing. It does not take an Aristotle to notice this, but it did take an Aristotle to construct a comprehensive ethics around it.

Each of the virtues is an end then, which means they are intrinsically valuable, which is to say beautiful and noble (*kalon*). The person who possesses them is also beautiful and noble, as are the actions he or she performs: "A man is noble [and/or beautiful] and good because those goods which are noble are possessed by him for themselves, and because he practices the noble and for its own sake, the noble being the excellences and the acts that proceed from excellence."[19] Though persons and their virtues can each be regarded as valuable, it is *kalon* activity that renders them so: "Now excellent actions are noble and done for the sake of the noble."[20] The most beautiful and noble of activities is that of God, the imitation of whose activity provides the ultimate standard by means of which a meaningful life is measured:

What choice, then, or possession of the natural goods—whether bodily goods, wealth, friends, or other things—will most produce the contem-

---

19. *Eudemian Ethics* VII 15, 1248^{b}34–36.
20. *NE* IV 1, 1120^{a}23.

plation of god, that choice or possession is best; this is the noblest standard, but any that through deficiency or excess hinders one from the contemplation and service of god is bad; this a man possesses in his soul, and this is the best standard for the soul—to perceive the irrational part of the soul, as such, as little as possible.[21]

To kalon is put to different uses by Aristotle, but here he uses it as a metaphysical cum aesthetic standard for human activity, a standard that in turn is measured against God's own activity.[22]

Aristotle's logic, only some of which explicitly appears in this passage at the conclusion of the *Eudemian Ethics*, seems to run something like this: God is most alive, most active, and the activity of thought is both life[23] and God.[24] The more perfected an activity is, the more godlike it is; the more noble and beautiful it is, the more godlike it is. Insofar as each ethically relevant virtue entails rational activity of soul, it shares in this godlike activity, from which it derives its nobility and beauty. God's activity serves as standard for our best

---

21. *Eudemian Ethics* VII 15, 1249^{b}21.

22. Several scholars have sought to untangle what exactly is entailed by Aristotle's use of *to kalon*. Kelly Rogers looks to how Aristotle uses the term in connection with what is proper (*to prepon*) as well as its connection to praise and self-respect in "Aristotle's Conception of Τὸ Καλόν," *Ancient Philosophy* 13 (1993): 355–71; and in "Aristotle on the Motive of Courage," *Southern Journal of Philosophy* 32 (1994): 303–13. John Milliken draws on the research of Rogers and argues for the advantages of the *to kalon* standard over Kantian and utilitarian standards in "Aristotle's Aesthetic Ethics," *Southern Journal of Philosophy* 44 (2006): 319–39. Terence Irwin connects *to kalon* with actions that benefit others in "Aristotle's Conception of Morality," in *Proceedings of the Boston Area Colloquium in Ancient Philosophy*, vol. 1, ed. John J. Cleary (Lanham, Md.: University Press of America, 1986), 115–43. Thomas Tuozzo explores the connection between *to kalon* and contemplation in "Contemplation, the Noble, and the Mean: The Standard for Moral Virtue in Aristotle's Ethics," in *Aristotle, Virtue and the Mean*, ed. John Bosley (Edmonton, Canada: Academic Printing and Publishing, 1996), 129–54. John Cooper explores the connection between *to kalon* and one of the two types of nonrational desire, *thumos*, in "Reason, Moral Virtue, and Moral Value," chapter 11 of his *Reason and Emotion: Essays on Ancient Moral Psychology and Ethical Theory* (Princeton N.J.: Princeton University Press, 1999), 253–80. I am particularly indebted to Joseph Owens's arguments in "The ΚΑΛΟΝ in the Aristotelian *Ethics*," in *Studies in Aristotle*, ed. D. J. O'Meara (Washington, D.C.: The Catholic University of America Press, 1981), 261–77.

23. *NE* IX 9, 1170^{a}15–19.

24. *Metaphysics* XII 7, 1072^{b}14–31.

activity (contemplation of God), which in turn serves as standard for our other good activities (all other virtuously performed activities), which in turn serve as standards for our good traits of character (all the ethically relevant virtues). The hierarchy of the virtues takes its cue from the hierarchy of best activities, and each of the virtues is itself an end because of their active share in rational activity *and* because of their conduciveness to good activities.

It is not enough—measured from the perspective of our complete end or, what amounts to the same, measured from the standard of beauty and nobility—to perform the sorts of activities that are virtuous. For progress to be made in the fulfillment of the purpose of our lives, those virtuous activities need to be performed virtuously.[25] This insight is a central point of contact between the two threads of teleological reflection Aristotelian ethics pursues with respect to the virtues and virtuous activity: the virtues are ends that serve as means to the successful completion of virtuous activity.

No activity, simply qua activity, is necessarily virtuously performed. Consider two examples, playing basketball and leading a prayer service. Playing the game of basketball, a practice, can be done virtuously or viciously. Someone can play the game very effectively and yet play it in order to put off doing more important things, or to flaunt her skills in such a way as to embarrass somebody else. Conversely, someone can choose to play it at the right time (when other duties are not put off), for the right reason (to relax and socialize), and in the right way (playing her best, but without striving to flaunt her abilities). The same goes for leading prayer, another practice. Someone can call a prayer service when he ought to be doing other things. He can engage in prayer to make unworthy demands of God, or to appear holier than others. But someone can also engage

---

25. This is a point emphasized throughout, but especially in chapter 2, Eugene Garver's *Confronting Aristotle's Ethics: Ancient and Modern Morality* (Chicago: University of Chicago Press, 2006). One of the virtues of this book is its attempt not simply to interpret Aristotle's ethics, but to treat contemporary ethical discussions in light of Aristotle's ethics.

in the activity of leading others in prayer at the right time, in the right manner, and for the right reasons. What is striking about these activities, however, is that they are not neutral in and of themselves. Both have intrinsic value, both are worthwhile activities, the worth of which is measured by the intrinsic and beneficial goods they offer to those who engage in them virtuously. Yet, they can be done well—in the sense in which one can play basketball or lead others in prayer effectively even when the player seeks self-glorification and the pray-er is engaged in histrionics for profit—without the one doing them doing well. So, it takes more than great performances to constitute fully virtuous actions. What is required for the best sorts of actions is that the actors performing them do so well and for the sake of their intrinsic beauty, which is to say for the sake of what MacIntyre calls the goods intrinsic to the practices.

It stands repeating that even though no activity, qua activity, is necessarily virtuously done, it is the case that only some activities are intrinsically valuable insofar as they afford opportunities in which they can be done virtuously.[26] There is no way to beat children virtuously, or to murder virtuously, or to commit adultery virtuously, or to bilk money from others by running a Ponzi scheme virtuously. But there are ways virtuously to punish children, to redress wrongs, to socialize with those with whom we are not married, and to invest money.

Happiness

A clear account of happiness is a primary goal of Aristotelian ethical inquiry, and yet an account of happiness is also presupposed from the outset of the inquiry. Aristotelian ethics presupposes an

---

26. See Kevin L. Flannery, SJ's *Acts amid Precepts: The Aristotelian Logical Structure of Thomas Aquinas' Moral Theory* (Washington, D.C.: The Catholic University of America Press, 2001) for a defense of the position that Aristotle's ethics recognizes the binding force of moral absolutes, and that the structure of Aquinas's moral theory is structurally Aristotelian.

account of happiness insofar as the account of the nature of virtue, and the account of any particular virtue, are each made intelligible only through a teleological framework that looks to at least a vague conception of fulfillment. And yet, the Aristotelian definition of happiness in *NE* I. 13 presupposes an understanding of virtue, if not an articulated account of virtue. And so it is that on the one hand the hope of a coherent and comprehensive account of happiness motivates inquiry into the virtues, and on the other, making sense of the virtues presupposes central features of that full account of happiness. Aristotle's method avoids the charge of circularity, however, by utilizing distinctions between more and less comprehensive accounts of happiness and virtue: it is one thing to recognize that every action and inquiry aims at some end, and another to define the content of that end, just as noting that children and even nonanimals can model natural virtue does not imply the presence in them of virtue in the full sense. Aristotle begins with but a vague notion of human fulfillment, and as he makes progress in pursuing other lines of teleological inquiry into the nature and structure of human action and the virtues that enable us to perform those actions well, the account of happiness continuously develops a more definite content.

One difference between happiness and the virtues is that whereas virtues are both ends and means, happiness is not. In fact, this feature of never-being-sought-after-for-the-sake-of-some-further-end is held up as one of the definitive features of happiness. Early in his investigation, Aristotle tells us that if we can arrive at an understanding of this preeminent good, that knowledge will serve us like a target serves an archer and we will know what it is at which we are aiming.[27] *That* we all aim at some self-sufficing good Aristotle takes as necessary; *what* we conceive such a good to be is where the work needs to be done. Though much of that specification is achieved in his *NE*, it is Aristotle himself who insists from the outset that the

27. *NE* I 2, 1094^a 23–25.

reflections which compose his *NE* are a contribution to his political philosophy, and indeed, the last chapter of the work is incoherent if we do not see it as a part of Aristotle's political philosophy.[28]

In that larger inquiry of politics the central question becomes how to structure one's polity in such a fashion as to enable the flourishing of its citizens, where, again, such flourishing is understood in terms of virtuous actions virtuously done. It turns out that happiness is not a matter of individual, but of communal, accomplishment, the mutually enriching activity of dependent rational animals:

> It is clear then that a state is not a mere society, having a common place, established for the prevention of mutual crime and for the sake of exchange. These are conditions without which a state cannot exist; but all of them together do not constitute a state, which is a community of families and aggregations of families in well-being, for the sake of a perfect and self-sufficing life. Such a community can only be established among those who live in the same place and intermarry. Hence there arise in cities family connexions, brotherhoods, common sacrifices, amusements which draw men together. But these are created by friendship, for to choose to live together is friendship. The end of the state is the good life, and these are the means towards it. And the state is the union of families and villages in a perfect and self-sufficing life, by which we mean a happy and honorable life.[29]

To be sure, the notion of the state as a local polity has long been swallowed by larger conglomerates with strong central authorities. In fact, the localized and uniformed polis Aristotle imagines was but an ideal even in Aristotle's time, and certainly contrary to the experiences of his Macedonian fellow countrymen. But whatever the possibilities are for the sorts of local polities Aristotle recommends, his claim that human beings can flourish only within a polis is worthy of serious consideration. I would also argue that Aristotle's observa-

---

28. Peter Simpson makes a compelling case for this in the first chapter, "Introduction to the *Politics: Nicomachean Ethics* 10.9," in *A Philosophical Commentary on the Politics of Aristotle* (Chapel Hill: University of North Carolina Press, 1998).

29. *Politics* III 9, 1280^{b}29–1281^{a}2.

tions regarding the common good as achievable within a polis have significance for less comprehensive communities.

Aristotle has described well what is necessary for a thriving local community, and if he is right, then it is only within such communities that we can work out our own happiness among friends and family. These communities can take many forms, such as neighborhoods, universities, parishes, and so forth, and experience shows that indeed they can succeed as, so to speak, gardens in which virtuous activities can plant themselves and grow, and this despite the constant pressure of absorption into the faceless and centralized institutions of governing organizations. If Aristotle is right that the only way to thrive as the communal beings we are is in communities of political friendship, then struggling to maintain such local communities presents us with one of the central challenges of our lives.

The tension that Aristotle exposes in *NE* X. 7–8 between happiness-as-contemplative-activity and happiness-as-fully-engaged-and-virtuous-communal-activity seems ineliminable. In the Thomistic tradition of Aristotelianism it is complicated still further by Aquinas's insistence that complete happiness is possible only beyond our natural lives. Like Aristotle, Aquinas argues that primary happiness is a sort of contemplative activity,[30] the contemplation of God,[31] but we can "see" God and so contemplate him directly only in heaven.[32] Aquinas's discussion of charity in *ST* II-II qq.23–26 gives more flesh to what can seem a rather cold activity of contemplation, and that discussion also points the way toward a better understanding of how our happiness is tantamount to a special type of friendship, that with God, out of which all other friendships flow. Yet, even if we accept the positions that Aquinas adds to Aristotle's description of happiness, we are still left with some basic questions about how to organize our lives in the here and now.

---

30. *ST* I-II, q.3, a.5, *respondeo*.
31. Ibid., q.3, a.8, *respondeo*.
32. *ST* I, q.12, a.11, *respondeo*.

How does one structure one's life in such a way as to engender opportunities for achieving happiness of both the primary and secondary sorts? We would be at a total loss in answering this question if we were behind a veil of ignorance, or considered ourselves autonomous individuals, or men in the state of nature, or in any other sort of fabricated position. But we are not, and it is here we feel the wisdom of Aristotelian ethics with particular poignancy. For Aristotle and those who follow him know that we do not begin from a fictitious ground zero. By the time we are wondering about how best to structure our lives, how best to achieve our own flourishing, we are already educated about the virtues. Our narrative, in the MacIntyrean sense, is already well under way. We already know who are the heroes and who the villains, who the sinners, who the saints, what sorts of actions are beautiful and noble, and which ugly and ignoble. We know all this simply from being born, being raised, and experiencing much of life before beginning philosophical inquiry. As we begin to make further progress as reflective adults in pursuing that quest for happiness which is our ongoing reflection on what the good life for man is, our story is already shaped by the countless stories of others. To be sure, the rest of the story is ours to write, but our situation is more like picking out an intricate path along a map of life than like staring at blank pages.

And so, though much more can and should be said about the sort of happiness achievable by beings such as ourselves than I have said here, the particular details of any fine-grained account can never be fully anticipated. What can be anticipated are the general contours of happy lives. Whether we are uncomfortable about the endeavor or not we can, and if we are to be happy we must, take up that question concerning the overall purpose of our lives and attempt to supply substantive answers to it.

Chapter 8

NATURAL LAW IN ARISTOTELIAN ETHICS

Every Virtuous Action Needs Its Reason

> *Of political justice part is natural, part legal,—natural, that which everywhere has the same force and does not exist by people's thinking this or that; legal, that which is originally indifferent, but when it has been laid down is not indifferent, e.g. that a prisoner's ransom shall be a mina, or that a goat and not two sheep shall be sacrificed.*
>
> Aristotle, *NE* V7, 1134^b18-22.

※

Making sense of the virtue of practical wisdom requires a fairly robust account of the foundations of moral principles. Making sense of the role and scope of the natural law in moral philosophy requires a robust account of the virtues. Virtue theorists on the one hand and natural law theorists on the other would seem to stand in need of each other's support. They are two branches sharing the same Aristotelian trunk, share a connatural friendship, and would seem to have everything to gain by uniting. And in point of fact, one certainly finds both branches intertwining in Aquinas's virtue-laced and natural-law-based moral philosophy. Moreover, with the example of

Aquinas to rely on, and because of Anscombe's admiration for the work of Aquinas, an admiration that Foot reports sharing in *Virtues and Vices* and that one still finds a few echoes of in Hursthouse,[1] one expects to find serious interest in natural law theory among contemporary virtue ethicists. One also expects to find serious interest in contemporary virtue ethics among enthusiasts of Aquinas's natural law. Surprisingly, this is not the case. For a variety of reasons one rarely finds collaboration between natural lawyers and contemporary virtue ethicists.[2] What are the reasons?

Why Natural Lawyers and Contemporary Virtue Ethicists Have Not Been Friends

On the part of natural law theorists, one reason has to do with what has been at the center of attention in their literature for the last half century—a dispute about how we arrive at the first precepts of the natural law—which, at least with respect to foundational issues in natural law theory, has left little room for attention to other matters.[3] Of course, new natural law theorists like Germain Grisez, John Finnis, and Alfonso Gomez-Lobo, as well as more traditional natural law theorists like Ralph McInerny, Joseph Koterski, SJ, and Thomas Hibbs, do discuss virtue in their writings, but not in a way that seeks to engage recent contemporary virtue ethical discussions about the virtues. On the part of some of these thinkers, the sort of attention

---

1. For example, see 112n2 of *On Virtue Ethics*.
2. MacIntyre's work might seem an exception to this. He has done extensive work on the virtues and on the natural law. His work has also garnered the attention of both natural law theorists and contemporary virtue ethicists. However, as I have already argued, he neither counts himself, nor should he be regarded as, a contributor to the mainstream contemporary virtue ethics movement.
3. I am distinguishing here between questions of foundations and questions of applications. There has been a great deal of attention given to questions of the applications of the natural law in recent years.

that contemporary virtue ethicists seek to bring to virtues—stressing their importance for moral philosophy—has not been seen as significant simply because natural lawyers are thoroughly entrenched in a tradition that already gives a certain pride of place to the virtues. Some natural law theorists, regarding themselves as members already of that choir, have concluded that not much is to be gained from paying attention to contemporary virtue ethical preaching, and this suggests a second reason for why natural lawyers have not paid much attention to the movement.

Where natural lawyers have perhaps taken contemporary virtue ethics too lightly as a sort of younger sibling who has yet to become very interesting, contemporary virtue ethicists have tended to see in natural law theory an overbearing and oppressive father. Natural law reasoning is used to advance positions on abortion, contraception, homosexual acts, divorce, and other controversial matters in which the conclusions arrived at by natural law theorists on these important matters are, in almost every case, opposed to the conclusions of contemporary liberals whose views compose the orthodox ideology that serves as the common framework for discussions in contemporary moral philosophy, of which, as I have taken pains to show in this book, mainstream virtue ethics forms a part. Insofar as natural law theory necessarily leads to the conclusions that it is always morally impermissible to kill unborn children, that contraception distorts the conjugal act and depersonalizes couples and should not be used except for non-pregnancy-avoiding medical reasons, that homosexual acts are physically and emotionally harmful to the persons engaged in them and so should not be performed, and that the majority of divorces are legal fictions but with real and deleterious consequences for children, then it is not surprising that mainstream contemporary virtue ethicists want little to do with it.[4] Ultimately,

---

4. The fact that the most noticeable contemporary home for natural law reasoning is the Roman Catholic magisterium is no doubt a negative factor in some secularist virtue ethicists' considerations.

the lack of connection between the two parties has most to do with the secularist divide between natural law theorists and contemporary virtue ethicists, a division that functions something like a watershed: superficially, both sides look similar, but the water flows in opposite directions. The dividing mark between the two approaches perhaps becomes most manifest in the practical conclusions drawn from them, but these of course follow from what is going on beneath the surface: leading voices in the contemporary virtue ethicist movement embrace secularism and the sort of naturalism that excludes any consideration of what might be beyond nature, whereas no natural lawyers embrace secularism or that sort of naturalism.

It is of course lamentable that there has been so little conversation between these two camps, but no limp and vapid appeal to both parties to lay aside their differences and find some way to get along will be effective. The critical review of mainstream contemporary virtue ethics advanced in this book is not of such a nature as to encourage natural law theorists to start incorporating virtue ethical ideas wholesale into their work; in fact, if anything, these criticisms serve to make a natural law theorist wary of future collaboration. But we have also learned that it is a mistake to treat contemporary virtue ethics as a unified moral theory, and there are no doubt many points of collaboration open for natural lawyers of the Thomistic variety and some contemporary virtue ethicists to pursue.

Whatever divisions there have been between the natural law tradition and the virtue ethical movement in recent years, the fact remains that virtue theory and natural law theory still need each other. In the last two chapters we have looked at the basic structural and telic requirements of virtue theory; in this chapter we consider the normative under the aegis of natural law theory. What is natural law theory? Straw-man depictions of the theory abound in contemporary ethical handbooks, with ideas from Hobbes, Locke, Rousseau, and out-of-context notions from Aquinas often found mashed together into a supposedly representative theory called the natural law.[5] The theory, however, is not the convoluted and facile ideology it is sometimes supposed to be.

What Is Natural Law Theory?

Natural law theory is a theory about practical reasoning. The goal of the theory is not simply to lay out the principles by means of which we might reason rightly—though it does seek to do that—but its primary goal is to explain *how* we, any human being that is, reason about things to be done. That is to say, the theory is primarily descriptive rather than prescriptive, for its claim is that it is by means of the precepts of the natural law that any of us reason about any practical projects. It tells us that, most basically, we recognize that good is to be done, and evil to be avoided, and this basic insight guides all other discursive undertakings. This most basic precept does not yet tell us *what* is good, and what evil. That requires further insight and reasoning, and here the insights, again at a very basic level, are telic. We practically reason about what is good for us, where "good" is taken to mean something like "the fulfillment of our most basic, natural, desires." What are those desires? They are those desires for continued existence and the goods that foster its preservation, and the rejection of those things harmful to our existence; they are those desires for the things that promote the good of our animal natures, like sexual intercourse and the nurturing of our young, and the rejection of those

---

5. For a particularly egregious and recent example of this sort of thing, see chapter 6 of Russ Shafer-Landau's *The Fundamentals of Ethics*. Here Hobbes and Rousseau are the only two named natural law theorists (76). Natural law theorists will no doubt be surprised to hear of the company they have been keeping. Shafer-Landau's basic mistake seems to be in running together thinking about laws of nature with natural law reasoning. By the end of the chapter, Shafer-Landau races through a series of arguments intended to show that natural law arguments against suicide, contraception, homosexual activity (all three on 81), abortion (82), and homosexual marriage (84) are all specious. He does show that the confused theory he calls natural law does not support these positions, but he neither describes nor argues against natural law theory as it is found in the Aristotelian-Thomistic tradition.

evils that threaten those goods; they are also those desires for those things that are particularly good for us because we are not just animals, but dependent rational animals, like the desire for friendship, for knowledge, and for living in society with others, and so include a recognition that ignorance and hatred of others threaten our good or overall well-being.[6]

Natural law, then, pertains to the sort of reasoning about goods and evils that dependent rational animals, animals not only who have ends proper to them but who think about those ends in such a way as to establish a plan for their lives in conversation with others, have. It is distributed as widely as human nature is distributed.[7] To be human, in other words, is to think about what is good and evil for oneself and those others with whom we interact.[8] Natural law reasoning, then, is not a formal mechanism by means of which we seek to produce directives for action; it is rather, and simply, thinking about what is good and bad for creatures like ourselves. As with all our powers, as Aristotle's analysis makes plain, we can do this well or poorly. Reasoning well about what is good or bad for us is to exercise that virtue of practical wisdom that Aristotle names *phronēsis* and Aquinas calls *prudentia*.

Reasoning well about what is good and evil for us, moreover, enables us to see that all of the virtues are good for us, which is to say that they are perfective of our nature, which is to say they are prescribed by the natural law. Aquinas explains:

---

6. Aquinas, *ST,* I-II, q.94, a.2, *respondeo*.
7. Ibid., q.94, a.4, *respondeo*.
8. "Nature, as we often say, makes nothing in vain, and man is the only animal who has the gift of speech. And whereas mere voice is but an indication of pleasure or pain, and is therefore found in other animals (for their nature attains to the perception of pleasure and pain and the intimation of them to one another, and no further), the power of speech is intended to set forth the expedient and inexpedient, and therefore likewise the just and the unjust. And it is a characteristic of man that he alone has any sense of good and evil, of just and unjust, and the like, and the association of living beings who have this sense makes a family and a state" (*Politics* I 2, 1253^{a}9–18).

Now each thing is inclined naturally to an operation that is suitable to it according to its form: thus fire is inclined to give heat. Wherefore, since the rational soul is the proper form of man, there is in every man a natural inclination to act according to reason: and this is to act according to virtue. Consequently, considered thus, all acts of virtue are prescribed by the natural law: since each one's reason naturally dictates to him to act virtuously.[9]

The connections between our nature, our ends, the virtues, and natural law reasoning are all evident in this passage. At this level of the theory, it is difficult to see what all the consternation concerns when the natural law is identified for condemnation by its contemporary opponents. Though there are, of course, objectors to the theory at this level of generality, particularly on the issue of what is to count as a natural desire, whether we can deliberate about natural ends, and what it is to reason about means to ends, the most heated disagreements have to do with applications of natural reasoning to particular cases.[10]

Aquinas, in the continuation of the passage just quoted, begins to give us some indication of the reasons for our controversies today. To be sure, he argues the natural law prescribes every virtuous action. This is clear when we reflect on the connection between virtuous actions and the fulfillment of our natural powers. However, that connection is, in many cases, not immediately obvious, and it is only through a sometimes very difficult sequence of discursive reasoning, the success of which depends on the exercise of acquired virtues, that we arrive at the conclusion that a particular action *is* a virtuous action. And so Aquinas continues: "But if we speak of virtuous acts,

---

9. *ST*, I-II, q.94, a.3, *respondeo*.
10. MacIntyre examines the reasons for disagreements about the natural law, on both general and more specific levels, in "Intractable Moral Disagreements," in *Intractable Disputes about the Natural Law: Alasdair MacIntyre and Critics*, ed. Lawrence S. Cunningham (Notre Dame, Ind.: University of Notre Dame Press, 2009), 1–52. This work is particularly helpful for its explication of what is required for successful deliberation with others.

considered in themselves, i.e., in their proper species, thus not all virtuous acts are prescribed by the natural law: for many things are done virtuously, to which nature does not incline at first; but which, through the inquiry of reason, have been found by men to be conducive to well-living."[11] We are not virtuous by nature, as Aristotle emphasizes, and neither are we naturally inclined to every virtuous action. Moral education is necessary for honing those traits of character necessary for successful reflections on right action. It is, then, when we move from the general to the more particular levels of practical reasoning that hard cases begin to emerge, and where other variations of social circumstances, personality traits, prior obligations, and all the rest come to have a great bearing on our attempts at reasoning clearly through to the practical conclusions we hope to achieve. It is on this level of practical reasoning that disagreements abound, and do so not just between those who possess and those who lack the virtues, but between men and woman of more or less similar character and intelligence.

I do not need to wade through the various controversies about the natural law and how it is to be applied to individual hard cases to make the main point of this chapter. That point is that, in every case, what we seek to do when we consider what the most virtuous, which is to say best, course of action is on any occasion is to think about what is the most rational course of action. To consider what is the most rational course of action is to consider what is most perfective of ourselves and those others with whom we share our lives, in every circumstance. To think about the virtues and virtuous actions, in other words, is to engage in natural law reasoning. I attempt to help further my case for this claim with a consideration of natural law reasoning as it pertains to discussions about one of the virtues, justice. It just so happens that justice, the central virtue for Platonic and Aristotelian virtue theory, is a virtue that has been ne-

---

11. *ST*, I-II, q.94, a.3, *respondeo*.

glected in contemporary virtue ethical literature, but has received a great deal of attention from other contemporary moral and political philosophical quarters. Because of the importance of justice in the lives of the dependent rational animals we are, some consideration about conflicts over what exactly justice is, what role it ought to play in our lives, and what type of natural law reasoning ought to be exercised in thinking about justice, lends further insight into natural law reasoning as the outgrowth, so to speak, of the sort of creatures we are. To do this, I contrast what I will call classical natural law reasoning—most identified with Thomistic thought, against contractarian natural law reasoning—to which Hobbes and Rawls are two of the most important contributors, in an effort to make the case that classical natural law reasoning has the greater explanatory power.

The Natural Law: Justice and the Common Good

Loosely considered, theorizing about the natural law stretches as far back at least as the Pre-Socratics with Heraclitus's *logos*, the principle of order amid the flux, and his call to live in accord with it.[12] Plato has a major part to play in it with his defense of justice and the just life against the unjust effort to outdo everyone, *pleonexia*, and the tyrannical life,[13] and it is in Plato that we first see two different

---

12. "All things come to be in accordance with this *logos*" (22B1); "For this reason it is necessary to follow what is common. But although the *logos* is common, most people live as if they had their own private understanding" (22B2); "Right thinking is the greatest excellence, and wisdom is to speak the truth and act in accordance with nature, while paying attention to it" (22B112); "Those who speak with understanding must rely firmly on what is common to all as a city must rely on law and much more firmly. *For all human laws are nourished by one law, the divine law*; for it has as much power as it wishes and is sufficient for all and is still left over" (22B114, my emphasis). Translations of these fragments are taken from "Heraclitus," in *Readings in Ancient Greek Philosophy: From Thales to Aristotle*, 2nd ed., ed. S. Marc Cohen, Patricia Curd, and C. D. C. Reeve (Indianapolis, Ind.: Hackett Publishing, 2000), 25 and 29.

13. The challenge to defend an account of justice that fulfills our nature is made and accepted in *Republic*, II, 358b–368b.

traditions of theorizing about the natural law sharply contrasted. It is, however, Aristotle, and especially Aquinas, who have done the most to forge the categories with which the classical tradition of natural law reasoning addresses the problem of justice and the common good.

Natural Law Reasoning in the Aristotelian Tradition

Let us briefly review some of the things we have already seen about justice in the Aristotelian tradition. In the fifth book of the *Nicomachean Ethics* Aristotle argues that justice has several interconnected senses. The common thread between all senses of justice is that justice is always concerned with another's good. Justice as complete virtue (*telia arête*) is all the moral virtues *insofar* as they are in relation to other persons: "What the difference is between virtue and justice in this sense is plain from what we have said, they are the same but being them is not the same; what, as a relation to others, is justice is, as a certain kind of state without qualification, virtue."[14] It is this sort of justice that most emphatically promotes the common good because it directs all other virtues in the service to other members of our community. Aristotle refers to this sort of justice as lawful or legal justice because "the things that tend to produce excellence taken as a whole are those of the acts prescribed by the law which have been prescribed with a view to education for the common good."[15] Aristotle, of course, knows that not every positive law is necessarily just, and it is for this reason that he qualifies his sense of law to mean those laws that do in fact promote the common good.[16] The common good that general justice promotes is the

---

14. *NE* V 1, 1130^{a}11–13.
15. *NE* V 2, 1130^{b}25–27.
16. See *Politics* III 6, 1279^{a}17–21: "Governments which have a regard to the common interest are constituted in accordance with strict principles of justice, and are therefore true forms; but those which regard only the interest of the rulers are all defective and perverted forms, for they are despotic, whereas a state is a community of freemen."

happy life lived by each of the citizens, which is to say the noble and beautiful life of virtue.[17] Incidentally, it is general or legal justice that seems to be meant by "social justice" when the term comes to be adopted within this tradition more than two millennia after Aristotle.

There are two other sorts of justice, each of which is particular in relation to general justice. Each of these still concerns the good of another, but they do not have the same scope as general justice in promoting the common good, and, although they are parts of justice, the combination of these two species of particular justice does not constitute the whole of general justice. The first species of particular justice concerns the distributions of the goods of society (money, honors, etc.) to those who have made extraordinary contributions to the common good, and so is usually called distributive justice.[18] This sort of justice implies a certain inequality in distribution, since some citizens are more worthy of external goods, the best of which are honors, than others. One must take care not to confuse Aristotelian distributive justice with the way in which "distributive" is often used in contractarianism as a distribution or redistribution according to the principle of fairness—where distribution according to fairness is often taken as tantamount to social justice. Nonetheless, there is still a principle of equality at work in Aristotle's distributive justice, the equality according to merit: "The only stable principle of government is equality according to merit, and for every man to enjoy his own."[19] What constitutes meritorious service on the part of the citizens is the extent to which they promote the common good.[20] The basic natural law principle at work here is that one ought to promote the goods of one's community, and that it helps to promote

---

17. *Politics* VII 13, $1332^{a}28-38$; see also, *Politics* III 9, $1280^{b}4-14$, $1280^{b}38-1281^{a}8$; VII 3, $1325^{b}14-32$.
18. *NE* V 2, $1130^{b}30-35$; V 3, $1131^{a}10-1131^{b}24$.
19. *Politics* V 7, $1307^{a}27-28$.
20. *Politics* III 9, $1281^{a}3-7$.

the good of community to offer rewards to those who do this in an exemplary way.

The second species of particular justice concerns rectification in various transactions between individuals, and this is called rectificatory or corrective justice.[21] This is the sort of justice that is binding in all transactions, both voluntary—such as in commercial exchanges and business contracts, and involuntary—such as in theft or injury. It is this sort of justice that is most often associated with the work of courts of law, where the aim is to restore according to strict equality what has been wrongly withheld or taken. Here questions of merit do not come into play: "For it makes no difference whether a good man has defrauded a bad man or a bad man a good one, nor whether it is a good or bad man that has committed adultery; the law looks only to the distinctive character of the injury, and treats the parties as equal."[22] One often finds casual readers of Aristotle confusing corrective justice with legal justice since corrective justice is often obtained through an application of the law in legal settlements. But legal settlements are not what Aristotle, or Aquinas, has in mind when speaking of legal justice, but rather justice in all its manifestations as that virtue which promotes the common good.[23]

Aquinas retains these Aristotelian categories in his discussions of justice not only when commenting on Aristotle's *Nicomachean Ethics*,[24] but also in his own treatments of justice. Nevertheless, well beyond merely Latinizing Aristotle's terminology, Aquinas deepens and expands Aristotle's treatment of justice in at least three significant ways.

First, Aquinas provides a more thoroughgoing account of justice

---

21. *NE* V 2, 1130^{b}30–1131^{a}9; V 3–5, 1131b–1134^{a}16.
22. *NE* V 4, 1132^{a}2–5.
23. *NE* X 9, 1180^{b}22–28; *Politics* III 6, 1278^{b}16–30; 12, 1282^{b}15–23; *ST* I-II, q.90, a.3.
24. *In decem libros Ethicorum Aristoteles ad Nicomachum* (Taurini: Marietti, 1934). Aquinas's commentary is most easily found in the *Opera Omnia*, Tomus XLVII (Rome, 1968), but C. I. Litzinger's translation (*Commentary on Aristotle's Nicomachean Ethics* [Notre Dame, Ind.: Dumb Ox Books, 1993]) is of the Marietti edition.

as both natural and universal. In Aristotle we find a few comments about natural justice, and about justice in the unqualified sense,[25] but not the systematic account we find in Aquinas.[26] The overarching structure of Aquinas's treatment of the natural law in the *prima secundae* is overlooked when, as often happens, questions 90–94 are treated in isolation. In fact, those remarks on the natural law provide the last stage in a general treatment of the elements composing moral action, an analysis that includes reflection on the virtues, the nature of habit, the passions, the sources of the distinction between good and bad actions, and a detailed reflection on our final good. In the next section of the *Summa theologiae*, the *secunda secundae*, Aquinas deepens his account of the natural law in connection to his reconsideration of the cardinal virtues in the light of the supernatural virtues of faith, hope and charity. It is there that he argues that the fundamental precept to do good and avoid evil is entailed by general justice,[27] and that just as general justice includes all the virtues, so too does the fundamental precept of the natural law direct us to every virtue.[28] General justice pertains to that special aspect of the good that is in accord with divine and human law, which, as in the case of Aristotle, enables us to speak of general or complete justice as legal justice.[29] The dictates of justice are ultimately grounded in eternal law, since natural law is, when viewed from some distance from a consideration of the specific features of our nature, our participation in the eternal law.[30] It is, moreover, these considerations that undergird Aquinas's claim that all the elements of justice are demanded both by the dictates of right reason and by the Decalogue.[31]

Second, Aquinas provides a much more thorough treatment of

---

25. *NE* V 7, 1134b18–35
26. See especially *ST*, II-II, q.79, a.1; but also *ibid.*, q.57, aa.1–2, and *ST*, I-II, qq.90–94.
27. *ST* II-II, q.79, a.1.   28. Ibid., q.58, aa.5–6.
29. Ibid., q.79, a.1
30. "talis participatio legis aeternae in rationali creatura *lex naturalis* dicitur" (*ST* I-II, q.91, a.2).
31. *ST* II-II, q.122, a.1.

the ways in which justice ought to be manifest in political society.[32] Through carefully examining the demands of justice placed on rulers and judges involved with the applications and maintenance of law in the current political circumstances of his day, Aquinas actively seeks to adopt Aristotle's notion of justice, whose first home is in the polis, to the very different political circumstances of the thirteenth century.[33] In this he points the way for how we might similarly fit the classical account of justice to our own very different contemporary political circumstances.[34]

Third, Aquinas radically expands the extension of justice to include every member of society as full and naturally equal partners joined together in the effort to pursue the common good. He argues, for instance, that although Jews and Gentiles are to be compelled by the faithful in a Christian community to refrain from blasphemies, evil persuasions, and persecutions, they cannot be compelled to accept the faith since believing is an act of the will,[35] and compulsion is repugnant to the will.[36] Nor are the children of Jews or Gentiles to be baptized without parental consent since this would be an abrogation of justice, which necessarily respects parental authority.[37] So long as unbelievers do nothing to undermine the faith they are to be tolerated, and can even continue to exercise political authority over believers in communities whose existence precedes the Church's life in it, since human law—nurtured as it is ultimately by the eternal

---

32. Ibid., qq.63–78.

33. MacIntyre reflects on this in "The Natural Law as Subversive: The Case of Aquinas," in *Ethics and Politics: Selected Essays Volume 2* (Cambridge: Cambridge University Press, 2006): 41–63. See also John Finnis's treatment of such issues in *Aquinas: Moral, Political, and Legal Theory* (Oxford: Oxford University Press, 1998), especially 1–19, 219–74.

34. For a treatment of Aquinas's political philosophy that seeks as well to show its applicability to our contemporary circumstances see again Finnis's *Aquinas: Moral, Political, and Legal Theory*. See also Paul E. Sigmund's "Law and Politics," in *The Cambridge Companion to Aquinas*, ed. Norman Kretzman and Eleonore Stump (Cambridge: Cambridge University Press, 1993), 217–31.

35. *ST* II-II, q.10, a.8.   36. *ST* I, q.82, a.1; I-II, q.6, a.5.

37. *ST* II-II, q.10, a.12.

law—is not vitiated by the divine law, which is the law of grace.[38] This contrasts sharply with Aristotle, who recognized the full and equal status of relatively few members of society, the citizens (adult free native-born males), and gave only secondary consideration to others. This change has everything to do with Aquinas being a Christian, and, as MacIntyre notes, makes Aquinas's task one of incorporating Aristotle into a Pauline and Augustinian system rather than vice versa.[39]

Though there are plenty of differences in status that persist in society, and ought to persist, according to Aquinas, there are no differences in regard to the common humanity of each member of society. It is this radical expansion by Aquinas that makes possible the natural law tradition's incorporation of the Aristotelian framework for thinking about justice, for without it, or something very like it, it is difficult to see how one might claim to be an Aristotelian with respect to political theory, and a Christian.

Natural Law Reasoning in the Modern Contractarian Tradition

It is profitable to turn to Plato to begin to make sense of a tradition of natural law reasoning that is in conflict with that tradition of which Plato is the founder and Aquinas is the most important figure, even though the contractarian position did not receive significant philosophical support until the modern period. It is against a contractarian view of justice, one that claims that the promotion of justice is a consequence of the weakness of those unable to live the best life of tyranny, that Socrates wages war throughout the *Republic*. Plato's main concern in this work is to defend the position that the life of justice is the best life and that justice is a supreme virtue in and of itself. This is an effort in arguing that true justice is grounded in nature, rather than by convention.

38. Ibid., q.10, a.10.
39. MacIntyre, *Whose Justice? Which Rationality?*, 182.

It is Plato's brother, Glaucon,[40] who as interlocutor in the *Republic* takes over and deepens the sophist Thrasymachus's claim that what is best by nature is to pursue unbridled acquisition.[41] Glaucon, playing devil's advocate, argues that the best thing is to be unjust because through acts of injustice you get whatever you want—and presuppose that happiness, whatever its content turns out to be, must at least include the fulfillment of desire. The worst thing, Glaucon continues, is to suffer injustice because being the recipient of injustice robs you of whatever you have. The majority, who are too weak to do what they really want, find a way at least to avoid suffering injustice. They "decide that it is profitable to come to an agreement with each other neither to do injustice nor to suffer it. As a result, they begin to make laws and covenants, and what the law commands they call lawful and just.... [Justice] is intermediate between the best and the worst."[42] Justice is then not the best state of affairs, and it does not make us happy, for it is neither natural nor in accord with our human nature so that it might promote our best end.

The just man is not, on Glaucon's score, the happy man; but at least he is not suffering at the hands of the happiest of men, the tyrant. Though not itself natural, this contractual view of justice has some connection to nature, for it is necessary for the relatively peaceful living of those weaker natures who represent the bulk of humanity.

---

40. Glaucon claims that he is pursuing this line for the sake of argument so that he might more wholeheartedly promote the life of justice as the best: "My ears are deafened listening to Thrasymachus and countless others. But I've yet to hear anyone defend justice in the way I want, proving it is better than injustice. I want to hear it praised *by itself*" (*Republic* I, 358d). Quotations from *Republic* are taken from G. M. A. Grube's translation in *Plato: Complete Works*, ed. John M. Cooper (Indianapolis, Ind.: Hackett Publishing, 1997).

41. Thrasymachus argues in Book I that "justice is really the good of another, the advantage of the stronger and the ruler, and harmful to the one who obeys and serves. Injustice is the opposite, it rules the truly simple and just ... they make the one they serve happy, but themselves not at all" (*Republic* I, 343c) and that "a person of great power outdoes everyone else.... This is tyranny.... So, Socrates, injustice, if it is on a large enough scale, is stronger, freer, and more masterly than justice" (*Republic* I, 344a–c).

42. *Republic* II, 358e–359a.

This contract theory of justice promotes justice as a compromise between our conflicting desires to do injustice but not to suffer injustice. Socrates sees immediately what is at stake in this view of justice: it represents a concession rather than a virtue, and as a founding principle in a social body it vitiates the possibility of achieving a true common good, replacing it instead with a tense sort of peace. This sort of justice, as perhaps Nietzsche most forcibly shows, promotes the life of mediocrity rather than nobility.[43]

But perhaps mediocrity is not so bad given the alternative in a fallen world. So answers the Hobbesian. It is Plato who first describes a contractarian account of justice, but Hobbes is its first champion. Confronted with the chaos of political upheaval in his native England, Hobbes sought to find a surer basis for government.[44] In working out the details of a contractual basis of society he subverted the classical natural law tradition's understanding of human nature, virtue, justice, and the common good.

For Hobbes, we are by nature each equal to one another insofar as any individual can kill another: "Nature hath made men so equal in the faculties of body and mind.... For as to the strength of body, the weakest has strength enough to kill the strongest."[45] In our natural condition we each have the right of nature, the right to do whatever we want to preserve our lives: "The RIGHT OF NATURE ... is the liberty each man hath to use his own power, as he will himself, for the preservation of his own nature, that is to say, of his own life, and consequently of doing anything which, in his own judgment and reason, he shall conceive to be the aptest means thereunto."[46] In the state of

---

43. See, for example, Nietzsche, *Beyond Good and Evil*, sections 199–203.

44. His explicit aim was to develop a theory that legitimizes sovereignty and centralized authority, such as the English monarchy, though his theory has served as groundwork (in large part through the effort of more subtle philosophical successors) for the modern democratic state.

45. Thomas Hobbes, *Leviathan*, ed. Edwin Curley (Indianapolis, Ind.: Hackett Publishing, 1994), XIII 1, 74

46. *Leviathan* XIV, 1, 79.

nature Hobbes describes, each individual is his or her own sovereign, his or her own law. This is a *jus naturale* altogether indifferent to considerations of justice, and so altogether different from Aquinas's understanding of natural law. In exercising our natural right to all, our natural state amounts to a state of war of all against all, a war in which questions of right and wrong are irrelevant: "To this war of every man against man, this also is consequent: that nothing can be unjust. The notions of right and wrong, justice and injustice, have there no place. Where there is no common power, there is no law; where no law, no injustice."[47] Such is our natural condition, and in it life is bereft of any fruit of social intercourse and filled with the fear of having others exercise their natural right over ourselves.[48]

We need a way out of this state of nature, and it is reason that directs us to it. Reason grasps the law of nature, "by which a man is forbidden to do that which is destructive of his life or taketh away the means of preserving the same, and to omit that by which he thinketh it may be best preserved."[49] Peace, not war, is that condition in which our lives are best preserved, which suggests to reason that we ought to form contracts with other men in order to preserve ourselves: "This [is] the second law: *that a man be willing, when others are so too, as far-forth as for peace and defence of himself he shall think it necessary, to lay down this right to all things, and be contented with so much liberty against other men, as he would allow other men against himself.*"[50] This social contract is then the origin of society, and so too of justice, injustice, right, and wrong. It marks the termination of natural right, and the origin of all morality. It is the product of a reason that is bound in service to our passion for self-preservation.

---

47. *Leviathan* XIII, 13, 78.
48. "In such condition there is ... no arts, no letters, no society, and which is worst of all, continual fear and danger of violent death, and the life of man, solitary, poor, nasty, brutish, and short" (*Leviathan* XIII, 9, 76).
49. *Leviathan* XIV, 3, 79.
50. *Leviathan* XIV, 5, 80.

In accord with its origin, then, society has as its end nothing definite except the preservation of peaceful living.[51]

Rather than our natures finding fulfillment in the promotion of the common good of society, as the natural law tradition would have it, the contractarian tradition conceives of society as something that keeps our natures in check, that prevents us from doing what we would do, should we, like the shepherd who finds the ring of Gyges,[52] discover a means to "have it all." Society, in this tradition, is something of a compromise between what is best and worst by nature. Justice is a matter of exercising our reason, understood narrowly as rational self-interest, in such fashion that we find a way to help ourselves by not harming each other.

Hobbes's story is told in harsh tones, but it is the starkness of his reasoning that helps lay bare the principles at the core of contemporary political liberalism. If Strauss is right that Locke is Hobbes in sheep's clothing,[53] still more benignly appareled, and much more palatable to contemporary sensibilities, is Rawls's version of Hobbes's story. The institutional repository for the contractarian tradition is the modern state, but Rawlsianism can be regarded as its theoretical headquarters.[54]

Rawls, like Aristotle, speaks of justice in a general sense, calling it "social justice":[55] "Our topic, however, is that of *social justice*. For us the primary subject of justice is the basic structure of society, or more exactly, the way in which the major social institutions *distribute* fun-

---

51. Hobbes argues that this end is best served by investing all power in a single sovereign, a leviathan (*Leviathan* XVII, 13, 109).

52. *Republic* II, 359c–360a.

53. Strauss, *Natural Right and History*, 202–51.

54. One sign of this enshrinement can be found in the prominence of Rawls in Michael Slote's entry, "Justice as a Virtue," in *Stanford Encyclopedia of Philosophy*, ed. Edward N. Zalta, Fall 2010 ed., http://plato.stanford.edu/entries/justice-virtue/. In this entry, Rawls is presented as *the* voice for a contemporary account of justice.

55. This helps to explain why "social justice" means such radically different things to its different users: some are thinking of it insofar as it has been developed in the classical tradition, others insofar as it has been developed in the contractarian.

damental rights and duties and determine the division of advantages from social cooperation."[56] The word "distribute" in this quotation is telling: general or social justice becomes in this tradition a matter of the distribution of goods by institutions of the state.[57] According to the Rawlsian characterization it is the institutions, not nature, not God, not the members of society, that establishes justice by properly distributing *our* rights and duties; in other words, by properly forming *us* insofar as we come to acquire social selves.[58]

We of course, in keeping with the contractarian tradition, are not merely the product of the state; in fact, we are its parents, but only insofar as we are *not* social by nature. What drives Rawls's theory is the thought experiment of thinking ourselves in an original asocial position in which we construct the sort of society we would want by applying rational choice (rational self-interest) behind a "veil of ignorance," that is, without knowing what or who we would be in society: "The idea of the original position is to set up a fair procedure so that any principles agreed to will be just.... Somehow we must

---

56. John Rawls, *A Theory of Justice* (Cambridge, Mass.: Harvard University Press, 1971), 7, my emphases.

57. For the connection between social justice and distribution/redistribution see Bernard Williams's "Social Justice," *Journal of Social Philosophy* 20 (1989): 68–73, especially 72; David Johnston's "Is the Idea of Social Justice Meaningful?" *Critical Review* 11(1997): 607–14; Martha C. Nussbaum's "Human Functioning and Social Justice: In Defense of Aristotelian Essentialism," *Political Theory* 20 (1992): 202–46, especially 205 and 232 (Nussbaum's argument here has features of both traditions, but she assumes throughout that social justice is a matter of proper distribution); Thomas W. Pogge's "Human Flourishing and Universal Justice," *Social Philosophy and Policy* 16 (1999): 333–61, especially 337 and 343; and David Miller, *Principles of Social Justice* (Cambridge, Mass.: Harvard University Press, 1999), especially 3, 33, and 233. With these references I suggest not that all these are Rawlsian in the same way, but that all are Rawlsian insofar as they conceive of general social justice as the basic and proper distribution of rights, duties, and goods by state institutions.

58. On this point, one again finds the enshrinement of Rawls's theory of justice as the definitive theory of justice in contemporary moral and political theory. See Julian Lamont and Christi Favor's entry, "Distributive Justice," in the *Stanford Encyclopedia of Philosophy*, ed. Edward N. Zalta, Spring 2013 ed., http://plato.stanford.edu/entries/justice-distributive/. Aristotle's account of distributive justice has but a small role in their discussion, and only in a section on merit as grounds for distribution.

nullify the effects of specific contingencies which put men at odds and tempt them to exploit social and natural circumstances to their advantages. Now in order to do this I assume that the parties are situated behind a veil of ignorance."[59] This construction allows us to establish justice as fairness:[60] "The general conception of justice as fairness requires that all primary social goods be distributed equally unless an unequal distribution would be to everyone's advantage."[61] What establishes fairness is a matter of exercising our rational self-interest in the absence of knowledge concerning our particular circumstances:

I have assumed throughout that the persons in the original position are rational. In choosing between principles each tries as best he can to advance his interests. But I have also assumed that the parties do not know their conception of the good. This means that while they know that they have some rational plan of life, they do not know the details of this plan, the particular ends and interests which it is calculated to promote.[62]

To be rational, for Rawls, is to advance one's own self-interest, rather than as Aristotle would have it, to deliberate with those others with whom one lives about what is best and right.

Repeatedly in his work Rawls exhorts us to see that while rational self-interest is driving the social contract wagon, so to speak, his theory is not egoistic.[63] He insists it is not so because one does not know any specifics about one's personal situation, and so serving one's interest is a matter of serving the interest of all others. Put another way, in respecting the rights and duties of others you are respecting your potential self. This, to many of his admirers, seems the strongest point of Rawls's doctrine; it approximates Kant's kingdom of ends. Justice is then realized by promoting social institutions and

---

59. Rawls, *A Theory of Justice*, 136.
60. See Rawls's description of the priority of this conception of justice in ibid., 11–17.
61. Ibid., 150.
62. Ibid., 142.
63. See especially ibid., 147–50, 488–89, 567–69.

personal practices that treat all others as you yourself would want—given your own interest in living peacefully so that you can promote your interests—to be treated. Justice in this tradition entails an emphasis on institutional distribution of social goods rather than the personal discharging of responsibilities.

Two Justices: Aristotelian-Thomistic versus Contractrian Natural Law Reasoning

There are many areas in which these two traditions overlap with respect to the ends they promote. Both can claim, for instance, that social justice mandates what Rawls terms "fair play" and what Aristotle terms "corrective justice" in relationships between employers and employees to achieve that right balance between owner profits and a living wage. Both can agree that justice implies due process, universal suffrage, and the power for persons to possess private property. But there are a number of areas in which these two traditions find themselves at loggerheads, and most notably on life and death issues. Englehardt, for one, thinks the opposition between the two traditions on these issues is so great and the dominance of contractarianism so pronounced that those who call for justice from within the context of the natural law tradition cannot but be misunderstood: "In a post-Christian social context, calls for social justice will be understood as calls for a post-Christian social justice: in such a context Christian understandings of justice will in many areas appear unjust."[64] I am not yet convinced that our social context is quite so dominantly post-Christian, but I do think Englehardt

---

64. H. Tristam Engelhardt Jr., "Roman Catholic Social Teaching and Religious Hospital Identity in a Post-Christian Age," *Christian Bioethics* 6 (2000): 295–300, 295. Consider also the following: "If one appeals to concerns for social justice in a way that can claim a place in the public forum of a secular society, then one will support post-Christian forms of social justice. If one appeals to concerns for social justice in a way that is true to one's religious commitments, then one's appeals will be marginalized as sectarian. The second choice appears morally unavoidable. It is unjust for Christians to call for social justice in secular terms when, given the character of the society, social justice will take on a character in opposition to Christian commitments" (ibid., 297).

is right about the opposition often evident between calls for justice from the two respective traditions.[65] The reason for this opposition arises from the different answers given by the respective traditions to the pivotal questions of what a human being is, what a person's good is, what the common good is, what the purpose of government is, and what it is for a person to work for the common good.[66]

The differences between the two traditions on anthropology are starkly drawn. The one sees the person as incorrigibly individualistic insofar as he or she is naturally driven to promote his or her own interests above all else;[67] the other sees the person as originally and naturally already part of a social nexus. This makes all the difference when considering the question of whether or not justice is a virtue; that is, virtue classically understood as a habituated excellence of a person whereby a person has achieved a concentrated perfection with respect to his or her natural *telos*. Justice in the natural law tradition is a virtue, and precisely that virtue that works for the good of other persons. This cannot be so for the contractarian tradition, for there is no natural *telos* that might be perfected in this fashion. Indeed, for this tradition, there is no sense of good or bad according to nature.

---

65. It is, of course, the contractarians themselves who first claim the incompatibility of their approach to that of classical natural law theorists: modern political philosophy is born from opposition to the classical. Consider, for example, Hobbes's rejection of the classical understanding of the greatest good in *Leviathan* XI, 1; or Rawls's rejection of Aquinas's conception of the best life: "Although to subordinate all our aims to one end does not strictly speaking violate the principles of rational choice (not the counting principles anyway), it still strikes us as irrational, *or more likely as mad*." (*A Theory of Justice*, 554, my emphasis).

66. For an argument that Rawlsianism and the social teaching of the Church are theoretically incompatible see Franz-Josef Bormann's "Was von der Fairness übrig blieb: Zur Bedeutung von John Rawls 'Theorie der Gerechtigkeit für die katholische Soziallehre," *Theologie und Philosophie* 78 (2003): 384–405, especially 401–5.

67. Consider MacIntyre on this point: "My thesis is not that the procedures of the public realm of liberal individualism were cause and the psychology of the liberal individual effect nor vice versa. What I am claiming is that each required the other and that in coming together they defined a new social and cultural artifact, 'the individual.' ... In the practical reasoning of liberal modernity it is the individual *qua* individual who reasons" (*Whose Justice? Which Rationality?* 339).

Justice is created by us through a contract that seeks to promote the ultimately unsatisfiable goal of preserving our lives and whatever other goals might emerge as parts of what Rawls calls our "plan of life." Justice in the contractarian tradition is a compromise, not a virtue. Just as this tradition claims the origin of society is to be found in the mediation of competing desires, so too are subsequent calls to justice by the holders of this tradition so many exhortations for compromises between the competing desires of various individuals.

The common good as classically conceived is a common life of virtue, the promotion of noble and righteous living. Neither Aristotle nor Aquinas thinks this means legally prohibiting every vice;[68] you cannot force people to be virtuous, but you can encourage them to be so. Moreover, this is not a conception of the common good that disregards such goods as peace and the preservation of life, as Aquinas shows by arguing that general justice entails promotion of the precepts of the natural law. What is, nevertheless, particularly objectionable to Rawls and his followers is that the natural law tradition does make a definite commitment to a conception of the best sort of life. The common good as conceived by contract theorists, on the other hand, is minimalistic: it is the enforcement of peace by means of preventing harm, and further aims to create room for one to pursue happiness in whatever way one thinks best just so long as this does not interfere with others in their pursuit of happiness. This common good is noncommittal on the issue of which sort of life is best. Indeed, it is impossible to make evaluative judgments regarding how one lives that extend beyond the reasons for which society was founded, security. These differing conceptions of the common good lead to different ways of viewing the role of government in society: the classical natural law tradition takes government's task to be the promotion of the best, the contractarian to be safeguard against the worst. The classical natural law tradition views government like a

---

68. See *ST* I-II, q.96, aa.2–3.

natural father who encourages us in our moral education and hopes to see us become all we naturally can be. The contractarian tradition views government as a political god who creates social rights and obligations and keeps us from doing what we naturally want to do.[69] These different conceptions of what counts as the good of another and why one ought to promote the good of another in the theoretical frameworks of these two traditions often makes for a vast difference in practice, which points again to why classical natural law theory comes in for such abuse in contemporary moral philosophy. For instance, Aristotelian-Thomistic natural law theory prescribes against the killing of innocent human beings (even the unborn) in all circumstances (including when killing an innocent person might serve some other good), and against certain sorts of sexual activities (like adulterous and bestial ones). Despite attempts to portray such prescriptions as arbitrary, they are in fact grounded on a deep concern for the good of each person who could potentially be involved in such unlawful activities. Such prescriptions are grounded, in other words, in political friendship—in an abiding love for others in one's community, which is to say in willing both to promote the good of others and to live in harmony with them. Justice in the contractarian tradition, on the other hand, is formalistic and abstract, the procedural arm of secularism. It leaves all sorts of room for the exercise of personal preferences within an individualistically grounded sphere of privacy, to be sure, but it does not arise from political friendship. Much to the contrary, and ironically given its identification with some social causes, the grounding presuppositions of contractarianism are driven by a rational self-interest that is incorrigibly individualistic, for such is the nature of reasoning behind a veil of ignorance.

---

69. "This is the generation of that great LEVIATHAN, or rather (to speak more reverently) of that *Mortal God*" (*Leviathan* XVII, 109) This mortal god, the sovereign, enforces peace through terror, and his right to do so is inalienable. See Jacques Maritain's criticism of the notion of sovereignty in chapter 2, "The Concept of Sovereignty," of *Man and the State* (Chicago: University of Chicago Press, 1951), 28–53.

Ultimately, the question of which sense of justice one adheres to has much to do with the account one tenders of *why* justice ought to be promoted, and this comes down to what one takes a human being to be, and how one conceives such beings to go about the business of reflecting upon good and bad actions. Contract theorists contend we ought to promote institutional justice because it is in our own best interests. As Rawls argues, we ought to promote justice because others are, when we think about them through the hypothetical machinery of the original position, really ourselves. We agitate on behalf of others because it is rational to work for our own individualistic interests. Natural law theorists in the Aristotelian-Thomistic tradition argue we ought to promote the good of others because they are our fellows, our brothers and sisters. We are to work for justice like we work for the good of our family. The contractarian tradition seeks to promote the good of another as oneself, the Aristotelian-Thomistic tradition seeks to promote the good of other as other. The contractarian is motivated to serve others once they are conceived in abstraction, the Aristotelian-Thomistic insofar as they are concrete. The contractarian utilizes a hypothetical fabrication based on an extrapolation of our fears to generate its principles; the Aristotelian-Thomistic postulates no state of nature, no original position, but rather takes human beings as they are found in communities and reflects on how best to encourage the flourishing of those communities.

※

Aristotelian-Thomistic natural law reasoning is superior to modern contractarian natural law theory ultimately because it regards human beings as they truly are: dependent rational animals whose own ends are always wrapped up in the goods of others. It is only this tradition of moral reasoning that can make sense of justice as a virtue, and only it that provides the path by means of which we can render intelligible those other traits of character we regard as virtues.

The Natural Law: Virtues, Virtuous Actions, and Reasons

Natural law reasoning is reasoning about what is good or bad for us to do. It does not represent a restricted means of analysis that can be brought to bear on those special occasions that fall within a special sphere of "the moral." It is, simply, our thinking about what we are to do, and as such it provides standards against which we can judge progress toward our ends. We can think well about what we are to do only because we are rational creatures whose practical reflections can be guided by principles that make themselves manifest in the very framework of our multifaceted natures. Being dependent rational animals with the capacity to practically reason well is no guarantee that we will do so, for doing so implies achievements of the sort we call virtuous, where the intellectual virtue of practical wisdom is supported by those other traits of character designated as moral virtues, and those moral virtues in turn are supported by practical wisdom. Making sense of the virtues requires natural law theory, this theory is indelibly teleological in character, and acting virtuously requires a certain perfection of natural law reasoning.

The considerations of natural law reasoning pursued in this chapter in such a fashion as to include considerations of conflicting accounts of what it entails yield several important conclusions. First, it makes a great deal of difference what one considers a human being to be when it comes to considering principles for action. Second, a coherent account of the virtues, and one that does justice to our intuitions about the virtues and their significance for our lives, requires some version of an Aristotelian anthropology, an anthropology that includes a vivid teleological framework, a framework that incorporates the facts of our communal and rational nature, and a robust account of the good. Third, it indicates one of the reasons why the virtue of justice, which is so central to the Aristotelian-Thomistic tradition, has received little or no attention in the contemporary virtue ethics movement. This is because justice, as it is treated in contemporary moral philosophy, is a formalistic virtue that is tied to the contractarian framework of moral reasoning, and mainstream contemporary virtue ethicists, often seeking to eschew a robust and teleologically rich anthropology, have deprived themselves of the means to come to the defense of the traditional understanding of justice in the face of its contemporary and formalistic defenders. Though the fate of the traditional understanding of justice is the most obvious example of this, it is not only justice whose meaning becomes tenuous in the absence of Aristotelian answers to the fundamental questions of ethics, but so too the other virtues.

Chapter 9

VIRTUE ETHICS, AFTER AND BEFORE

Now I am not able to do the philosophy involved—and I think that no one in the present situation of English philosophy can do the philosophy involved—but it is clear that a good man is a just man; and a just man is a man who habitually refuses to commit or participate in any unjust action for fear of any consequences, or to obtain any advantage, for himself or anyone else.

G. E. M. Anscombe, "Modern Moral Philosophy"

The aim of this book has been to appraise the contemporary virtue ethics movement, and ultimately to measure it against the rich tradition of Aristotelian ethics. The movement has been discovered to be multifaceted and complex, far more complex than many of its descriptions suggest. In taking a historical approach to making sense of contemporary virtue ethics, I have given a great deal of attention to its literature. The point of this attention has been not simply to provide a review of that literature, but to consider its content from the perspective of its supplying the best available evidence for determining what precisely the status of the movement is. The evidence yields the conclusion that although contemporary virtue ethics is a movement with a certain historical unity, it does not provide a substantive moral theory that is cohesive, comprehensive, or coherent. A consideration of the basic elements of Aristotelian ethics and a comparison of it to the contemporary virtue ethics movement has, moreover, shown contemporary virtue ethics, despite claims to the contrary, not to be on the whole a substantive revival of Aristotelian ethics. Underlying the whole analysis runs a consideration of the most basic questions of moral philosophy, and from a consideration of those, Aristotelian ethics succeeds in ways that at least mainstream contemporary virtue ethics fails. This and other conclusions arrived at in this study are on many points contrary to some of the central themes, assumptions, presuppositions, and status quo methodological criteria in mainstream contemporary virtue ethics as well as moral philosophy at large. Be that as it may, it has not been my intention to stake out a contrarian position for its own sake, but rather to follow the evidence wherever it may lead.

In some respects, what I have argued in this book is relatively modest: contemporary moral philosophy is in disarray, which is a conclusion to which many an unconventional philosopher has born witness; mainstream contemporary virtue ethics is not the unified movement it is often regarded to be by both its adherents and its detractors, which is a conclusion to which a representative survey of its diverse literature, such as has been brought forth in these pages, bears witness; the neo-Aristotelianism of contemporary virtue ethicists is often only thinly Aristotelian when compared against the basic elements of Aristotelian ethics itself; and Aristotelian ethics presents the most viable means to answer the foundational questions of ethics, which is a judgment with a long history, a history that includes as well at least the genesis of the contemporary virtue ethics movement. The conclusions this book arrives at are generated not by a novel methodology, but rather by historical considerations in which the tradition of Aristotelian-Thomistic philosophy is given precedence.

As much as I have relied on MacIntyre's project, the fecundity of which, I think, will take generations to appreciate, it is ultimately Anscombe's insights in "Modern Moral Philosophy" that I have sought to champion throughout this book. It was this essay of Anscombe's that proved the genesis of the contemporary virtue ethics movement, and the lessons of this essay that the movement in a variety of ways has not sufficiently heeded. What, among other things, Anscombe has taught us in that work is that if we are to put moral philosophy back on its rails, we need a revitalization of Aristotelian ethics. Such revitalization requires more than simply bringing Aristotelian answers to bear on the central problems of modern moral philosophy, but reenvisioning the central problems of moral philosophy as well. Anscombe directs us to develop again the language of virtue, but she warns us that doing so is impossible without the creative recovery of what she calls an adequate philosophical psychology. A coherent and comprehensive virtue theory requires a system that has wrestled successfully with the fundamental questions of ethics—those questions pertaining to our nature, to our ends, and to the means by which we reflect profitably upon our nature and ends.

I have sought to argue, again following Anscombe's lead, that it is the Aristotelian ethical tradition that proves the most successful in providing the framework by means of which these more basic questions can be answered. It is not that we need philosophy to be instructed in virtue, for that is a matter best learned at one's mother's knees. But if it is virtue treated philosophically that we are after, we do need to rest any such account in a sufficiently rich anthropology, one that includes an explicit teleology and a robust theory of practical reasoning. And so, I hope to have gone some way toward giving reasons for why it is not simply that the Aristotelian tradition of moral philosophy supplies the most coherent account of the virtues and that contemporary moral philosophers ought to turn their attention to it, but that the Aristotelian tradition of the virtues is coherent precisely because of its sufficiently rich anthropology.

BIBLIOGRAPHY

Ackrill, J. L. "Aristotle on *Eudaimonia.*" In *Essays on Aristotle's Ethics*, edited by A. Rorty, 15–33. Berkeley: University of California Press, 1980.
Adams, Robert M. "Saints." In *The Virtues: Contemporary Essays*, edited by Robert B. Kruschwitz and Robert C. Roberts, 153–60. Belmont, Calif.: Wadsworth Publishing, 1987. Originally published in *Journal of Philosophy* 81 (1984): 392–401.
———. *Finite and Infinite Goods.* Oxford: Oxford University Press, 1999.
———. *A Theory of Virtue: Excellence in Being for the Good.* Oxford: Oxford University Press, 2006.
Alderman, Harold. "By Virtue of a Virtue." In *Virtue Ethics: A Critical Reader*, edited by Daniel Statman, 145–64. Washington, D.C.: Georgetown University Press, 1997. Originally published in *Review of Metaphysics* 36 (1982): 127–53.
Allard-Nelson, Susan K. *An Aristotelian Approach to Ethical Theory: The Norms of Virtue.* Studies in the History of Philosophy 77. Lewiston, N.Y.: Edwin Mellen Press, 2004.
Annas, Julia. "Plato and Aristotle on Friendship and Altruism." *Mind* 86 (1977): 532–54.
———. "Self-Love in Aristotle." *Southern Journal of Philosophy*, supplement 27 (1988): 1–18.
———. *The Morality of Happiness.* Oxford: Oxford University Press, 1993.
———. "Virtue and Eudaimonism." *Social Philosophy and Policy* 15 (1998): 37–55
———. *Platonic Ethics, Old and New.* Ithaca, N.Y.: Cornell University Press, 1999.
———. "Moral Knowledge as Practical Knowledge." In *Moral Knowledge*, edited by E. E. Paul, F. D. Miller, and J. Paul, 236–56. Cambridge: Cambridge University Press, 2001.

———. "My Station and Its Duties: Ideal and the Social Embeddedness of Virtue." *Proceedings of the Aristotelian Society*, new series 102 (2002): 109–23.

———. "Being Virtuous and Doing the Right Thing." In *Ethical Theory: An Anthology*, edited by Russ Shager-Landau, 735–45. Oxford: Blackwell Publishing Ltd, 2006. Originally published in *Proceedings and Addresses of the American Philosophical Association* 78 (2004): 61–74.

———. "Virtue Ethics: What Kind of Naturalism?" In *Virtue Ethics, Old and New*, edited by Stephen M. Gardiner, 11–29. Ithaca, N.Y.: Cornell University Press, 2005.

———. "Virtue Ethics." In *The Oxford Handbook of Ethical Theory*, edited by David Copp, 515–40. New York: Oxford University Press, 2006.

———. *Intelligent Virtue*. Oxford: Oxford University Press, 2011.

Anscombe, G. E. M. *Intention*. Oxford: Basil Blackwell, 1957; 2nd ed., 1963.

———. "Modern Moral Philosophy." In *Virtue Ethics*, edited by Roger Crisp and Michael Slote, 26–44. Oxford: Oxford University Press, 1997. Originally published in *Philosophy* 33 (1958): 1–19.

———. *Ethics, Religion, and Politics*. Vol. 3 of *The Collected Papers of G. E. M. Anscombe*. Minneapolis: University of Minnesota Press, 1981.

———. "Morality." In *Faith in a Hard Ground: Essays on Religion, Philosophy, and Ethics*, edited by Mary Geach and Luke Gormally, 113–16. Charlottesville, Va.: Imprint Academic, 2008. Originally published in *Pro Ecclesia et Pontifice* (1982): 16–18.

———. *Human Life, Action, and Ethics*. Edited by Mary Geach and Luke Gormally. Charlottesville, Va.: Imprint Academics, 2005.

Appiah, Kwame Anthony. *Experiments in Ethics*. Cambridge, Mass.: Harvard University Press, 2008.

Aquinas, Thomas. *In decem libros Ethicorum Aristoteles ad Nicomachum*. Taurini: Marietti, 1934.

———. *Commentary on Aristotle's Nicomachean Ethics*. Translated by C. I. Litzinger. Notre Dame, Ind.: Dumb Ox Books, 1993.

Aristotle. *The Complete Works of Aristotle*. 2 vols. Edited by Jonathan Barnes. Princeton, N.J.: Princeton University Press, 1984.

———. *Aristotelis Ethica Nicomachea*. Edited by I. Bywater. Oxford Classical Text. Oxford: Clarendon Press, 1894.

Athanassoulis, Nafsika. "Virtue Ethics." In *Internet Encyclopedia of Philosophy*. http://www.iep.utm.edu/virtue/.

Baier, Annette. *Postures of the Mind: Essays on Mind and Morals*. Minneapolis: University of Minnesota Press, 1985.

Baron, Marcia. *Kantian Ethics Almost without Apology.* Ithaca, N.Y.: Cornell University Press, 1995.
Baron, Marcia W., Philip Pettit, and Michael Slote. *Three Methods of Ethics.* Oxford: Blackwell, 1997.
Bartlett, Robert C., and Susan D. Collins, eds. *Action and Contemplation: Studies in the Moral and Political Thought of Aristotle.* Albany, N.Y.: SUNY Press, 1999.
Bejczy, István, ed. *Virtue Ethics in the Middle Ages: Commentaries on Aristotle's Nicomachean Ethics, 1200–1500.* Leiden, Netherlands: Brill Publishers, 2007.
Bennett, William. *The Book of Virtues: A Treasury of Great Moral Stories.* New York: Simon and Schuster, 1996.
Blum, Lawrence A. "Compassion." In *The Virtues: Contemporary Essays,* edited by Robert B. Kruschwitz and Robert C. Roberts, 225–36. Belmont, Calif.: Wadsworth Publishing, 1987. Originally published in *Explaining Emotions,* edited by Amélie O. Rorty, 507–18. Berkeley: University of California Press, 1980.
———. "Moral Exemplars: Reflections on Schindler, the Trocmes, and Others." *Midwest Studies in Philosophy* 13 (1988): 196–221.
———. "Community and Virtue." In *How Should One Live?* edited by Roger Crisp, 231–50. Oxford: Oxford University Press, 1996.
Bormann, Franz-Josef. "Was von der Fairness übrig blieb: Zur Bedeutung von John Rawls 'Theorie der Gerechtigkeit für die katholische Sozialehre.'" *Theologie und Philosophie* 78 (2003): 384–405.
Brewer, Talbot. "Virtues We Can Share: Friendship in Aristotle's Ethical Theory." *Ethics* 115 (2005): 721–58.
———. *The Retrieval of Ethics.* Oxford: Oxford University Press, 2009.
Broadie, Sarah. *Ethics with Aristotle.* Oxford: Oxford University Press, 1991.
Casey, John. *Pagan Virtue: An Essay in Ethics.* Oxford: Clarendon Press, 1990.
Chappell, Timothy, ed. *Values and Virtues: Aristotelianism in Contemporary Ethics.* Oxford: Clarendon Press, 2006.
———. "Virtue Ethics in the Twentieth Century." In *The Cambridge Companion to Virtue Ethics,* edited by Daniel C. Russell, 149–71. Cambridge: Cambridge University Press, 2013.
Clark, Stephen L. *Aristotle's Man.* Oxford: Oxford University Press, 1984.
Coleman, Janet. "MacIntyre and Aquinas." In *After MacIntyre: Critical Perspectives on the Work of Alasdair MacIntyre,* edited by John Horton and

Susan Mendus, 65–90. Notre Dame, Ind.: University of Notre Dame Press, 1994.

Conly, Sarah. "Flourishing and the Failure of the Ethics of Virtue." *Midwest Studies in Philosophy* 13 (1988): 83–96.

Coope, Christopher Miles. "Modern Virtue Ethics." In *Values and Virtues: Aristotelianism in Contemporary Ethics*, edited by Timothy Chappell, 20–52. Oxford: Clarendon Press, 2006.

Cooper, John. *Reason and Human Good in Aristotle*. Cambridge, Mass.: Harvard University Press, 1975.

———. "Contemplation and Happiness: A Reconsideration." *Synthese* 72 (1987): 187–216.

———. "Reason, Moral Virtue and Moral Value." In *Reason and Emotion: Essays on Ancient Moral Psychology and Ethical Theory*, ch. 11, 255–80. Princeton, N.J.: Princeton University Press, 1999.

Copp, David, and David Sobel. "Morality and Virtue: An Assessment of Some Recent Work in Virtue Ethics." *Ethics* 114 (2004): 514–54.

Cottingham, John. "Partiality and the Virtues." In *How Should One Live? Essays on the Virtues*, edited by Roger Crisp, 57–76. Oxford: Oxford University Press, 1996.

Crisp, Roger, ed. *How Should One Live? Essays on the Virtues*. Oxford: Clarendon Press, 1996.

———. "Modern Moral Philosophy and the Virtues." In *How Should One Live? Essays on the Virtues*, edited by Roger Crisp, 1–18. Oxford: Clarendon Press, 1996.

Crisp, Roger, and Michael Slote, eds. *Virtue Ethics*. New York: Oxford University Press, 1997.

Cunningham, Lawrence S., ed. *Intractable Disputes About the Natural Law: Alasdair MacIntyre and Critics*. Notre Dame, Ind.: University of Notre Dame Press, 2009.

Darwall, Stephen, Alan Gibbard, and Peter Railton. "Toward *Fin de siècle* Ethics: Some Trends." *Philosophical Review* 101 (1992): 115–89.

Darwall, Stephen, ed. *Virtue Ethics*. Oxford: Oxford University Press, 2003.

Davis, Michael. "Civic Virtue, Corruption, and the Structure of Moral Theories." *Midwest Studies in Philosophy* 13 (1988): 352–66.

DePaul, Michael, and Linda Zagzebski, eds. *Intellectual Virtue: Perspectives from Ethics and Epistemology*. Oxford: Clarendon Press, 2003.

Deshpande, Sharad. "Kant and the Revival of Virtue Ethics." In *Reason, Morality, and Beauty: Essays on the Philosophy of Immanuel Kant*, edited by Bindu Puri, 11–25. Oxford: Oxford University Press, 2007.

Diamond, Cora, "The Dog That Gave Himself the Moral Law." *Midwest Studies in Philosophy* 13 (1988): 161–79.
Doris, John M. "Persons, Situations and Virtue Ethics." *Nous* 32 (1998): 504–30.
———. *Lack of Character: Personality and Moral Behavior.* Cambridge: Cambridge University Press, 2002.
Driver, Julia. "The Virtues and Human Nature." In *How Should One Live? Essays on the Virtues,* edited by Roger Crisp, 111–29. Oxford: Clarendon Press, 1996.
———. *Uneasy Virtue.* New York: Cambridge University Press, 2001.
———. "Virtue Theory." In *Contemporary Debates in Moral Theory,* edited by James Dreier, 113–23. Oxford: Blackwell Publishing, 2006.
———. "Gertrude Elizabeth Anscombe." In *Stanford Encyclopedia of Philosophy,* edited by Edward N. Zalta. Winter 2011 ed. http://plato.stanford.edu/archives/winter2011/entries/anscombe.
Engelhardt, H. Tristam, Jr. "Roman Catholic Social Teaching and Religious Hospital Identity in a Post-Christian Age." *Christian Bioethics* 6 (2000): 295–300.
Everitt, Nicholas. "Some Problems with Virtue Theory." *Philosophy* 82 (2007): 275–99.
Finnis, John. *Aquinas: Moral, Political, and Legal Theory.* Oxford: Oxford University Press, 1998.
Flannery, Kevin L., SJ. *Acts amid Precepts: The Aristotelian Logical Structure of Aquinas's Moral Theory.* Washington, D.C.: The Catholic University of America Press, 2001.
Foot, Philippa. "Euthanasia." *Philosophy and Public Affairs* 6 (1977): 85–112.
———. *Virtues and Vices, and Other Essays and Other Essays in Moral Philosophy.* Oxford: Clarendon Press, 1978.
———. *Natural Goodness.* Oxford: Oxford University Press, 2001.
Frankena, William. "Prichard and the Ethics of Virtue: Notes on a Footnote." *Monist* 54 (1970): 1–17.
Frede, Dorothea. "The Historic Decline of Virtue Ethics." In *The Cambridge Companion to Virtue Ethics,* edited by Daniel C. Russell, 124–48. Cambridge: Cambridge University Press, 2013.
Fritz-Cates, Diana. *Aquinas on the Emotions: A Religious-Ethical Inquiry.* Washington, D.C.: Georgetown University Press, 2009.
Gardner, Stephen M, ed. *Virtue Ethics, Old and New.* Ithaca, N.Y.: Cornell University Press, 2005.
Geach, Peter. *The Virtues.* Cambridge: Cambridge University Press, 1977.

George, Robert. "Moral Particularism, Thomism, and Traditions." *Review of Metaphysics* 42 (1989): 593–605.

Gilson, Étienne. *From Aristotle to Darwin and Back Again: A Journey in Final Causality, Species, and Evolution.* Translated by John Lyon. San Francisco, Calif.: Ignatius Press, 2009 (1984).

Girard, René. *Violence and the Sacred.* Translated by Patrick Gregory. Baltimore, Md.: Johns Hopkins University Press, 1977.

———. *The Scapegoat.* Translated by Yvonne Freccero. Baltimore, Md.: Johns Hopkins University Press, 1986.

———. *I See Satan Fall Like Lightning.* Translated by James G. Williams. Maryknoll, N.Y.: Orbis Books, 2001.

Hadot, Pierre. *Philosophy as a Way of Life: Spiritual Exercises from Socrates to Foucault.* Edited by Arnold I. Davidson. Translated by Michael Chase. Oxford: Blackwell Publishing, 1995.

———. *What Is Ancient Philosophy?* Translated by Michael Chase. Cambridge, Mass.: Harvard University Press, 2002.

Haldane, John. "MacIntyre's Thomist Revival: What Next?" In *After MacIntyre: Critical Perspectives on the Work of Alasdair MacIntyre,* edited by John Horton and Susan Mendus, 91–107. Notre Dame, Ind.: University of Notre Dame Press, 1994.

———, ed. *Mind, Metaphysics, and Value in the Thomistic and Analytic Traditions.* Notre Dame, Ind.: University of Notre Dame Press, 2002.

Hardie, W. F. R. "The Final Good in Aristotle's Ethics." *Philosophy* 40 (1965): 277–95.

Harman, Gilbert. "Moral Philosophy Meets Social Psychology: Virtue Ethics and the Fundamental Attribution Error." *Proceedings of the Aristotelian Society* 99 (1999): 316–31.

Hartman, Edwin. "The Virtue Approach to Business Ethics." In *The Cambridge Companion to Virtue Ethics,* edited by Daniel C. Russell, 240–64. Cambridge: Cambridge University Press, 2013.

Hauerwas, Stanley. *Character and the Christian Life.* San Antonio, Tex.: Trinity University Press, 1975.

Hauerwas, Stanley, and Charles Pinches. *Christians among the Virtues: Theological Conversations with Ancient and Modern Ethics.* Notre Dame, Ind.: University of Notre Dame Press, 1997.

Heraclitus. "Heraclitus." In *Readings in Ancient Greek Philosophy: From Thales to Aristotle,* 2nd ed., edited by S. Marc Cohen, Patricia Curd, and C. D. C. Reeve, 24–34. Indianapolis, Ind.: Hackett Publishing, 2000.

Herdt, Jennifer A. *Putting on Virtue: The Legacy of the Splendid Vices*. Chicago: University of Chicago Press, 2008.

Hobbes, Thomas. *Leviathan*. Edited by Edwin Curley. Indianapolis, Ind.: Hackett Publishing, 1994.

Hooker, Brad. *Ideal Code, Real World*. Oxford: Oxford University Press, 2000.

———. "The Collapse of Virtue Ethics." *Utilitas* 14 (2002): 22–40.

Hurka, Thomas. *Virtue, Vice, and Value*. Oxford: Oxford University Press, 2001.

Hursthouse, Rosalind. "Virtue Theory and Abortion." *Philosophy and Public Affairs* 20 (1991): 223–46.

———. "Normative Virtue Ethics." In *How Should One Live? Essays on the Virtues*, edited by Roger Crisp, 19–36. Oxford: Oxford University Press, 1996.

———. "Virtue Ethics and the Emotions." In *Virtue Ethics: A Critical Reader*, edited by Daniel Statman, 99–117. Washington, D.C.: Georgetown University Press, 1997.

———. *On Virtue Ethics*. Oxford: Oxford University Press, 1999.

———. "Virtue Ethics vs. Rule-Consequentialism: A Reply to Brad Hooker." *Utilitas* 14 (2002): 41–53.

———. "Are Virtues the Proper Starting Point for Morality?" In *Contemporary Debates in Moral Theory*, edited by James Dreier, 99–112. Hoboken, N.J.: Blackwell Publishing, 2006.

———. "Discussing Dilemmas." *Christian Bioethics* 14 (2008): 141–50.

———. "Virtue Ethics." In *Stanford Encyclopedia of Philosophy*, edited by Edward N. Zalta. Fall 2007 ed. http://plato.stanford.edu/archives/fall2007/entries/ethics-virtue/.

Irwin, T. H. "Aristotle's Conception of Morality." In *Proceedings of the Boston Area Colloquium in Ancient Philosophy*, vol. 1, edited by John J. Cleary, 115–43. Lanham, Md.: University Press of America, 1986.

———. "The Virtues: Theory and Common Sense in Greek Philosophy." In *How Should One Live? Essays on the Virtues*, edited by Roger Crisp, 37–55. Oxford: Oxford University Press, 1996.

Ivanhoe, Philip J. "Virtue Ethics and the Chinese Confucian Tradition." In *The Cambridge Companion to Virtue Ethics*, edited by Daniel C. Russell, 49–69. Cambridge: Cambridge University Press, 2013.

Jefferson, Mark. "What Is Wrong with Sentimentality?" In *The Virtues: Contemporary Essays*, edited by Robert B. Kruschwitz and Robert C.

Roberts, 186–93. Belmont, Calif.: Wadsworth Publishing, 1987. Originally published in *Mind* 92 (1983): 519–29.

Johnston, David. "Is the Idea of Social Justice Meaningful?" *Critical Review* 11 (1997): 607–14.

Justin, Martyr. *Dialogue with Trypho.* In *Justin, Philosopher and Martyr: Apologies,* edited by Denis Minns and Paul Parvis. Oxford: Oxford University Press, 2009.

Kamtekar, Rachana. "Ancient Virtue Ethics: An Overview with an Emphasis on Practical Wisdom." In *The Cambridge Companion to Virtue Ethics,* edited by Daniel C. Russell, 29–48. Cambridge: Cambridge University Press, 2013.

Kenny, Anthony. *The Aristotelian Ethics.* Oxford: Clarendon Press, 1978.

———. *Aristotle on the Perfect Life.* Oxford: Oxford University Press, 1992.

Kotva, Joseph J., Jr. *The Christian Case for Virtue Ethics.* Washington, D.C.: Georgetown University Press, 1996.

Kraut, Richard. *Aristotle on the Human Good.* Princeton, N.J.: Princeton University Press, 1989.

Kultgen, John. "The Vicissitudes of Common-Sense Virtue Ethics, Part I: From Aristotle to Slote." *Journal of Value Inquiry* 32 (1998): 325–41.

Lamont, Julian, and Christi Favor. "Distributive Justice." In *Stanford Encyclopedia of Philosophy,* edited by Edward N. Zalta. Spring 2013 ed. http://plato.stanford.edu/entries/justice-distributive/.

Langston, Douglas C. *Conscience and Other Virtues: From Bonaventure to MacIntyre.* University Park: Pennsylvania State University Press, 2001.

Lockwood, Thornton C. "A Topical Bibliography of Scholarship on Aristotle's *Nicomachean Ethics:* 1880–2004." *Journal of Philosophical Research* 30 (2005): 1–116.

Lombardo, Nicholas E. *The Logic of Desire: Aquinas on Emotion.* Washington, D.C.: The Catholic University of America Press, 2010.

Louden, Robert B. "On Some Vices of Virtue Ethics." In *Virtue Ethics,* edited by Roger Crisp and Michael Slote, 201–16. Oxford: Oxford University Press, 1997. Originally published in *American Philosophical Quarterly* 21 (1984): 227–36.

———. "Kant's Virtue Ethics." *Philosophy: The Journal of the Royal Institute of Philosophy* 61 (1986): 473–89.

Lutz, Christopher Stephen. *Tradition in the Ethics of Alasdair MacIntyre: Relativism, Thomism, and Philosophy.* Lanham, Md.: Lexington Books, 2004.

MacIntyre, Alasdair. *After Virtue.* 2nd ed. Notre Dame, Ind.: University of Notre Dame Press, 1984.
———. "*Sōphrosunē:* How a Virtue Can Become Socially Disruptive." *Midwest Studies in Philosophy* 13 (1988): 1–11.
———. *Whose Justice? Which Rationality?* Notre Dame, Ind.: University of Notre Dame Press, 1988.
———. *Three Rival Versions of Moral Enquiry: Encyclopaedia, Genealogy, and Tradition.* Notre Dame, Ind.: University of Notre Dame Press, 1990.
———. "Plain Persons and Moral Philosophy: Rules, Virtues, and Goods." In *The MacIntyre Reader,* edited by Kevin Knight, 136–52. Notre Dame, Ind.: University of Notre Dame Press, 1998. Originally published in *American Catholic Philosophical Quarterly* 66 (1992): 3–19.
———. "The Return to Virtue Ethics." In *The Twenty-Fifth Anniversary of Vatican II: A Look Back and a Look Ahead,* edited by Russell E. Smith, 239–49. Braintree, Md.: Pope John Centre, 1992.
———. "Virtue Ethics." In *Encyclopedia of Ethics,* edited by Lawrence C. Becker and Charlotte B. Becker, 1276–82. New York: Garland Publishers, 1992.
———. "A Partial Response to My Critics." In *After MacIntyre: Critical Perspectives on the Work of Alasdair MacIntyre,* edited by John Horton and Susan Mendus, 283–304. Notre Dame, Ind.: University of Notre Dame Press, 1994.
———. "Moral Relativism, Truth, and Justification." In *Moral Truth and Moral Tradition: Essays in Honor of Peter Geach and Elizabeth Anscombe,* edited by Luke Gormally, 6–24. Dublin: Four Courts Press, 1994. Reprinted as the third chapter of the first volume of *Selected Essays: The Tasks of Philosophy.* Cambridge: Cambridge University Press, 2006.
———. "First Principles, Final Ends and Contemporary Philosophical Issues." In *The MacIntyre Reader,* edited by Kevin Knight, 171–201. Notre Dame, Ind.: University of Notre Dame Press, 1998. Originally published as an Aquinas Lecture. Milwaukee, Wis.: Marquette University Press, 1990.
———. *Dependent Rational Animals: Why Human Beings Need the Virtues.* Paul Carus Lecture Series 20. Chicago, Ill.: Open Court, 1999.
———. "The Ends of Life, the Ends of Philosophical Writing." In *The Tasks of Philosophy, Selected Essays,* vol. 1, 125–42. Cambridge: Cambridge University Press, 2006.
———. "The Natural Law as Subversive." In *Ethics and Politics: Selected Essays,* vol. 2, 41–63. Cambridge: Cambridge University Press, 2006.

———. *God, Philosophy, Universities: A Selective History of the Catholic Philosophical Tradition.* Lanham, Md.: Rowman and Littlefield, 2009.

———. "Intractable Moral Diagreements." In *Intractable Disputes about the Natural Law: Alasdair MacIntyre and Critics,* edited by Lawrence S. Cunningham, 1–52. Notre Dame, Ind.: University of Notre Dame Press, 2009.

Maritain, Jacques. *Man and the State.* Chicago, Ill.: University of Chicago Press, 1951.

McAleer, Sean. "An Aristotelian Account of Virtue Ethics: An Essay in Moral Taxonomy." *Pacific Philosophical Quarterly* 88 (2007): 208–25.

McDougall, Rosalind. "Acting Parentally: An Argument against Sex Selection." *Journal of Medical Ethics* 31 (2005): 601–5.

———. "Parental Virtue: A New Way of Thinking about the Morality of Reproductive Actions." *Bioethics* 21 (2007): 181–90.

———. "Impairment, Flourishing and the Moral Nature of Parenthood." In *Disability and Disadvantage,* edited by K. Brownless and A. Curenton. Oxford: Oxford University Press, 2009.

McDowell, John. "The Role of *Eudaimonia* in Aristotle's Ethics." In *Essays on Aristotle's Ethics,* edited by Amélie Oksenberg Rorty, 359–76. Berkeley: University of California Press, 1980.

———. "Eudaimonism and Realism in Aristotle's Ethics." In *Aristotle and Moral Realism,* edited by Robert Heinaman, 201–18. London: University College London Press, 1995.

———. "Virtue and Reason." In *Virtue Ethics,* edited by Roger Crisp and Michael Slote, 141–62. Oxford: Oxford University Press, 1997. Originally published in *Monist* 62 (1978): 331–50.

McInerny, Daniel. "Deliberation about Final Ends: Thomistic Considerations." In *Recovering Nature: Essays in Natural Philosophy, Ethics, and Metaphysics in Honor of Ralph McInerney,* edited by Thomas Hibbs and John O'Callaghan, 105–25. Notre Dame, Ind.: University of Notre Dame Press, 1999.

McKinnon, Christine. *Character, Virtue Theories, and the Vices.* Peterborough, Canada: Broadview Press, 1999.

Meilander, Gilbert. *Theory and Practice of Virtue.* Notre Dame, Ind.: University of Notre Dame Press, 1984.

Milliken, John. "Aristotle's Aesthetic Ethics." *Southern Journal of Philosophy* 44 (2006): 319–39.

Miller, David. *Principles of Social Justice.* Cambridge, Mass.: Harvard University Press, 1999.

Miner, Robert. *Thomas Aquinas on the Passions: A Study of Summa Theologiae, 1a2ae 22-48*. Cambridge: Cambridge University Press, 2009.
Montague, Phillip. "Virtue Ethics: A Qualified Success Story." In *Virtue Ethics: A Critical Reader*, edited by Daniel Statman, 194–204. Washington, D.C.: Georgetown University Press, 1997. Originally published in *American Philosophical Quarterly* 29 (1992): 53–61.
Nietzsche, Friedrich. *Beyond Good and Evil*. In *Basic Writings of Nietzsche*, translated by Walter Kaufmann. New York: Modern Library, 1968.
———. *Ecce Homo*. In *Basic Writings of Nietzsche*, translated by Walter Kaufmann. New York: Modern Library, 1968.
Nussbaum, Martha C. *The Fragility of Goodness: Luck and Ethics in Greek Tragedy and Philosophy*. Cambridge: Cambridge University Press, 1986.
———. "Non-Relative Virtues: An Aristotelian Approach." *Midwest Studies in Philosophy* 13 (1988): 32–53.
———. "Human Functioning and Social Justice: In Defense of Aristotelian Essentialism." *Political Theory* 20 (1992): 202–46.
———. "Virtue Ethics: A Misleading Category?" *Journal of Ethics* 3 (1999): 163–201.
Oakley, Justin. "Virtue Ethics and Abortion." In *The Cambridge Companion to Virtue Ethics*, edited by Daniel C. Russell, 197–220. Cambridge: Cambridge University Press, 2013.
Oakley, Justin, and Dean Cocking. *Virtue Ethics and Professional Roles*. Cambridge: Cambridge University Press, 2001.
O'Neill, Onora. "Kant's Virtues." In *How Should One Live? Essays on the Virtues*, edited by Roger Crisp, 77–97. Oxford: Oxford University Press, 1996.
———. *Towards Justice and Virtue: A Constructive Account of Practical Reasoning*. Cambridge: Cambridge University Press, 1996.
Owens, Joseph. "The ΚΑΛΟΝ in the Aristotelian *Ethics*." In *Studies in Aristotle*, edited by D. J. O'Meara, 261–77. Washington, D.C.: The Catholic University of America Press, 1981.
Pelligrino, Edmund D. *For the Patient's Good: The Restoration of Beneficence in Health Care*. Oxford: Oxford University Press, 1988.
———. "Toward a Virtue-Based Normative Ethics." *Kennedy Institute of Ethics Journal* 5 (1995): 253–77.
Pellegrino, Edmund D., and David C. Thomasma. *A Philosophical Basis of Medical Practice*. Oxford: Oxford University Press, 1981.
Pence, Gregory E. "Recent Work on Virtue." *American Philosophical Quarterly* 21 (1984): 281–98.

Peterson, Christopher,; and Martin E. P. Seligman. *Character Strengths and Virtues*. Oxford: Oxford University Press, 2004.

Plato. *Plato: Complete Works*. Edited by John M. Cooper. Indianapolis, Ind.: Hackett Publishing, 1997.

Pogge, Thomas W. "Human Flourishing and Universal Justice." *Social Philosophy and Policy* 16 (1999): 333-61.

Pojman, Louis P. *Ethics: Discovering Right and Wrong*. Belmont, Calif.: Wadsworth Publishing, 1990.

Porter, Jean. *The Recovery of Virtue: The Relevance of Aquinas for Christian Ethics*. Louisville, Ky.: Westminster/John Knox Press, 1990.

———. *Moral Action and Christian Ethics*. Cambridge: Cambridge University Press, 1999.

———. "Virtue Ethics in the Medieval Period." In *The Cambridge Companion to Virtue Ethics*, edited by Daniel C. Russell, 70-91. Cambridge: Cambridge University Press, 2013.

Purinton, Jeffrey S. "Aristotle's Definition of Happiness (*NE* I, 7, 1098a16-18)." *Oxford Studies in Ancient Philosophy* 16 (1998): 259-97.

Putnam, Ruth Anna. "Reciprocity and the Virtues." *Ethics* 98 (1988): 379-89.

Rawls, John. *A Theory of Justice*. Rev. ed. Cambridge, Mass.: Harvard University Press, 1999 [1971].

Rieff, Philip. *Triumph of the Therapeutic*. New York: Harper & Row, 1966.

———. *Sacred Order/Social Order: My Life among the Deathworks*. Charlottesville: University of Virginia Press, 2006.

Rist, John M. *Real Ethics: Rethinking the Foundations of Morality*. Cambridge: Cambridge University Press, 2002.

———. *On Inoculating Moral Philosophy against God*. Aquinas Lecture. Milwaukee: University of Wisconsin Press, 2000.

Rogers, Kelly. "Aristole's Conception of Τὸ Καλόν." *Ancient Philosophy* 13 (1993): 355-71.

———. "Aristotle on the Motive of Courage." *Southern Journal of Philosophy* 32 (1994): 303-13.

Rorty, Amélie. *Essays on Aristotle's Ethics*. Berkeley: University of California Press, 1980.

———. "Virtues and Their Vicissitudes." *Midwest Studies in Philosophy* 13 (1988): 136-48.

Russell, Daniel C. *Practical Intelligence and the Virtues*. Oxford: Oxford University Press, 2009.

———. *Happiness for Humans*. Oxford: Oxford University Press, 2012.

———, ed. *The Cambridge Companion to Virtue Ethics*. Cambridge: Cambridge University Press, 2013.

———. "Virtue Ethics, Happiness, and the Good Life." In *The Cambridge Companion to Virtue Ethics*, edited by Daniel C. Russell, 7–28. Cambridge: Cambridge University Press, 2013.

Russell, Paul. "Hume's Anatomy of Virtue." In *The Cambridge Companion to Virtue Ethics*, edited by Daniel C. Russell, 92–115. Cambridge: Cambridge University Press, 2013.

Santas, Gerasimos X. "Does Aristotle Have a Virtue Ethics?" In *Virtue Ethics: A Critical Reader*, edited by Daniel Statman, 260–85. Washington, D.C.: Georgetown University Press, 1997. Originally published in *Philosophical Inquiry* 15 (1993): 1–32.

Scheler, Max. *Ressentiment*. Translated by Lewis B. Coser and William W. Holdheim. Milwaukee, Wis.: Marquette University Press, 1998.

Schneewind, Jerome B. "The Misfortunes of Virtue." In *Virtue Ethics*, edited by Roger Crisp and Michael Slote, 178–200. Oxford: Oxford University Press, 1997. Originally published in *Ethics* 101 (1990).

Shafer-Landau, Russ. *The Ethical Life: Fundamental Readings in Ethics and Moral Problems*. Oxford: Oxford University Press, 2009.

———. *The Fundamentals of Ethics*. Oxford: Oxford University Press, 2009.

Sherman, Nancy. "Common Sense and Uncommon Virtue." *Midwest Studies in Philosophy* 13 (1988): 97–114.

Sigmund, Paul E. "Law and Politics." In *The Cambridge Companion to Aquinas*, edited by Norman Kretzman and Eleonore Stump, 217–231. Cambridge: Cambridge University Press, 1993.

Sim, May. *Remastering Morals with Aristotle and Confucius*. Cambridge: Cambridge University Press, 2007.

Simon, Yves. *The Definition of Moral Virtue*, ed. Vukan Kuic. New York: Fordham University Press, 1986.

Simpson, Peter. *Goodness and Nature: A Defense of Ethical Naturalism*. Dordrecht, Netherlands: Martinus Nijhoff Publishers, 1987.

———. "Contemporary Virtue Ethics and Aristotle." *Review of Metaphysics* 45 (1992): 503–24.

———. *A Philosophical Commentary on the* Politics *of Aristotle*. Chapel Hill: University of North Carolina Press, 1998.

———. *Vices, Virtues, and Consequences*. Studies in Philosophy and the History of Philosophy 35. Washington, D.C.: The Catholic University of America Press, 2001.

Slote, Michael. *From Morality to Virtue*. Oxford: Oxford University Press, 1992.

———. "Virtue Ethics, Utilitarianism, and Symmetry." In *How Should Live? Essays on the Virtues*, edited by Roger Crisp, 99–110. Oxford: Oxford University Press, 1996.

———. "Agent-Based Virtue Ethics." In *Virtue Ethics*, edited by Roger Crisp and Michael Slote, 239–262. Oxford: Oxford University Press, 1997. Originally published in *Midwest Studies in Philosophy* 20 (1995): 83–101.

———. *Morals from Motives*. Oxford: Oxford University Press, 2001.

———. Review of *Natural Goodness*, by Philippa Foot. *Mind* 112 (2003): 130–39.

———. "Justice as a Virtue." In *Stanford Encyclopedia of Philosophy*, edited by Edward N. Zalta. Fall 2010 ed. http://plato.stanford.edu/entries/justice-virtue/

Solomon, David. "Internal Objections to Virtue Ethics." *Midwest Studies in Philosophy* 13 (1988): 428–41.

———. "Keeping Virtue in Its Place: A Critique of Subordinating Strategies." In *Recovering Nature: Essays in Natural Philosophy, Ethics, and Metaphysics in Honor of Ralph McInerney*, edited by Thomas Hibbs and John O'Callaghan, 83–104. Notre Dame, Ind.: University of Notre Dame Press, 1999.

———. "Virtue Ethics: Radical or Routine?" In *Intellectual Virtue: Perspectives from Ethics and Epistemology*, edited by Michael DePaul and Linda Zagzebski, 57–80. Oxford: Clarendon Press, 2003.

Solomon, Robert C. "The Virtue of Love." *Midwest Studies in Philosophy* 13 (1988): 12–31.

Sreenivasan, Gopal. "Errors about Errors: Virtue Theory and Trait Attribution." *Mind* 111 (2002): 47–68.

———. "Character and Consistency: Still More Errors." *Mind* 117 (2008): 603–12.

———. "The Situationist Critique of Virtue Ethics." In *The Cambridge Companion to Virtue Ethics*, edited by Daniel C. Russell, 290–314. Cambridge: Cambridge University Press, 2013.

Statman, Daniel, ed. *Virtue Ethics: A Critical Reader*. Washington, D.C.: Georgetown University Press, 1997.

Stocker, Michael, "Emotional Identification, Closeness and Size: Some Contributions to Virtue." In *Virtue Ethics: A Critical Reader*, edited by Daniel Statman, 118–27. Washington, D.C.: Georgetown University Press, 1997.

———. "The Schizophrenia of Modern Ethical Theories." In *Virtue Ethics*, edited by Roger Crisp and Michael Slote, 66–78. Oxford: Oxford University Press, 1997. Originally published in *Journal of Philosophy* 73 (1976): 453–66.

Stohr, Karen. "Contemporary Virtue Ethics." *Philosophy Compass* 1 (2006): 22–27.

Strauss, Leo. *Natural Right and History*. Chicago: University of Chicago Press, 1953.

Swanton, Christine. "Virtue Ethics and Satisficing Rationality." In *Virtue Ethics: A Critical Reader*, edited by Daniel Statman, 82–98. Washington, D.C.: Georgetown University Press, 1997. Revision of "Satisficing and Virtue." *Journal of Philosophy* 90 (1993): 33–48.

———. *Virtue Ethics: A Pluralistic View*. Oxford: Oxford University Press, 2003.

———. "The Definition of Virtue Ethics." In *The Cambridge Companion to Virtue Ethics*, edited by Daniel C. Russell, 315–38. Cambridge: Cambridge University Press, 2013.

Taylor, Gabriele. *Deadly Vices*. Oxford: Clarendon Press, 2006.

Taylor, Jacqueline. "Virtue and the Evaluation of Character." In *The Blackwell Guide to Hume's Treatise*, edited by Saul Traiger, 276–95. Malden, Mass.: Blackwell Publishers, 2006.

Taylor, Richard. *Virtue Ethics: An Introduction*. Amherst, N.Y.: Prometheus Books, 2002.

Teichmann, Roger. *Nature, Reason, and the Good Life: Ethics for Human Beings*. Oxford: Oxford University Press, 2011.

Trianosky, Gregory. "What Is Virtue Ethics All About?" In *Virtue Ethics: A Critical Reader*, edited by Daniel Statman, 42–55. Washington, D.C.: Georgetown University Press, 1997. Originally published in *American Philosophical Quarterly* 27 (1990): 335–44.

Tuozzo, Thomas. "Contemplation, the Noble, and the Mean: The Standard for Moral Virtue in Aristotle's Ethics." In *Aristotle, Virtue and the Mean*, edited by John Bosley, 129–54. Edmonton, Canada: Academic Printing and Publishing, 1996.

Van Hooft, Stan. *Understanding Virtue Ethics*. Chesham, UK: Acumen Publishing, 2006.

Van Zyl, Liezl. *Death and Compassion: A Virtue-Based Approach to Euthanasia*. London: Ashgate Publishers, 2000.

———. "Virtue Ethics and Right Action." In *The Cambridge Companion to Virtue Ethics*, edited by Daniel C. Russell, 172–96. Cambridge: Cambridge University Press, 2013.

Walker, Rebecca L., and Philip J. Ivanhoe. *Working Virtue: Virtue Ethics and Contemporary Moral Problems*. Oxford: Oxford University Press, 2007.

Wallace, James D. *Virtues and Vices*. Ithaca, N.Y.: Cornell University Press, 1978.

Watson, Gary. "On the Primacy of Character." In *Virtue Ethics: A Critical Reader*, edited by Daniel Statman, 56–81. Washington, D.C.: Georgetown University Press, 1997. Originally published in *Identity, Character, and Morality: Essays in Moral Psychology*, edited by Owen Flanagan and Amélie O. Rorty, 449–70. Cambridge, Mass.: MIT Press, 1990.

Welchman, Jennifer, ed. *The Practice of Virtue: Classic and Contemporary Readings in Virtue Ethics*. Indianapolis, Ind.: Hackett Publishing, 2006.

White, Richard. *Radical Virtues: Moral Wisdom and Ethics in Contemporary Life*. Lanham, Md.: Rowman and Littlefield, 2008.

Wiggins, David. "Natural and Artificial Virtues: A Vindication of Hume's Scheme." In *How Should One Live? Essays on the Virtues*, edited by Roger Crisp, 131–40. Oxford: Oxford University Press, 1996.

Wilkes, Kathleen. "The Good Man and the Good for Man in Aristotle's Ethics." In *Essays on Aristotle's Ethics*, edited by Amélie Oksenberg Rorty, 341–58. Berkeley: University of California Press, 1980.

Williams, Bernard. *Ethics and the Limits of Philosophy*. Cambridge, Mass.: Harvard University Press, 1985.

———. "Social Justice." *Journal of Social Philosophy* 20 (1989): 68–73.

Wolf, Susan. "Moral Saints." In *Virtue Ethics*, edited by Roger Crisp and Michael Slote, 79–98. Oxford: Oxford University Press, 1997. Originally published in *Journal of Philosophy* 79 (1982): 419–39.

Woodcock, Scott. "Philippa Foot's Virtue Ethics Has an Achilles' Heel." *Dialogue* 45 (2006): 445–68.

Wright, G. H. von. *The Varieties of Goodness*. London: Routledge & K. Paul, 1963.

Yu, Jiyuan. *The Ethics of Confucius and Aristotle: Mirrors of Virtue*. London: Routledge, 2007.

Zwolinski, Matthew, and David Schmidtz. "Environmental Virtue Ethics: What It Is and What It Needs to Be." In *The Cambridge Companion to Virtue Ethics*, edited by Daniel C. Russell, 221–39. Cambridge: Cambridge University Press, 2013.

INDEX

Ackrill, J. L., 217n18
act and potency, 195–96
Adams, Robert Merrihew, 29, 41
altruism, 16n23, 108, 121, 124, 169
Annas, Julia, 6n12, 16n24, 51–52, 57, 83n4, 88, 90, 94–99, 105, 111, 117, 119, 124–25, 131, 144, 157n23, 160n28, 170
Anscombe, G. E. M., 1, 5–11, 13, 25, 27, 45–46, 54n6, 58–74, 77n52, 78, 80–81, 85, 87, 93, 106, 109, 111–14, 136, 141–43, 151, 153, 167–68, 175, 183–86, 208–10, 212, 228, 257
Aquinas, St. Thomas, 18–19, 29, 34–35, 44, 54–56, 59, 67n38, 97, 117, 140, 144, 152, 168–70, 176, 189, 191–93, 195–97, 199, 200, 203–4, 211, 222n26, 225, 227–28, 230, 232–33, 236, 238–41, 244, 249n65, 250
Appiah, Kwame Anthony, 8n15, 17n25, 29, 88n11, 91n17, 124n22
applied ethics and contemporary virtue ethics: abortion, 77n52, 79, 138, 229, 231n5; euthanasia, 78–79, 138; homosexuality, 133, 135, 138, 229
Aristotelian ethics, 6–7, 14–18, 20, 56–57, 73, 112–13, 142: and anthropology, 183–204; and natural law, 227–54; and teleology, 205–26; and virtue ethics, 142–50; not a virtue ethics, 151–81
Aristotle, 3–6, 16–20, 28–31, 34–35, 42, 52, 54–56, 59, 65, 68, 71–72, 92, 98, 103, 117, 127, 129, 131, 135, 140–50: biology, 19; *kalon*,154, 219–20, 237; naturalism, 95n24; neo-, 6, 15, 116–17, 130–31, 141; philosophical psychology, 11, 142; physics, 39, 59; Thomism, 10n18, 54–57; tradition, 14, 44–45, 48, 50, 93–94; virtue theory, 50, 65, 98, 141. *See also* Aristotelian ethics
Athanassoulis, Nafiska, 118n6, 144
Augustine of Hippo, St., 5, 29, 97, 117, 152

Baier, Annette, 57n13, 103, 118n6
Baron, Marcia, 91n16
Bennett, William, 88n11
Blum, Lawrence, 179
Bormann, Franz-Josef, 249n66
Brewer, Talbot, 9, 33n11, 171n54, 192n10, 207–8, 216n13

INDEX

Chappell, Timothy, 8n14, 9n17, 57n14, 131–32
character, 3, 8, 12, 17, 20, 37, 72n44, 73–75, 84–85, 86n10, 88, 101, 119–20, 123, 125n24, 126, 128, 130, 135, 140, 147, 157–64, 166–67, 172, 181, 194, 198, 205–6, 212–14, 216, 221, 234, 252. *See also* habit; situationism; virtue theory
charity: as a theological virtue, 56, 203–4, 225, 239; as benevolence, 66, 68, 78, 87, 117n3, 167, 175–76; Christian versus secular, 67–69, 79, 167–68, 170, 176
Clark, Stephen L., 217n18
Coleman, Janet, 199n23
compassion, 79, 136–38, 203–4
Conly, Sarah, 22, 82n2, 83–84, 86n10, 139
consequentialism, 2, 15, 24, 32, 48–49, 53, 67–80, 90, 92, 107, 112, 115, 118n5, 122, 126n27, 133–34, 151, 175, 206
contemplative wisdom, 16n23, 154–56, 161, 171–72, 177, 195, 221, 225. *See also* Aristotelian ethics; happiness
Coope, Christopher Miles, 9n17, 49, 60–62, 66, 69, 75–76, 83n4, 167–68, 174
Cooper, John, 217n18, 220n22, 242n40
Copp, David, 82n2, 126n27, 174
courage, 136, 140, 154, 155n17, 165, 190, 193
Crisp, Roger, 24n2, 82n3, 120n12

Darwall, Stephen, 34n12
deontology, 2, 15, 23, 48–49, 53, 63, 92, 96, 107, 112, 115, 119, 121–22, 126, 130, 137, 151, 164
Deshpande, Sharad, 91n16
disposition. *See* habit
Doris, John, 124n22
Driver, Julia, 4, 53n3, 60, 82n2, 86n10, 91n17, 139

emotion. *See* passion
end: as good, 19, 32, 48, 105, 134, 140–41, 158–60, 181, 186, 189–190, 194, 196, 204–06, 211–13, 215–16, 219, 221, 223, 232–33, 242, 245, 248–49, 253, 257. *See also* Aristotelian ethics: teleology; good; happiness
Engelhardt, Jr., H. Tristam, 248
eudaimonia. See happiness
Everitt, Nicholas, 117n5
exceptionless moral norms. *See* moral absolutes

Favor, Christi, 246n58
Finis, John, 54, 228, 240n33
Flannery, S.J., Kevin L., 222n26
Foot, Philippa, 1, 7, 8n14, 10, 15, 47, 54, 58–59, 78–80, 82n2, 100n37, 102n41, 103–5, 109–10, 117, 126n27, 174n61, 210, 228
Frankena, William, 82n2
Frede, Dorothea, 57n14
friendship, 16n23, 67, 145–46, 168–73, 176–77, 225, 227, 232, 251
Fritz-Cates, Diana, 193n13

Gardner, Stephen M., 82n3
Garver, Eugene, 221n25
Geach, Mary, 46n29, 60–61
Geach, Peter, 47, 54n6, 58–59, 66, 109, 117, 136, 168, 170, 175, 208

INDEX 277

George, Robert P., 199n23
Gibbard, Alan, 34n12
Gilson, Ettiene, 38
Girard, René, 41
good: action, 34, 71, 116, 158, 164, 196, 206, 221, 231; and virtue, 49, 61, 136–38, 147, 190, 194, 217; as end, 205–6; attributive adjective, 136–38; common, 75, 173, 225, 235–52; for a person, 49, 70, 75, 79, 88, 147, 158, 164, 173, 201, 216, 219, 222, 231–32; life as a whole, 204–5, 207–9, 211–15, 217, 219, 226; modern sense of, 46n30, 63, 66–67, 69, 80, 136–38. *See also* Aristotelian ethics: natural law theory, teleology; end; happiness

habit, 133–35, 140, 162, 188, 190–91, 194–95, 213–15, 239, 249. *See also* character
Hadot, Pierre, 41, 188n4, 210
Haldane, John, 55n8, 199n23
happiness, 16n23, 17, 47, 52n2, 57n13, 66, 92, 97, 147, 149, 156–61, 171, 178, 181, 193n14, 212–13, 216–18, 222–226, 242, 250. *See also* Aristotelian ethics; virtue ethical varieties: eudaimonistic
Hardie, W. F. R., 217n18
Harman, Gilbert, 124n22
Hartman, Edwin, 2n2
Hauerwas, Stanley, 56
Heraclitus, 235
Hobbes, Thomas, 92, 178, 230, 231n5, 235, 243–45, 249n65
Hooker, Brad, 91n17, 132–35, 138–39
human nature, 16n23, 31, 35, 37, 48, 56, 96, 128, 141, 158–59, 177–79, 185, 200–202, 204–6, 211–13, 231–35, 239, 243–46, 253, 257. *See also* Aristotelian ethics; anthropology
Hume, David, 3, 8, 16, 52, 57, 63–64, 69, 91–92, 103–04, 110, 112, 117, 124, 127, 131, 140, 144, 176, 202
Hursthouse, Rosalind, 12n21, 15, 48, 54, 66, 69, 75–79, 80n63, 82n3, 90–100, 105, 109, 115–21, 124–25, 126n27, 129, 130n34, 131–40, 144–46, 151, 157, 163n34, 165–68, 170, 174–76, 181, 199n21, 210, 228

Irwin, Terrence, 220n22
Ivanhoe, Philip J., 3n5, 55n9, 83n4, 86n10, 127n28

Johnston, David, 246n57
justice, 16n23, 28, 37, 40, 65, 67n37, 100, 120n12, 140, 170, 173–79, 190, 195, 234–54

Kamtekar, Rachana, 3n4
Kant, Immanuel, 8, 16, 31, 47, 52, 58, 64, 91, 101–3, 112, 117, 130, 140, 202, 247
Kenny, Anthony, 217n18
Kraut, Richard, 217n18

Lamont, Julian, 246n58
Lockwood, Thornton, 54n4, 149n11
Lombardo, OP, Nicholas, 193n13
Louden, Robert B., 82n2, 91n16
Lutz, Christopher Stephen, 199n23

MacIntyre, Alasdair, 1, 5–10, 18–19, 24n2, 27–28, 33n10, 34n13, 41, 47, 54, 64n28, 65, 82n1, 93–94, 100n37, 103–6, 109–10, 117, 135n45, 142,

MacIntyre, Alasdair (*cont.*)
 159n25, 175, 179, 186, 199–204,
 208–15, 222, 226, 228n2, 233n10,
 240n33, 241, 249n67, 257
Maritain, Jacques, 54, 251n69
Martyr, St. Justin, 41–42
McAleer, Sean, 83n4, 99n35
McDougall, Rosalind, 79n62
McDowell, John, 103, 160n28
McInerny, Ralph, 54, 228
McKinnon, Christine, 82n3
Meilander, Gilbert, 56
metaphysics: in relation to moral philosophy, 22, 30, 37–45, 95, 201
Mill, John S., 8, 16, 47, 52, 92, 101, 112, 117, 127, 130, 140, 157, 202, 206
Miller, David, 246n57
Milliken, John, 220n22
Miner, Robert, 192n12, 193n13
misericordia. *See* compassion
Montague, Phillip, 82n2
moral: modern and contested sense of the term, 63–65, 85, 137–39. *See also* Anscombe; obligation: in modern moral philosophy
moral absolutes, 42–43, 70–80, 100, 112, 153, 167, 175, 222n26
moral dilemma, 12, 35, 75–77, 124, 165–67
moral theory: basic questions for any, 17–19, 31–37, 39, 41, 44–45, 50, 185–186, 257; standards for judging any, 115, 126–42

natural law. *See* Aristotelian ethics
naturalism, 39, 95, 156, 230
nature, 34, 40, 177, 226, 230, 241–44, 246, 249, 252

Nietzsche, Friedrich, 19, 27, 69, 91–94, 117, 127, 129, 131, 140, 168, 243
normativity. *See* rule(s)
Nussbaum, Martha, 1, 7, 10, 15, 36n14, 49, 82n2, 98–106, 111, 117, 119, 127, 131, 199n21, 246n57

Oakley, Justin, 2n2, 78–79, 80n63
obligation, 79, 179, 234, 251: in modern moral philosophy, 18, 60, 62–65, 67, 69, 107
Owens, Joseph, 220n22

passion: of the soul, 103, 140, 149, 187, 191–95, 198, 205, 239, 244
Pellegrino, Edmund D., 80n63
Pence, Gregory, 82n1, 86n10
Peterson, Christopher, 88n11
phronesis. *See* practical wisdom
Plato, 3–4, 29, 31, 35–36, 42, 52, 71–72, 92, 95, 97–98, 111, 117, 140, 144, 153, 155–56, 164n38, 167, 187, 190, 234–35, 241–43
Pogge, Thomas W., 246n57
Pojman, Louis P., 148
Porter, Jean, 3n6, 56
practical wisdom, 3, 16n23, 19, 61, 77n53, 92, 94, 95n29, 96–97, 119, 140, 141n51, 144, 149, 155, 161–65, 181, 195, 216, 227, 232, 253
prudence. *See* practical wisdom
Purinton, Jeffrey S., 217n18

Railton, Peter, 34n12
Rawls, John, 27–29, 92, 106, 235, 245–50, 252
Rieff, Philip, 34n13, 41
Rist, John, 29, 34n12
Rogers, Kelly, 220n22

Rorty, Amélie O., 83n4
rule(s): -based ethics, 8, 15, 47, 74, 115, 121, 183 ; consequentialism, 117n5, 133–35; the role of in moral philosophy, 23, 34, 37, 102, 107, 122, 151, 162–63, 181; Virtue/V, 109n59, 116, 118, 124, 163n34, 175
Russell, Daniel, 2n1, 3–5, 6n12, 16n24, 47, 83n5, 84n8, 95n29, 99n35, 118n6, 119, 122n17, 125n23, 129, 131–32, 141n51, 160n28, 163n34
Russell, Paul, 3n7

Santas, Gerasimos X., 82n2, 148, 152, 161–62, 174
Scheler, Max, 168n47
Schmidtz, David, 2n2
Schneewind, Jerome B., 82n2
Seligman, Martin E. P., 88n11
sentimentalism, 23, 48–49, 68, 124. *See also* Slote
Shafer-Landau, Russ, 118–19, 231n5
Sigmund, Paul E., 240n34
Sim, May, 55n9
Simon, Yves, 54
Simpson, Peter, 16n22, 49, 82n2, 148, 152, 157–58, 159n25, 174, 213n6, 224n28
situationism, 12, 119, 123–25
Sobel, David, 82n2, 126n27, 174
Solomon, David, 8–9, 13, 83n4, 84, 106–11, 121–23, 125, 148, 184
sophia. See contemplative wisdom
speculative wisdom. *See* contemplative wisdom
Slote, Michael, 8n15, 10n19, 17n25, 24n2, 48, 62n26, 63n27, 66–69, 74–75, 83n4, 91n18, 98, 109, 116–17, 118n6, 120–21, 124–25, 126n27, 131, 140, 163n35, 168, 174n61, 245n54
Sreenivasan, Gopal, 125n23
Statman, Daniel, 82n1, 159n27, 161–62
Stohr, Karen, 82n1, 127–28
Strauss, Leo, 24n2, 34n13, 245
Swanton, Christine, 3, 4n10, 6n12, 8n13, 57n14, 83n5, 91n19, 99n35, 128–29, 131

Taylor, Charles, 8n14, 34n13
Taylor, Gabrielle, 15, 166n43, 170
Taylor, Jacqueline, 91n18
Taylor, Richard, 57n13
teleology. *See* Aristotelian ethics
telos. See end
temperance, 140, 162, 188, 195
Thomism. *See* Aristotle
Trianosky, Gregory, 82n1, 148
Tuozzo, Thomas, 220n22

utilitarianism, 23, 74, 97, 101–03, 105–6, 110–12, 119, 121–22, 125–27, 130, 157, 159, 170, 172, 176, 206

Van Hooft, Stan, 82n3
virtue ethics: defining a contemporary virtue ethicist, 85–89, 131; difficulties defining, 3–5, 57n14, 82–83, 128–32, 147–48. *See also* Aristotelian ethics; virtue ethical varieties
virtue ethical varieties, 81–113: agent-based, 6, 68, 83n4, 109n59; agent-centered, 6, 101, 109n59, 167; Aristotelian, 15–16, 50, 92, 94, 97–98, 112–13, 118n6, 129, 142; classical versus contemporary/reduced versus unreduced, 52–53, 90, 94–98, 102, 105, 111, 119, 125;

virtue ethical varieties (*cont.*)
Confucian, 3, 56n9; eudaimonistic, 6, 16n24, 92, 97, 118n6, 120, 124, 147, 157; Hard Virtue Ethics, 3–4, 47, 95n29, 129, 141n51; Humean, 102–4, 111–12, 131, 141–42, 199n22; Kantian, 57, 91–92, 101–5, 110–12, 141; mainstream/conventional, 6, 9–14, 16, 18, 20, 47–49, 61, 66–67, 74, 78, 80, 106, 108–13, 117, 119, 121–143, 149, 151–52, 171n54, 175–76, 180, 184, 229–30, 254, 256; marginal/unconventional, 9–10, 14, 18, 48, 65, 67, 106, 109, 111, 121–22, 142, 208; Nietzschean, 57, 129, 131, 140–41; pure, 17, 109n59, 120, radical, 8–9, 13, 84, 106, 110, 148n9; routine, 8–9, 84, 106, 148n9, 171n54, 184; sentimentalistic, 68, 124; Soft Virtue Ethics, 3n8, 95n29; Stoical, 3, 57, 97, 99, 111, 127, 131, 140, 144, 192; utilitarian, 91, 96–97, 124n22
virtue theory: and the natural law, 230; Aristotelian, 161, 163, 180, as opposed to virtue ethics, 4, 7, 53n3, 86n10; classical, 53, 90, 95, 106, 234; coherent, 139–142, 257; definition of virtue, 187–98; ethical versus intellectual virtue, 194–95; unity of the virtues, 16n23, 47n35, 67, 119, 129, 164. *See also* Aristotelian ethics; MacIntyre; virtue ethical varieties

Walker, Rebecca L., 83n4, 86n10, 127n28
Wallace, James D., 46n28
Watson, Gary, 82n3, 99n35, 119, 148
Wiggins, David, 91n18, 102n41
Wilkes, Kathleen, 63n27
Williams, Bernard, 8n14, 28, 34n13, 47, 63n27, 100n37, 103, 108, 246n57
Wright, G. H. von, 46, 58n16
Yu, Jiyuan, 55n9

Zwolinski, Matt, 2n2
Zyl, Liezl van, 2n2, 79

Before Virtue: Assessing Contemporary Virtue Ethics was designed in
Minion and composed by Kachergis Book Design of Pittsboro, North Carolina.
It was printed on 60-pound Natures Natural and bound by
Thomson-Shore of Dexter, Michigan.

www.ingramcontent.com/pod-product-compliance
Lightning Source LLC
Chambersburg PA
CBHW051937290426
44110CB00015B/2012